MAIRZY DOTES
AND ANECDOTES

DON P. MARQUESS

Copyright © 2025 Don P. Marquess

ISBN (Hardback):   979-8-89381-119-3
ISBN (Paperback):   979-8-89381-120-9
ISBN (eBook):   979-8-89381-121-6

All rights reserved. No part of this book
may be Reproduced or transmitted in any form or by any means,
electronic or mechanical, including photocopying, recording, or by any
information storage and retrieval system, without permission
in writing from the copyright owner.

The views expressed in this work are solely those of the
author and do not necessarily reflect the views of the publisher, and the
publisher hereby disclaims any responsibility for them.

508 West 26th Street KEARNEY, NE 68848
402-819-3224
info@medialiteraryexcellence.com

There are many ways to define, to narrate, to track a life: humor and good feeling, warmth and conviviality, as in author Don P. Marquess' *Quickies Too,* are definitely the way to go.

Marquess writes from the admirable though sometimes daunting aerie of *looking back.*

Looking back at a life extraordinarily well lived. At age eighty-two, Marquess writes with the alacrity and expansive hindsight of a true citizen of the world. Lucky readers get to meet Marquess in full bloom: Marquess as a successful brick distributor, as a photographer, as a musician. This man is in love with life and it shows on every page.

For example: the writer's enthusiasm and love of baseball -- a lifelong passion for the St. Louis Cardinals, in his case -- is positively infectious. We are with Marquess when he photographs Mark McGwire's legendary 70th home run. The author marked the occasion by producing 70 autographed photographic prints of the illustrious baseball. Throughout, the writing is breezy, conversational; akin to the chatty dugout talk during an exciting World Series game.

The stories in this volume are practically edible! They are like Krispy Kreme donuts - they go down fast, one after the other, in rapid chortle-filled succession, including the author's childhood in Missouri; early wonder filled junkets in the pages of encyclopedias; the onus of being born lefthanded; the sheer miracle of owning one share of Berkshire Hathaway stock; poker games infamous and long; encounters with tornadoes and the awesome beauty of nature, including the Hawaiian Islands and the author's beloved dogs.

There is a long-standing tradition of memoir-by-anecdote. Comparisons with Damon Runyon and P.G. Wodehouse is fair. A similarly hilarious volume, *My Cousin, My Gastroenterologist,* also comes to mind. (Boswell's *Samuel Johnson* being perhaps the forerunner of this very delicious trope.)

My favorite chapter is Chapter 40, 'Some People Can't Tell A Joke.' Read an excerpt and weep! *A man was sitting on an airplane next to a very well-dressed elderly lady, and as the sun caught the ring on her finger the reflection of it was almost blinding. The man kept looking at the incredible diamond and just had to ask about it. He said, "Ma'am, I am a jeweler in Manhattan and I have never seen such an incredible diamond, it looks almost as big as the Hope Diamond." She says, "Yes, it is almost the same size, it is the Klopman Diamond, but like the Hope Diamond, it carries a curse." The jeweler says, "A curse? What is the curse?" She says "Mr. Klopman."*

The stories in *Quickies Too* have a tenderness and wistfulness entirely in keeping with the author's stated mission: to charm the reader with the best and brightest moments of a life well lived and worth remembering.

—Pacific Book Review

"With so much heartache, drama, and horrors filling our world on a day-today basis, it is easy to forget sometimes to just take small moments to find the joy and humor in life. Humor can be a great tool, not just in a writing or entertainment profession, but in everyday life as well. Being able to find humor not only fills our hearts with warmth, but allows us to really absorb life's lessons. As Hugh Sidney once said, "A sense of humor… is needed armor. Joy in one's heart and some laughter on one's lips is a sign that the person down deep has a pretty good grasp of life."

In author Don P. Marquess's Quickies: Don't You Just Love Quickies? the author uses humor and wit to explore everyday life and memories over the course of his life. From pranks involving old grave stones in his youth to he and his wife's attempt at becoming private investigators, bowling nights gone wrong and even his longtime friendship with legendary sportscaster Jack Buck and the memories they shared together, the author uses his unique charm and humor to bring a lifetime of memories to life.

A truly brilliant read, the author does a great job of infusing truth and realness into the overall humor of the memoir. Each story is short, yet packs a punch as the author manages to make himself relatable and the stories themselves pretty grand. Yet the stories are lined not just with humor, but with real-life memories and lessons that so many of us learn throughout our life's journeys. The first story of Jack Buck in particular includes some of life's more somber moments, from diagnosing many ailments to witnessing a nationwide and worldwide tragedy unfolding, and yet the stories take these moments and showcase how humor and the bonds we form with one another can overcome those darker moments in life.

This is the perfect read for those who enjoy memoirs, especially those which infuse those memories and moments in a memoir with humor, wit, charm, and brilliant storytelling that makes these very real moments feel like a perfect narrative. As a fan of memoirs, it was fascinating to see the author's expertise and skill turn his own life and journey into a vivid memoir, taking on elements of imagery which brought these incredible moments to life.

A funny, charming, and engaging memoir, author Don P. Marquess's Quickies is a must-read book. e remarkable way the author makes the reader feel connected to his life and the people he was fortunate to have in it, from his beloved family to celebrities like Jack Buck and Burt Reynolds, really created a welcoming atmosphere and tone in the narrative, taking readers on a new journey of their own."

—Pacific Book Review

Table of Contents

Preface i
The Value of Autographs 1
Eric and Tracey Tavener 4
Man Mountain Oscar 8
George C. Cockerel, may He Rest in Peace 11
The Book of Knowledge 15
Lobster, Anyone? 20
Creepy, Crawly Reptiles 25
The Evening That Almost ruined Our Lives 29
Left-Handed (Like It Or Not) 32
Jack Buck, My Partner & Friend 35
My Grandfather's Hearing Test 47
Mel Famie 50
The Parkmoor Disaster 52
Baseball 56
The Acolyte Aspirant 64
An Unforgettable Evening at Busch Stadium 68
Sister Bee and the Special Chorus 71
John Rooney, The Pro 74
The Incredibly Powerful 1957 Mercury 78
The Honeymoon (Almost) 81
Berkshire Hathaway 87
Burt Reynolds – Peachtree Plaza 90
Dr. Dick 93
Karen – Busch Stadium Attendant 96

Naja Karamaru 100
What Time is It? 103
April McIntire...107
The Most Incredible Day 110
The True Definition of Art...113
Trip to Shreveport 115
Liar's Poker..118
Ducks on Parade 120
Really Good . . . Then Really Bad 123
The Crushing of The Balls 126
We Hit the Big Time..128
Darlene Theusch (née Gardner).....................................131
The Presidential Suite 134
Garfield, the Wonder Goose 137
Susan's Delightful Grandmother 140
The Deutschland Experience 142
Ten Las Vegas Casinos in One Afternoon 147
Saturday Morning Breakfast...151
Pardon Me, What Did You Just Say? 154
My Mother, The Brilliant Lady......................................157
That is Not Exactly What I Meant, Ted........................161
My Brother, Robert Marquess 165
My Jaguar XKE 170
World-Record Gambling Conversation 173
Really Fun Afternoon 177
Twenty-Six? Why? 182
Bill Haslett and The Las Vegas Caper 187
English Is Hard 192
Linda Zorsch 195

Incredible Trust	198
Boarding House Audi	201
Mount St. Helens	204
The Killer Stalactite	208
1982 McDonnell Douglas Aero Classic	211
Breeders' Cup Gambit	217
OFB 2003	221
My Grandfather – The Indestructible	224
The Sparkling Hawaiian Rainbow	229
Beautiful Virginia Beach	235
The Remarkable Marty	240
Prom Night, 1958	245
Tornado Encounters	249
Popcorn	252
Wonderful Pranks	255
The World's Greatest Blackjack Dealer	259
Very Hot Stuff	263
Yankee Doodle Dixie	267
I Don't Gamble. I Play Poker	270
Three Quickies with Susan (I Just Loved Quickies with Susan)	274
Fernando Tatis and the Incredible Feat	277
The Great Gippo	281
Dogs Are Truly Man's Best Friend	286
Michael Barnes and The Seventieth Home-Run Ball	292
Some People Can Tell a Joke, Some People Can't	295
Las Vegas (We're Gonna Kill 'Em)	302
John Curry Marquess	306
Kennenbunkport, Maine	309

Hotel Colombi 314
The Fabled Waters of The Sea of Cortez 317
Henry Mancini, The Gentleman 325
What Happens in Port St. Lucie Doesn't Stay in
Port St. Lucie 328
The Cartier Watch 332
Oh Deer 334
Irving B. Mestman 337
What An Unbelievable Trip! 339
Why Black Coffee is Part of my Life 344
The unbearable being of weight 346
Jim Sullivan's Arrival 349
The Shortest Line at White Castle 352
Riding the Rapids 354
Bobby Kennedy 357
Smoking 359
Oysters, Oysters, Oysters, and more Oysters 362
Finally…a brilliant thought 365

Preface

Egad! I am eighty-two years old and writing my second book? My intention in writing these stories is only to entertain. There are no murders, no politics, no villains, no controversies, no sex (now that I mentioned all the things my book isn't, I wonder why anyone would want to read this book …), but anyway, you purchased it and there is no turning back!

These are all very true stories just written to make the reader smile. One of my English professors termed my writing a "conversational prose," sayin' that my stories are written as if I am talking directly to the reader.

As I approach the half way point of my life, I feel compelled to relate these very humorous events in my life. When I think of them again, I tend to chuckle and wish to share these moments with the reader. With all the unhappy and dramatic events occurring in our world today, I think of the funny things in life, and they take me away from the drama of the world and give me comfort and laughter. My good friend, Hall of Fame broadcaster, Jack Buck, every Saturday morning when I was with him in his kitchen, no matter what his ailments were (he had Parkinson's, a pacemaker, cancer, and was an insulin-dependent diabetic), he would always look at the funny side of life and keep me laughing with his take on whatever the situation happened to be. He told me he was anxious to get Alzheimer's because then he would forget he had Parkinson's. No matter what, Jack always found humor in the darkest situations

My only intention of writing these very short stories is that after a difficult day working, or even a bad day on the golf course, the reader will take a few minutes to read these true events and hopefully lighten a day's tensions. I am not preaching nor attempting to persuade you to do anything other than to take a few moments to read my stories, then relax and smile for a while.

******

As I write this, I am almost eighty years of age. With any luck at all, I will make it. All of the stories in this "Quickies" book are real-life experiences with no names changed in any way whatsoever. I have not attempted to protect the innocent. Why would an innocent person care anyway? Probably most of the people mentioned in this book have long since passed away and therefore can't refute nor complain about their names being used in this book, and the others would be disinclined to purchase this book anyway. I have loved telling these stories for years, and with urging of those who listened to them and apparently enjoyed them, I have been encouraged to put them in print. I have been told by several physicians and a few brainiacs that I have an eidetic memory, which is a "nearphotographic" memory, so all of these stories are exactly as I remember them. I researched these from the recesses of my mind. And they have been researched for accuracy and verified by me. They are all written just as I speak them.

These Quickies are presented in the hope that after a hard day at work or a difficult day doing nothing, these true-life stories will bring a smile to the readers' face.

My close friend, the late Rich Wolfe, writer of over fifty books, who used my photos on the covers of five of his books (four with my permission), all best sellers, termed my writings "Thurberesque" in homage to James Thurber. My stories are short and do not take a major commitment to read.

They are sort of like the Far Side Cartoons by Gary Larson. Read them, smile, and then turn to the sports page. ink Max Shulman and Jean Shepherd.

Also, I was encouraged to write all of these stories by the noted child psychiatrist, David Berland, MD, since my stories are somewhat childish in their simplicity.

The world's most honored professor of the piccolo, Jan Gippo, who wrote the bible of piccoloists, *The Complete Piccolo*, was on the faculty of Webster University and is currently teaching at the University of Missouri in Kansas City, and is also an avid reader, who strongly encouraged me to put these stories in print. Jan has always loved a great story.

I completed seven projects with Jack Buck, the Hall of Fame broadcaster, who every Saturday morning in his kitchen had me laughing at his sophistication in telling humorous anecdotes. Jack, in his later years, became a very prolific poet, and we incorporated his poems onto my photos. I spent many weekend mornings with him as he read his latest poem that would end up on one of my photos. Jack was a major source of my baseball related stories.

There are stories that mention encounters with Burt Reynolds, Henry Mancini, and a few other celebrities of note. All of these stories are absolutely true-life stories that have occurred in my (almost) eighty years.

Hopefully, you will read them and enjoy doing so . . . but keep the sports page handy.

The Value of Autographs

The Chicago Cubs call it the Cubs Convention, the Boston Red Sox call it the Red Sox Winter Weekend, the Yankees call it Yankee's Fan Fest—they are all mid-winter baseball fan gatherings. At these fests, baseball fans come together to get ready for the coming baseball season. Baseball fans are unrelenting in their desire to see and do anything connected with their favorite sport. At these events, anything even remotely concerned with baseball is on display in booths with vendors hoping to tempt fans to purchase their wares.

The St. Louis Cardinals call their fan fest the Winter Warmup. In 1999, which was after Mark McGwire broke the Roger Maris's record of sixty-one home runs, and totally shattering it with seventy home runs, we had a booth for our baseball "art." Mark McGwire was attending the Winter Warmup. What a terrific event for Cardinals's fans.

I was very fortunate in securing the exclusive art photographic rights to the seventieth home run baseball. I produced seventy Cibachrome 30" x 40" prints that sold for $2,500 each, and seven thousand 18" x 24" poster prints that were priced at $70.00 each. That ball was auctioned at Gurnsey's in New York and purchased by cartoonist Todd McFarlane for $3.14 million. With Mark McGwire in attendance and signing his autograph on items brought by fans, this was indeed a stand out event for Cardinals's fans. My prints were offered in our booth with Phil Ozersky (who caught the ball), and I am signing the prints. People lined up were twenty-five or so deep and anxious to get the print of the actual ball Mark McGwire hit for number 70.

Darlene Williams, our gallery curator, was assisting in the booth taking the money and placing the prints in the large envelopes to take to Mark McGwire for his autograph. This was indeed an event for the ages. Every purchaser seemed thrilled to have the photographer and the man who caught the ball signing the prints for Mark to sign.

With one exception . . .

The next person in line to purchase the print asked if I had to sign the print. I was amazed that someone wasn't thrilled that I was signing the photo that I created.

I said, "If I signed it, it would cost $70, if I didn't sign it, it would cost $130."

Darlene Williams heard me tell him that, and exploded with laughter.

The purchaser, who apparently had zero sense of humor, looked at me very seriously and said, "Well then, could you sign it on the back?"

It was then established that my autograph devalues anything I sign. (Think twice before getting a signed copy of this book.)

Eric and Tracey Tavener

Susan and I had been married for four months or so when she concocted this caper. Susan, by the way, was the most beautiful and intelligent person I ever met. She resembled a gorgeous combination of Barbara Feldon (Agent 99 in Get Smart), Marlo Thomas, and Cher, and she also possessed a delightful and devilish sense of humor. We were watching an old movie on TV called "After the in Man," or one of the six or seven versions with the same Nick and Nora Charles (William Powell and Myrna Loy) when Susan said that she thought the two of us could be private investigators. She even had our alias created. We would be Eric and Tracey Tavener. (She had apparently been harboring such thoughts for some time, because the names she mentioned were far too good to have been a spontaneous creation.) I immediately warmed to the idea and had thoughts that the Tavener Agency had a very reliable and distinguished sound.

I said, "Susan, that sounds great. However, neither one of us has any experience whatsoever. We need more than just a great sounding name for our private investigating rm. We don't even know how to secretly spy on anyone, much less tail anyone while being unnoticed." Herein is the origin of the caper.

Our apartment was in General Grant Colonial Village, a development that for a newlywed couple was just the most glorious complex we could imagine. (In reality, it was just nice, but to us, being newlyweds and goofy in love, it was absolute heaven.) It was named after the Civil War general whose farm was within shouting distance of the apartment complex. Also, the complex was in a slightly different direction of shouting distance from a very shady motel named "Coral Courts" that had a sign in front advertising "hourly rates." It also had individual cabins with single car parking garages with overhead doors to the units. We needed some experience in tailing someone without detections, so we decided to go there and kind of lurk in the shadows on the parking lot of the Marlboro Lanes Bowling Alley next to Coral Courts. We waited and huddled in the car with the engine and headlights off. We knew that anyone leaving there at 10:30 p.m. or so on a Friday night had probably been up to no good. Shortly, our thoughts materialized. We waited for fifteen minutes or so, then . . .

A white Eldorado Cadillac was leaving Coral Courts. In the passenger's seat was a woman with platinum blond hair. e driver was wearing a white hat with a black band. We imagined that he also had a pencil-thin mustache and a pinky ring, and probably looked very sleazy.

Susan, gleeful as she could be, said, "Let's get him."

So, we waited until he left the motel driveway and turned left on the major Watson Road thoroughfare. Quietly and very stealthily, we started our pursuit. We lagged back, knowing that the Taveners were undetected.

We continued behind, following a very safe one hundred or so yards behind. it was a great idea, and it was working. e Cadillac continued east to Jamieson Avenue and turned right, so we did the same, still knowing that we were invisible to our "perp." He turned left on Eichelberger Street, then went two blocks, and turned left. We laid back and did the same. He drove around Francis Park, and so did we, traveling safely behind. Then, when we saw the car again, we saw no blond in the front seat, and the driver accelerated very quickly. We assumed that he had discovered our tail, told the blond to duck down in the front seat (or maybe threw her out), and was going to elude our pursuit. We would have none of that. He took a right, then another right, and we were closer behind him. Then he turned left on Eichelberger and had upped his speed to 50 mph or so. We were unrelenting and did the same. He sped across Hampton Avenue (another major thoroughfare), and we were right behind, closer to him than ever. He saw an alleyway and turned on to it at his increased speed. I slowed up and didn't continue the pursuit.

Susan yelled and said, "He's getting away, why are you stopping?"

I said, "Susan, for God's sake, what will we do if we catch him?"

For the first time in a while, she was silent. Fortunately, we came to our senses and ended the chase. We both felt, however, that that man lived in fear for several days wondering who was pursuing him. I felt that he probably anticipated a wifely confrontation for a goodly (or badly) amount of time. Our foray into the private detective business failed, although we probably caused a man to live in fear for a while.

Man Mountain Oscar

We lived on a street named Oleatha in Southwest St. Louis that had many houses very close together with meticulously manicured lawns. This was 1950, and I was nine years old. Running behind all the houses on the block was an alley separating the houses on the next block from the houses on our block. Each house had an ashpit where the ashes from our coal furnaces were stored, and several times during the winter season, ashpit cleaners would come down the alley and empty the ashes for a $5.00 or so charge. An ashpit was a roughly 4' x 4' heavy-duty structure built with about 5" thick of concrete and stood about 4 1/2' tall. It was a very sturdy structure. My job was to fill the coal scuttle periodically with the ashes from the coal furnace and empty them in the ashpit. I also was charged with filling the hopper with coal from the coal bin to keep the coal cooking. I felt very proud that I had such important responsibilities. Our family could freeze if I didn't keep that hopper loaded.

Then in a very sad moment occurred, the city of St. Louis passed an ordinance that all ashpits had to be removed. My job was over. Then came a raft of carpetbaggers and scalawags offering to destroy and haul away the pits for some outrageous price, or at least that is what my daddy said. That was indeed "the pits" for me. I loved that pit and enjoyed my responsibility as well. My father had a man that worked for him named Oscar Jarret who said he would remove it for a much more reasonable price. His cousin had a flatbed truck that he could borrow and save my dad lots of money . . . deal done.

Oscar had deep blue-black skin with the most muscled arms and shoulders that I had ever seen. Hercules would be envious. It was a Saturday when Oscar the Giant came to destroy our ashpit, but our house was in the center of the block, and while driving down our alley, he got two more ashpit removing jobs. By the time he reached our house, he had already a couple of destroyed ashpits on his cousin's flatbed.

I was so excited to see Oscar and his unbelievable muscles. I told many of my friends on the block that they had to come and see this incredibly powerful man. I felt that Oscar could star in any movie and wipe out every villain, and then blow the smoke off his hands in victory. We all gathered around the ashpit, awaiting Oscar's arrival. When he got there, I could almost hear the trumpets heralding his arrival. Oscar was indeed a specimen of wonder. He was a star, as was I for bringing him.

Oscar smiled at his admiring audience of marveling ten-year-olds, and removed his sledgehammer of destruction and struck the first damaging blow. It took several swings, but the heavily reinforced concrete was no match for Oscar. The side of the pit started to give way. My neighborhood friends couldn't believe the strength that Oscar had. His muscles bulged, and the veins in his neck became enlarged with each piece of broken concrete that Oscar hurled on to his cousin's truck. The more we marveled and cheered, the bigger the chunk he hurled. Oscar, being a true showman and loving the cheering praise, grabbed the biggest piece of all, raised it over his sweat-glistening shoulders, grunted with an explosive oomph, and threw it high in the air to land on the concrete laden bed of the truck. It landed with a thundering thump, and as Oscar was taking additional bows for his performance, there was another thundering thump. The axle on the truck split in half and the flatbed crashed to the ground. Oscar was out of business the same day he entered it.

His fans, all of my friends, and some I had never seen before cheered and threw flowers to him, and yelled "Encore, Encore." Well, not really, but if we knew the word we would have. Alley traffic came to a halt for several days until the broken truck and broken concrete rubble were removed. To this day, that last piece of concrete exists in the Hall of Fame of Ashpit Chunks. Nevertheless, I remained the neighborhood hero for years for bringing Man Mountain Oscar to our alley. Every now and then, I still bask in the glory of my accomplishment!

George C. Cockerel, May he Rest in Peace

It was a somewhat sultry Sunday in August as Don Flaskamper and I exited the cool air-conditioning of the Redbirds Lanes Bowling Alley and stepped into the hot humid typical St. Louis summer breeze. As we were leaving the parking lot in my daddy's '56 mandarin orange and white Ford Victoria, we passed the rear of the Lucisic Monuments building where there were dumped and discarded tombstones. We supposed that the names were misspelled or the date of departure was incorrect or some other aw that had to be reengraved. There in the discarded pile of headstones was a large stone with the name George C. Cockerel who died in 1953. This was in 1958, so we figured he had been dead long enough to not catch us lifting his monument. It was somewhat strange that Don and I thought the same thing at the same time. at tombstone was ours!! We also had the same idea what we were going to do with it.

There were a group of guys that hung around together in high school. Actually, I was an outsider in the group (which highly inventively was called "The Group") due to the fact that I was Catholic and went to a private high school, while the rest of the group were heathens and went to a public high school. e oldest of this group (by several months) of five guys was Roger Goessling, a six-foot- five-inch 140 pounder. Tall and skinny, Roger who could devour six or seven Big Bevos in a single sitting. (In 1958, Big Macs had not hit the St. Louis market, but a restaurant named Schneithorst's had their version named the "Big Bevo.") At any rate, Roger, the tall and skinny, was not with us that afternoon, so he was the perfect candidate for our caper. We knew we were going to use that tombstone for a delightfully sinister prank.

We lifted that extremely heavy headstone into the trunk of the orange Victoria, and it made a resounding thump when it hit the trunk floor. We drove off to get the proper tools—two shovels and a bushel basket—so we could borrow (steal) dirt from a local construction site. Remember, this was a Sunday afternoon and no construction was going on. We filled the bushel basket to overflowing with dirt, placed it in the trunk next to good ol' George C., and headed to the rear of the florist shop. We assumed that the florists did the same as the monument folks did and threw dead or moldy flowers in the trash in the backs of their buildings. We were right, a florist in our neighborhood had done just that, and we gathered three dozen or so slightly and greatly withered red roses from the alley in the rear of the shop. We then had all of the necessary ingredients for our project.

It was almost seven o'clock at this time, so it was getting dark, not very dark but just dark enough not to be easily seen but yet light enough to see what we were going to do.

We drove to the alley behind Roger's house, opened the trunk, and struggled to take out the headstone. Don and I were both strong kids, but this damn thing was heavy, probably close to three hundred pounds. We lifted it out and took baby steps to place it in the perfect spot in Roger's backyard, placing it facing east so the morning sun would illuminate it adoringly. We brought the bushel basket of dirt and mounded it nicely in front of the tombstone just like it was a freshly dug grave. And then, just like the cartoon cat, Sylvester, we tiptoed our way back to the grave and placed the flowers. e red roses were the finishing touch, and it was a glorious sight.

Now, a freshly dug grave in one's backyard must conjure up many thoughts, none of which are fun. First of all, is it a real grave? A frightening thought at best. Also, why would someone bury someone in a private backyard? All of these thoughts were absolutely delicious, anticipating the wonderful reactions of one discovering a freshly dug grave in their backyard. We got into our orange hearse and quietly drove away.

The next morning, I received a call from our fish, Roger, the tall and skinny. He said that he was just waking up and he heard his mother from their bedroom say, "Gus, there is a grave in our backyard".

Gus then responded, "Go back to sleep, Edith."

"No, Gus, there really is a grave in our backyard." Roger said he heard his father's feet hit the floor and then a long pause. Then he heard both of them in unison yell, "Roger!"

Don and I were both reprimanded by our parents, but my mom and dad kept laughing when they told me what a hideous thing I had done.

The Book of Knowledge

The Conners family that lived across the street from our house had a full set of Encyclopedia Britannica. My elementary school, St. Joan of Arc, had the World Book Encyclopedia. Tommy Long's family had something called Americana, if I remember correctly. We had the Book of Knowledge encyclopedia, which my parents thought was the very accurate "Book of the Cat's Meow." I enjoyed reading the World Book Encyclopedia at school much more than any of the other publications. (I don't know if it was the type of printing, the font, or the layout, but it was my favorite to read during open time in the school day). Nevertheless, even as a fifth grader, I enjoyed reading useless information, and the encyclopedia at home was a good source for collecting information as well.

Our Book of Knowledge set was twenty plus volumes and contained many pages of interesting information. In later years, that information had gained the term "trivia," and I loved it then as I do today. One day as I was reading from our set of The Book of Knowledge, there was a story about how the ancient Egyptians measured the height of tall things that were too tall to measure with arms stretched to the max. I don't remember much about it other than it was done in Aswan or Alexandria with a pole of a known length. The information was that someone took that pole of which the length was known (let's say ten feet), placed it straight up in the ground, and measured the shadow it cast. So, if the shadow was two feet, one-fifth of the length of the known pole, then the shadow cast by any tall building or structure was simply five times the length of the shadow. How neat was that?

I have been worried and greatly fearful of tornadoes ever since I saw that deadly one in the Wizard of Oz. That and also the stories my grandmother told me about her brother, Douglas Chamblin, who was a detective with the St. Louis police force, and who, at the age of thirty-six, was killed in the line of duty in 1927 from a deadly tornado when it collapsed a tall building that crushed him. At my age of ten years old, I had several frightful dreams that I, like Dorothy and my great uncle, would be blown to the heavens, or crushed by a tornado while I was sleeping snugly in my bed.

There was a giant oak tree in our neighbor's backyard across the alley that had me worried that someday, during a tornado, it would fall onto my room. My room was a remodeled and closed-in sunporch in the back end of our house. I loved that room, and while it was being enclosed and created as a year-round room, my mom and dad let me pick out the knotty pine walls and the burgundy vinyl tile for the floor. It was the first time I had my very own and super special room. But what if that giant oak tree fell on it and crushed it along with me? I now had the information to simply determine just where that devastation from the giant oak tree would hit.

So, at two in the afternoon one day, I took a yardstick to our driveway and measured the length of the shadow. I didn't want to sink it in the ground because that would adversely affect the exposed length and mess up the equation. Fortunately, the concrete on our driveway was a flat surface, enabling me to get an accurate reading of the length of the shadow. I took several loose bricks from the garage (my dad was in the brick supply business, so we always had some laying around) and tried to support the yardstick. This took many attempts, as the yardstick needed support from at least three sides to keep it from falling over before I could measure the shadow. In the meantime, time was passing and it was no longer 2:00 p.m. It was getting close to 2:30 p.m., but I measured the shadow anyway and got my equation. Luckily the shadow was about one foot, approximately one-third of the length of the yardstick. Now I could determine the height of the Killer Oak and just how much peril my room and I were in.

I crossed our yard and searched for the end of the shadow of the tree. I found where the last leaf was located in the shadow and marked it with my pocketknife. That shadow ended at our side of the fence in our back yard. Now, all I had to do was measure the length of that shadow from the base of the tree, multiply it by three, and I would know what would happen to my room if the tornado hit that tree. My measuring tool was that yardstick, the length of which was constant; however, the time was not constant, as it was now close to 3:00 p.m., changing the length of that shadow. But that didn't matter to me . . . I had my equation.

As the shadow lengthened and the time passed, it changed the equation. But at ten years old, I didn't realize that and I proceeded. The tree was on the corner of the neighbor's property around seven or eight feet from their fence line. I had my yardstick for precise measurement, but I had to set the yardstick, starting at the base of the oak, going through the back fence, and going out their back gate to get to the yardstick, and continue my exact measurement.

I crossed the alley, set the yardstick through an opening at the base of our wire fence, and went around through the gate to reach the yardstick. It was the eighteenth yardstick, fifty-four feet so far. I looked for my pocketknife in the grass but couldn't locate it; and there on the other side of our backyard was my dog, Sarge nibbling on my pocket knife. Sarge was a great dog and behaved very well, so I called him to come to me and bring my knife. He brought it over. I asked him where he got it, but he didn't respond, so I just used my memory to find the exact spot for my "perfect" measurement. I determined that the shadow ended at about the twelfth yardstick, so that tree was 36' x 3', making the tree 108 feet tall, which is almost an eleven-story building. There must have been something wrong with my exact and very accurate measurements because that must have been a world record oak tree. Nevertheless, I continued. Now with this exact height of the mighty oak, I returned to the base of the tree and started measuring by thirty-six yardsticks to get to 108 feet inside our house. (This was also a great variable, as I had to go through the back steps and estimate just where that yardstick would land as it passed through the walls). I figured that if my measurement was correct (why wouldn't it be?), my room would be totally gone by that tree falling. That measurement took me inside our house, just past the dining room table. My measuring ended at around 6:00 p.m., and my quest was complete and very accurate(?). Whenever bad weather was forecast, I ran to the dining room past the table for safe harbor, and I knew that if my room was obliterated, I would survive whatever Mother Nature threw at our house. Recently I returned to my boyhood home, and the tree was still standing as well as my room in the back of our house. An entire afternoon of my childhood wasted!

At 2:00 a.m. on February 10, 1959, an F4 tornado hit St. Louis, killing twenty-one people, injuring 358 people, and leaving 1,400 people homeless, all about five miles from my room on the back of the house, and I, being eighteen years old and fast asleep in my bed, slept through it!

Lobster, Anyone?

Susan was born in New Jersey. She lived first in Woodbridge and then Woodbury, but always close to the Atlantic Ocean beaches. At least much closer to the Atlantic Ocean than a landlubber like me, being only from a river city, St. Louis, and miles and several days from either ocean. Susan, being so close to the ocean, thought of lobster and crab legs not as delicacies but just staples of lunch and dinner fare. I always felt that if anyone wanted to entice her, they could just drag a lobster behind them and she would follow them anywhere.

There is a seafood specialist grocer in St. Louis called Bob's Seafood that features live lobster and crab. I called them and asked for the largest live lobster he had in the tank. Bob said that he had a six-and-a-half pounder that was just ripe for steaming. This was Christmas Eve and I thought it would make a delightful surprise gift for "Lobster Susan." I bought it and had it packed in a box with seaweed. It was a very alive and active lobster and it kept popping the lid of the box on my drive home. This was Christmas Eve in St. Louis and the temperature was in the mid-thirties. We had an unheated garage, which was just perfect for storing the gift lobster.

I thought, what the hell, why not wrap it up as a gift and place it under the tree? I found the perfect shade of lobster red shiny paper and wrapped the live lobster box, leaving an open section in the wrapping so in the morning when I came downstairs to light the tree, it would be easy to seal the box while Susan and our two boys waited at the top of the stairs for me to say, "Santa came, come on down." I placed a big red satin bow on the box, sealed it, and added a tag that said, "For Susan . . . Open me first." I then gave the all clear, and Susan, Donny, and Danny came downstairs to view the wonders that Santa delivered. Susan and I decided that Santa would always only get credit for three unwrapped gifts that he usually brought. All of the other gifts were wrapped with their individual name tags saying, "From Mom and Dad."

I led Susan to the brightly lit and sparkling seven-foot Christmas tree and pointed to the box marked "Open Me First." Susan usually shakes a package and tries to determine what is in it before she unwraps it, which she did so this time wondering what could be so loose inside to be moving around so much. Her curiosity caused her to think maybe it was a jewelry box that I had wrapped in a bigger box, so she proceeded to unwrap it. Just when she was about to take the lid off, all the shaking awakened the lobster, and he was one mad crustacean. A giant claw shot out of the box, and Susan screamed and dropped the box. e lobster, one big fellow, fell on the floor, with Donny and Danny screaming and Susan laughing and screaming at the same time. It was indeed a challenge to capture the wild and maniacal lobster, but finally we got him! Our boys named the lobster "Ozzie," making it very difficult for Susan to cook something that had a name. Nevertheless, her appetite for lobster overcame her aversion to cooking a named animal, and we had that delicious "Ozzie" for dinner. e boys had no problem dipping the named morsels in the freshly drawn butter.

Just as an after statement, Susan, who cooked many a lobster, said that the more humane way of cooking one is, rather than placing the lobster in a boiling pot, which she said causes the lobster to stiffen and become tough, she put the lobster in a moderately warm pot and slowly raised the heat, lulling the lobster into a calm restful death. What a supremely humane method of dealing death to something edible. She was right, Ozzie was tender and delicious.

While on the Christmas subject, from the time I was eight or nine years old, around the middle of November, I became my grandmother's cookie sous-chef. (At eight years old, I just thought I was her helper. I learned the sous-chef term much later in life.) My grandmom was easily the greatest cookie baker on the planet, and it was a great adventure to assist in the creation of those delicious gems. She made date/walnut cookies, pfeffernüsse cookies which were some old German recipe (where my grandmother got it was questionable because she was all English and Irish without a trace of German), rum balls (I was not allowed to actively participate in the creation of those), some sort of licorice cookies which she called "Annie's cookies" (I learned later that these were anise cookies), and my favorite of all, her world-famous Scotch shortbread butter cookies, which I guess were immediate artery cloggers but nevertheless delicious. Toward the end of the batch of those, she let me roll out the leftover dough and make whatever shape and size I wanted. With my great creative abilities at that time of my life, they ended up as strange trapezoidal shapes of two to three bite sizes. My grandmom usually baked twenty dozen or so of each kind, so all members of our families could gorge on them until our buttons gave way and rocketed off. It was these great cookie memories that got me to implore the world's second-best cookie maker, my wife Susan, to make Christmas cookies. She kept delaying the baking of those, and I was getting anxious.

I was at the Missouri Botanical Gardens gift shop one afternoon and saw a spindle with various Christmas cards. One that particularly caught my eye was a card with a sweet-looking bear wearing an apron, a "Mother Hubbard" lacy hat, and holding a plate full of Christmas cookies. e bear's head was slightly tilted to the side and had a sweet grin on her face. Inside of the card was some sort of cheery message that I can't remember, but I signed the card saying, "Enough of this sweet Christmas drivel, where are my cookies?" I left that card leaning against the coffeepot as I left for work that morning.

I came home after work and opened the front door, and there was Susan wearing a Mother Hubbard hat, a burnt orange turtleneck sweater, and an apron. She was holding a plate of freshly baked cookies, had her head tilted slightly, and had a sweet smile on her beautiful face. She was a perfect replica of the card that I left for her that morning. She turned around and she was totally naked from the waist down.

Dinner and cookies that evening had a delightful delay!

Creepy, Crawly Reptiles

Not very far from our house was Kenrick Seminary, which occupied a very large tract of land with densely packed trees and many pathways. The property housed the lower school that had a very impressive dome and steeple, while the upper school had an extremely dignified appearance with several squared off towers of dusty orange brick. The entire property was enormous. As we kids in the area could get into the compound and ride bikes on the paths approaching the seminary buildings, there was a permanent hobo camp with five or six denizens of the sacred forest. That encampment was apparently just outside the seminary property line. It didn't matter to us kids. We crossed the line and entered at will. It was indeed a magical place that was really exciting for us to visit . . . as long as we didn't get caught. When we did get caught, we were told by a security guard that it was private property and we had to leave. Most of the time we didn't leave, and we continued to explore.

At the edge of this forest was a large pond surrounded with strange and exotic elephant ear plants, and those cat of nine tails things. Large black birds with bright red under wings, that I only saw there to this very day, made that pond a very special place indeed. Also, with patience and intense searching, baby toads and little squirmy garter snakes could be found.

On many occasions, I would catch a tiny toad or two and take them home as pets until they hopped away and escaped. My brother, ten years older and many inches taller, 6'5", was a big sissy about my captures and didn't want to see them at all. One day in my searching around this pond, I found four little garter snakes. And being eight years old—and I guess a little devilish regarding my brother—brought the four garter snakes home, wrapped them around my fingers, and went through the house, seeking my brother. He was in the air-conditioned room in the house reading. I had my snake-covered fingers behind my back, got his attention, brought my fingers to within inches of his face, and said, "Hi, brother." He screamed, jumped off his chair, and his 6'5" body almost hit the ceiling! It was such a wonderful moment for a little kid to control such a giant. I don't think he ever fully recovered.

One day, while playing in the alley behind our house, I found a turtle heading with the speed of a snail crossing the alley. That turtle became my pet. I picked him up (don't really know if it was a him or a her, I guess only another turtle could tell) and brought him to our basement. There is not much a boy can do with a turtle, except marvel at the uniqueness of such a helmeted beast. They don't meow or bark and mostly appear disinterested in the goings on around them. They just hide their heads in their shell and poke them out occasionally, get bored, and go back in their shell to do nothing. However, this was my turtle and I loved him.

Days later, while playing in the alley, I saw another turtle traveling at breakneck speed across the alley. I outran him, captured him, and took him to the basement! I now had a companion for my turtle. Maybe it was a female, and I would end up with a real flock of turtles. How great was that. A few days later, there was another turtle in our back yard, which I, now with such great experience in turtle capturing, grabbed him and carried him to our turtle haven in the basement. The two other turtles would have a new playmate! I was thrilled. The next day, I went downstairs to see my turtle harvest and couldn't find even one. I searched everywhere. No turtles. I looked in the coal bin, looked behind the washer and dryer, but not even one turtle to be found. My mom had a closet in the basement where she put her canned jams and jellies. I thought maybe the turtle family had somehow gotten in there and were feasting on crabapple jam, but no luck. My three turtles had vanished never to be seen again!

Years later, many years later, my brother's best friend, Attorney John Healy, told me what happened to my pet turtles. There was only one turtle! My big squeamish brother discovered my turtle, got the coal shovel, and scooped up my turtle and put him in the alley. I found him again, thought he was another turtle, and brought him downstairs. Same story once again. My brother found that damn turtle again and shoveled him off once more. My third turtle finally aggravated him to the point of shoveling him to neighborhoods unknown (or maybe even worse) and ended my turtle collection forever.

The Evening That Almost Ruined Our Lives

There was a bowling alley named Arway Lanes, which was on Arsenal Street just west of Kingshighway Boulevard that was a very popular bowling establishment. The Group," which was Dave Twist, Roger Goessling, Don Flaskamper, Ronnie Thoene, and yours truly, Don Marquess, decided to join a bowling league because we had a secret weapon . . . David Twist was a bowler on the "Little Budweisers." There was a bowling team called "The Budweisers," and if I remember correctly, Don Carter and Ray Blueth were on that team. It was a terrific team that won a lot. The "Little Budweisers" were formed by sons of Budweiser employees. Dave Twist's father was a brewmaster for Anheuser-Busch, so Dave became a member of that team. The "Little Budweisers" had five excellent bowlers, and our good friend and member of e Group was on the team. With Dave as the anchor on our team, we were golden!

Before the term "designated driver" was coined, I became one. Apparently, I wasn't born with the alcohol gene since neither of my parents ever drank. I think there was one bottle of alcohol in our house for the first eighteen years of my life until one night a guest dealt death to it, declaring "good old Guckenheimer ish besh ebber." e fact that I am a teetotaler is due to no great moral conviction, but due to the fact that I hate the taste of alcohol and I have a definite allergy to it. One sip and my lips get numb, and I have a brain-chilling pain right above my eyebrows, therefore, I don't drink at all. e rest of our team did, however.

We, as expected, were ruling our league since Dave Twist was carrying a 237 average. e rest of us carried 180s (except for me, I struggled to keep above 160), so we blew away all the other contending teams in the league . . . except for one night. Dave Twist, the magnificent, bowled 135 his first game. Unheard of!

Dave was livid (actually, I think his color was a light magenta) and he had several beers in him as he stated, "If I don't roll 210 my next game, I am taking my bowling ball and rolling it down Arsenal Avenue!" This was a ridiculous statement, and we all knew it. This was a Friday night and Arway Lanes was on Arsenal just above one of the busiest streets in St. Louis, and traffic was very heavy this time of night. However, we all felt comfortable that he would bowl over 210 his next game. He didn't. He barely made 200.

I should have known better since I was the only totally sober one of our team, but no, I was almost the premier taunter, saying, "Come on, Dave, let's see that old black beauty roll down Arsenal Street."

The other three team members had enough beer to cajole him into that stupid action. e bowling alley was on a street on a hill that led to a stoplight on the corner of Kingshighway, so the bowling ball would roll easily into that intersection. We all almost pushed Dave to fulfill his promise and went to the middle of Arsenal Street. Dave, with his usual approach, full of style and determination, took his ball and let it fly. Egad! As the ball started rolling, it gained speed and started to bounce in the air, first one foot and then two, gaining speed and height as it rolled toward Kingshighway. We all thought our lives were over as that sixteen-pound cannonball was surely going to smash the windshield of oncoming traffic on that very busy thoroughfare and kill several people. There is no way to stop a galloping bowling ball.

Fortunately, the light for Kingshighway traffic turned red, and it was like Moses parting the Red Sea. e ball bounced higher and higher across Kingshighway, split into two pieces, and landed in the corner of Tower Grove Park just across the intersection. No cars hit! Apparently, no one even noticed because no cars stopped with people getting out of their cars and looking for the bowling-ball halves, so we all went back into the bowling alley and played the third game. Dave just grabbed a ball from the rental rack and rolled a very respectable 231.

I don't think we all realized (at that moment at least) just how fortunate we all were that the light changed when it did. I could be writing this from my prison cell!

Left-Handed (Like It Or Not)

I was born in November 1940 on the twenty-sixth of the month as a surprise Thanksgiving gift to my parents. I have an excellent memory; however, I really don't remember much about that occasion in the hospital, other than it was very dark then very bright. Even in 1940, St. Luke's Hospital had a very bright lighting system. After several days of rest, my mom and dad drove me home in his 1936 Ford coupe. When we reached home, I was placed in my crib and given a blue rattle. (That, among other things, told me that I was a booming baby boy). I grabbed that noisy instrument with my left hand, and it was to remain there forever. I was lefthanded! A malady remaining to this very day.

My daddy was Methodist and my mother was Catholic, but according to the agreement between them, their children were to be raised and educated Catholic. I was to be baptized months later at a new church named St. Joan of Arc. As a matter of fact, I was to be the first baptism there. But according to my mom, I had some sort of bodily function mishap and some girl took my place. Nevertheless, l was the first boy baptized at St. Joan of Arc. Sadly, for the world, I remained left-handed. With the world population admitting that only 8 percent or so of the world contains the outcast lefties. (It is probably a little over 10 percent, but the World Census Organization doesn't wish to own up to that many shortcomings.) The Catholic Church and its educational nuns tried desperately to correct my malfunction.

Crayon and triangle instructors in Miss Fairbanks Nursery School seemed not to notice the affliction. I still received the coveted gold star on my forehead for my stick tapping and triangle musical accomplishments. However, when I became a first grader at St. Gabriel's Elementary, it was an entirely different situation as I was moving on to higher education. Sister Mary DeSales and all of the other nuns just would not tolerate such an affliction. The bloody messes of my left hand became very painful. The penmanship portion of my education became increasingly difficult. Anytime I was supposed to print anything, my right hand would not participate. If I were lucky enough to print an A, B, C, or the severely challenging T or F by using my left hand, everything was OK. However, if I were caught using such a devious method, Sister would demand that I would present my left hand for flogging with her yardstick.

Moving on to the next educational level of second grade, I became increasingly intolerant of such corporal punishment. One day, when Sister Mary Pure (I think that was her name, although I may have a cloudy recollection) stood with her disapproving glare while holding the yardstick of death and said, "Marquess, hold out your hand." I didn't. She said it even louder and much more threatening. "Marquess, hold out your hand NOW!" In a momentary loss of my mind, I grabbed the yardstick.

The entire second grade class said, "Ooogh."

I felt expulsion and great embarrassment that would no doubt ruin my educational process. Sister Mary Pure led me down the hall to see Father Steck. Yikes!

She took me into his office, sat me down in a chair, facing father, then left to return to the right-handed students.

I sat in fear as Father Steck looked at me and said, "Donny, you are lefthanded, don't worry about it, I will handle it with Sister."

Sister, sadly for her, had to break her daily habit of yardstick wielding. Fortunately, John McInroe, Stan Musial, Mark Twain, or Boomer Esiason never encountered Sister Mary Pure. By the way, I have heard that it is now permissible for priests to date nuns, as long as they don't get into the habit.

(Sorry about that, I just couldn't resist.)

My knuckles healed just fine (thanks to Father Steck), except for several remaining scars, and I never again was required to present my left hand for damage.

I am still left-handed, and no one ever swatted that sinister hand again.

Whew.

Jack Buck, My Partner & Friend

It may have been 1970 and the Cardinals starting pitcher may have been Reggie Cleveland, but, at the moment that is irrelevant. What is very relevant is Jack Buck was broadcasting the game. The Cardinals pitcher walked the first batter on four pitches and Jack Buck gave his traditional opening after the first batter by saying "And that's the way this one start". Then the next batter walked on five pitches. The next batter walked on six pitches loading the bases. The fourth batter walked on five pitches walking in the first run of the game. Jack said, "What an ignominious way to start a ball game!". It was then I realized that he was not the ordinary play by play announcer. He was indeed a highly sophisticated wordsmith.

I grew up listening to Harry Caray and his unique way of calling a game. Harry Caray could make a pop foul very exciting. If you tuned in the game in the later innings, you could just tell by the tone in Harry's voice whether the Cardinals were winning or losing. Many people thought he was the best ever, and many fans felt they were more Harry Caray fans than Cardinals fans. When Jack Buck became his partner is 1954, most people just thought of him as a rather nondescript shadow in the booth with Harry. How wrong they were.

Ron Jacober, Sports Director for KMOX, told me this story about a game at Wrigley against the Cubs. It was "Teen Night" and after the game there was to be a rock band playing with dancing in the aisles. During the game both Harry and Jack commented about one teen couple in the stands paying much more attention to each other than the game. In the middle of the third inning, Harry Caray said to Jack "I have been watching them throughout this game and I figured it out, he kisses her on the strikes and she kisses him on the balls!". Ron Jacober said that Jack Buck looked at Harry in total disbelief of what he said. Ron said that Jack's expression personified the word "incredulity". Harry then realized what he said, started laughing, pushed the "cough button" and pointed to Jack to continue. There was no way Jack could contain his laughter, push his cough button and point to Harry for him to continue. Dead Air ensued. The game was still progressing with neither of the announcers able to continue saying anything. Ron Jacober told me that in the middle of that inning with only one out, they broke for a commercial…. a really long commercial break. e next inning started, and Harry was still laughing and pointed to Jack to take over, he couldn't, so they broke for another commercial. Then the mikes went live again with one out in the top of the fourth when Jack finally takes the mike and says to Harry Caray "Why don't we just talk about what is going on in the game?".

Jack Buck broadcasted for the Cardinals for forty-seven years and captured the hearts of Cardinal Nation. He could have run for mayor and won in a landslide. Many prominent celebrities, if one was fortunate enough to meet one, really were somewhat distant when you were talking to them, and you got the feeling that they were in "program mode" and not really looking at you, nor caring about you…. but not Jack Buck. He seemed as interested in you as you were in him. He would always ask your name, where you were from, and what you were doing. Jack never turned down a request for an autograph or a few words of conversation. He was not only a gentleman, but a very considerate person who made you feel that he felt fortunate to meet you.

I met Jack due to my baseball art photography, and he also interviewed me several times, regarding a new photo I produced, on his dugout show prior to games. We, the entire Marty Hendin gang, including Fredbird, my wife,

Susan, and I, were at JBuck's Restaurant in Clayton, MO celebrating my 60th birthday when Jack came into our private room and started telling jokes and making everyone laugh. My celebration was indeed a great one. He then recited a poem that he had just written about baseball. It was titled "365", which meant that if you were a baseball fan, you were thinking about baseball every day of the year, and baseball was usually uppermost in your thoughts, whether during the season or not. It was a great poem and everyone loved it. For me there are only two sports seasons…baseball season and the off season, so I truly related to his poem.

Susan and I went on the Cardinals Cruise every year and on the cruise after my birthday, Marty Hendin read Jack's "365" poem and the entire theater (all Cardinals Fans) gave it a standing ovation. When we got back to St. Louis, I called Jack and told him about the reception his poem received and that we should produce it and offer it for sale. I had taken a photo of his bronze statue right after sculptor Harry Weber produced it and I told Jack that we should incorporate his poem on that photo and offer it to his fans. Jack loved the idea, and we went in partnership in the project.

Since it was for profit, and not for charity, Jack felt he couldn't promote it himself on the air as it would be using his airtime for personal pro t, so he arranged several interviews for me to speak about it. The Cardinals flagship station, KMOX, had a very successful hour long show in prime time called "Sports Open Line" hosted by Randy Karraker, and Jack arranged for me to be on the show. I thought it would be just for a few minutes, but I was on for the entire hour show. (Which probably amounted to $10,000 or so in free advertising)

During my appearance on the show Randy Karraker while looking at the Print with Jack's sculpture and the poem said, "There is a red background on the print and at the stadium and there is no red background, it is just a concrete block wall, how did you do that?" I responded, "I got the statue before it's erection and photographed it with a red cloth backdrop". Randy commented that it really looked great. Later in the show, I once again stated that "I got the statue before it's erection", which was grammatically correct.

I had left my phone in the car and after the show I went to my car and the call screen said I had missed thirteen calls. The first one was from my wife Susan who said, "Oh Jack is going to be so proud with everyone driving by that statue to see his erection!" It then dawned on me that I had said. Another of the calls was from my friend, Jan Gippo who said "It's ERECTION? It's ERECTION?.... and you said it TWICE!!. Boy oh boy, you got a great opportunity on the number one station in St. Louis, and you really messed it up!" e rest of the calls had the similar message, except for one of my friends who said "Nice interview".

After that photo project, Jack and I became partners in six more of projects of incorporating his poems onto my photos. Every print we produced sold very well. Jack was an outstanding broadcaster and in his last few years of life he became a very prolific and quite masterful poet. Jack was a major patriot and had a Purple Heart from WWII, and many of his poems reflected that patriotism. Perhaps one of his nest poems written was after September 11, 2001 when the Twin Towers were destroyed and 2,800 people lost their lives. After that tragedy all life seemed to stop. Baseball ceased play, as did every other sport and entertainment activity. America was stunned, and joy and happiness were missing from the lives of all Americans. Baseball took a one-week absence. The Cardinals game was the first game to return, which was an afternoon game carried nationally on ESPN. Before the game started, Jack Buck stood at home plate in Busch Stadium and said, "Many people wonder if it is time for baseball to return…I think we have the answer!". 44,000 stood and cheered. Jack Buck read the poem he wrote, and afterwards, the Lee Greenwood song "Proud to be an American" was played. You have heard this saying before, but there wasn't a dry eye in 40,000 plus fans.

Jack wrote a poem titled "What Would the World be without Music" for the St. Louis Symphony for the opening evening of their fund-raising season. It was to be a Black-Tie Event and Jack was the Master of Ceremonies. He asked me to print the poem for him and I found an old, yellowed music script and incorporated his poem on it. I gave it to Jack and he thought it looked terrific. I had gotten to think of Jack as my friend, as he could always make me laugh. He looked at my print of his poem and thought it was beautiful and then asked what the music behind the poem was. I said, "Jack, it is an early version of "Roll Me Over In e Clover". He laughed. It was then that I thought he thought of me as his friend also. Jack read that poem at Powell Hall and presented it to the Symphony for hanging in their administrative offices.

I have a very close friend with the St. Louis Symphony who has been their piccoloist (the guy who plays the piccolo) for 35 years or so named Jan (pronounced Yahn) Gippo who was present at the opening and asked me if it was possible to get Jack to sign one for the musicians of the symphony to hang in the lobby of Powell Hall. I asked Jack and he said, "Of course, also print one for you and Susan, and another one for Carole (Jack's wife)". I had them printed the next day and had them with me in my car to bring to Jack the following Saturday.

One Saturday morning at Jack's in his kitchen, I mentioned a Yogi Berra Quote that I thought was really funny regarding his remarking about a restaurant and saying, "Nobody goes there anymore, it's too crowded". Jack said that he felt that most of the Yogi quotes were massaged by the media to make them even funnier. But he said he knew two things that Yogi actually said, because Yogi said them to Jack. Jack said that the Astros (Yogi was a coach for them) had just finished a series with the Dodgers on the West Coast, and the Cardinals had just finished a series in New York with the Mets. e Cardinals and the Astros were meeting in Houston for a series. Jack said that in the corridor of the Astrodome he and Yogi met, they had the usual Hi's, and handshakes, when Yogi said to Jack, "When did you get here?" Jack replied, "Oh about an hour ago". Yogi said, "East Coast Time or Central Time?" Jack said he could think of no way to respond to that. e other time that Jack said Yogi truly said a Yogi ism was when they were both in Cooperstown going to a welcoming celebrity dinner. Yogi was on the bus when Jack got on, saw Yogi, and asked him, "Yogi, what time is it?" Yogi said, "You mean right now?" Once again, Jack was speechless.

Two of Yogi's statements that I know are true because I heard them both in the "This Week in Baseball Show" with Mel Allen being the host. Yogi, who at the time was a coach for the Mets, was asked by Mel Allen about the poor attendance at the Mets games. Yogi responded by saying, "If fans don't want to come to our games, how are you going to stop them?" In the very same interview Yogi said (being the true sage he was) "In baseball there are ONLY good times and bad times, and THIS is not one of those times."

I had the very fortunate honor of being the only art photographer to photograph and produce prints of Mark McGwire's 70th home run baseball. I have a multi-page document giving me those exclusive art photographic rights. e sports attorney, Michael Barnes, arranged for me to also photograph Sammy Sosa's 66th home run baseball. Sammy's 66th homerun ball was own to St. Louis and I photographed it. I had arrived at Jack Buck's home for a meeting one afternoon when Michael Barnes called and said that he would be offering a contract to whoever caught Barry Bonds 71st home run baseball and wanted me, probably for continuity, to photograph that ball in a contract similar to the one I had for McGwire's and Sosa's record-breaking home runs. I declined. I explained to him that the only way that I covered my expenses in photographing and producing prints was by the sales thereof. Everyone in the country seemed to love mark McGwire, and certainly Chicago Cubs fans loved Sammy Sosa. Recouping my expenses and making a pro t was an easy task regarding those two. However, I had never met anyone who even liked Barry Bonds, much less loved him. The proposal from Michael Barnes was indeed a compliment, but I saw no financial future in the deal. I then went in to Jack Buck's kitchen (through the garage, where he told me that is how his good friends enter) and being somewhat late for our meeting, I told him of the Michael Barnes proposal, and at the time, I think that Barry Bonds was within 5 or so home runs from breaking Mark McGwire's record of 70 home runs. Jack said to me "Do you want Barry Bonds to break McGwire's record?" I said, "Of course not, Jack", he said, "Neither do I, you know for $3,000 we could get Tonya Harding to break his kneecaps!" I said, "Count me in!"

Sometimes my mind wanders and I go off on a different tangent, so getting back to the "What would the World be Without Music" poem that Jack asked me to print for the musicians of the St. Louis Symphony. On Wednesday night I was the guest of Mary Hendin at a "Braggin' Rights" Illinois/Missouri basketball game at the Savvis Center when my phone rang. It was Jack calling, however, for every play on the court there was cheering with an equal number of Mizzou and Illini fans. It was very much like a Cards/Cubs game. e crowd noise was so loud I couldn't hear what he was saying. I said that I would call him back after the game.

I called him back after the game and noticed he had called four more times. Jack answered and asked if I had the symphony prints with me and asked me to come to his house on my way home. I said that I would be there shortly. When I got there, he was wearing his black silk pajamas and looked frailer than I had ever seen him. He said, "I've got cancer, and I am going into the hospital tomorrow morning, and I don't know if I'm coming out, so I wanted to sign these prints for you". Good grief, he was just diagnosed with cancer, yet it was very important for him to follow through on a promise of signing his poems. Not many people would think of that responsibility after receiving such devastating information.

Jack looked at the three prints, signed one for Carole, one for Susan and me, and asked how to sign the one for the orchestra players. I said, "Please sign it "For e Musicians of the St. Louis Symphony Orchestra". Jack said, "I can't do that, I don't know how to spell musicians". I said, "I don't either, let's ask Carole". He said, "No, you don't want to do that, she is sleeping and becomes rather surly when awakened". Anyway, he signed it and thanked me for bringing the prints over at such a late hour. It is hard to imagine anyone but Jack having that incredible sense of responsibility.

Jack Buck had a heart monitor, Parkinson's Disease, was an insulin dependent diabetic, and was just diagnosed with cancer, lung cancer. He told me he was looking forward to getting Alzheimer's Disease because then he would forget he had Parkinson's. Saturday morning after he returned home from his cancer operation that removed 40% from his right lung, called me and said, "Where are you? Come on over, I wrote another poem". e poem was titled "Wake Up" a poem to discourage people from smoking and probably losing lung portions, just like what happened to him. I went over and entered through his garage (and being a good friend that's where I entered) and saw him in his kitchen really looking weak and frail. I said to him, "I hope that all of what you have gone through hasn't affected your sense of humor". He paused a moment, looked at me with those very beady eyes of his, and started slowly maneuvering his right arm and pointed in my direction and said, "UP YOURS!" I said to him, "Jack, I will always cherish that moment."

He said, "Look what they have done to me" and took his shirt off his very skinny torso and revealed the incision on his back where the section of his lung was removed. At the incision there was a fluid sack hanging. He saw that I was looking at it and he said, "I told my doctor about that fluid sack this morning and he asked me how big it was…I told him it was about a 34B". at was Jack, never losing his sense of humor.

My Grandfather's Hearing Test

My grandfather, Albert F. Froussard, who got his thirtieth patent when he was eighty years old, was in his early nineties, and his hearing was almost gone. He had survived years earlier from a big bell-shaped object that fell off a large machine and crushed him against a truck. He was in a coma for three weeks, and when he came out of it, I was in the hospital room with him. He blinked his eyes several times and looked at me and said, "It's a damn good thing it happened to me, it would have killed anyone else."

That was my grandfather. He felt he was a super being with no flaws. However, he was fast approaching total deafness. This didn't appear to bother him as much as it totally aggravated his family and all who attempted conversation with him.

At his office when the phone would ring, he would answer the phone (he was quicker at that than anyone else in the office) and say at the top of his ninety-year-old lungs, "Hello. Hello . . . Hello . . . Who is this?" and "Speak up, we must have a bad connection."

My grandfather, since he was a highly successful inventor and businessman, felt he knew all, not unlike Al Capp's General Bullmoose (what is good for General Bullmoose is good for the USA), my grandfather felt that he was pretty much an infallible being. He was not very receptive to suggestions from anyone. I am not saying that he was disliked at all, but his hearing deficiency was definitely disturbing to those around him. He had sixty-five machinists at one time or another and most had been with him for twenty years or more, and they respected him much; however, to put it as gently as possible, his hearing loss was driving everyone goofy! I worked in his drafting department, making catalogs and other miscellaneous tasks, every summer between semesters. I was going to come to the rescue and help my grandfather hear again.

I made an appointment with a hearing center on Hampton Avenue close to his home in St. Louis Hills. My grandfather and I always got along very well, so I convinced him that a hearing test would make his life much more enjoyable. He seemed to understand and agreed to let me take him there for a hearing exam. That was to be a wonderful event for my grandfather (and everyone else in his life), so I picked him up one Saturday morning for the exam I had scheduled.

We arrived in plenty of time. The audiologist was very friendly and highly complementary to my grandfather, saying that he was amazed that he was in his nineties, but he certainly didn't look it. After all those pleasantries, he entered the booth (the cone of silence), and my granddaddy sat for the test. Well, it was determined after the test that his hearing was several degrees worse than Beethoven's, (well, actually at that time, it wasn't nearly as bad. Beethoven couldn't hear at all since he was dead), and the audiologist had the perfect hearing solution with a state-of-the-art hearing device for that time in the seventies. The hearing expert placed the hearing aids on my grandfather, and I could see from his facial expression that he could hear clearly for the first time in a decade or so. I had accomplished my goal, and the earth would be thrilled! Then the hammer dropped!

My grandfather said they were nice and asked how much they were. Bad question. As I remember, the audiologist told him around $500. My grandfather got up out of the chair, pointed his finger at the man, and screamed at the top of his lungs (I think the building actually shook), "YOU ARE A GODDAMN CROOK!"

My grandfather was serious. He was about six feet tall and considerably taller than the audiologist who looked at me with a very nervous expression and gently said, "Please take your grandfather away, and don't bring him back." I agreed and understood.

In the car taking him back home, he was still steaming from that hearing aid "crook" and said loudly, "If God wanted me to hear, he would let me hear."

I looked at his cane next to him on the seat and said to him, "Well, God wanted you to fall down, but you went against his wishes and bought a cane!" My grandfather looked at me and said even louder than he screamed at the hearing guy, "AW HELL!"

My grandfather passed away at 101 still not hearing.

Mel Famie

I was in Jack Buck's kitchen for another Saturday morning regarding his latest poem and the incorporation of such on one of my photos when he mentioned an incident regarding the pitcher, Mel Famie. I thought I was familiar with most baseball players, both past and present, but I had never heard of Mel Famie. Jack then said that he was a short relief pitcher for the Milwaukee Braves before they moved to Atlanta. Mel Famie was an alcoholic and while in the bullpen, he always brought a very large thermos container that he filled with beer. When he emptied it, Mel would go down the stairs, grab a couple more beers, and reload the thermos. On this particular day during the game between the Chicago Cubs and the Braves, Mel Famie had reloaded his thermos far too many times. e manager called to the bullpen for Mel to warm up so he could come in to pitch the eighth inning. Mel Famie warmed up (it didn't take much as he was already pretty loose) so he could come in.

Jack continued, "So Mel came in and walked the first batter, then the second, then the third, and then the fourth, scoring the eventual winning run. It was discovered after the game that Mel had been totally drunk from so many thermos bottles of beer that the Cubs referred to that beer in the container as 'The beer that made "Mel Famie walk us'!"

I was totally roped in and believed Jack until that punch line.

On another occasion with Jack, I was called to assist with the final preparation of several prints that Jack had commissioned as a fund raiser for the Backstoppers, (an organization to help support spouses of fallen re fighters and policemen). It was a print with Mark McGwire's autograph as well as Bob Gibson's, Lou Brock's, Stan Musial's, Red Schoendienst's, and Jack Buck's autographs. Two hundred prints were to be produced to sell for $2,500 each, raising $500,000. David Pratt, part owner of the Cardinals, matched the $500,000, and the print sold out the first day raising $1,000,000 for the Backstoppers. Jack Buck and Lou Brock had to resign three damaged prints. Marty Hendin asked me to be there since our gallery was packaging them and sending them out. We met in the Cooperstown Room at Busch Stadium II for the signing.

Marty Hendin said to Jack, "Jack, you need to thank Don for being here. He should be home packing. He is leaving for Hawaii tomorrow morning."

Jack then looked at me and said, "You are going to Hawaii? While you are there, will you find out if the hula is an ass . . . set to music?"

I asked Jack how long he had been saving that one up. He said this was his first opportunity.

The Parkmoor Disaster

I had my daddy's 1956 orange and white Ford Victoria for a date with Joan and two other couples. We were all classmates at Bishop DuBourg High School and we were going to dinner and a movie. There was a St. Louis favorite drive-in restaurant named The Parkmoor where the orange jacketed carhops delivered the food. (Remember carhops?) They had great malts and burgers, and we were all hungry.

The carhop hopped to my car, and we all ordered our burgers, fries, sodas, and malts. The order was delivered to my side window on a tray with all of the burgers and fries, while the malts and sodas were delivered to Joan's door. Judy in the back seat decided that she had to go to the ladies' room, and she had to exit from the car by Joan's door that had all the drinks. The Ford Victoria was a two door, so Joan scooched even closer to me (nice) to allow the back of her seat to lean forward to allow Judy's egress. She climbed over Jim, and Dolores got out on Joan's side, then with the brains of a grape, she slammed the door. Yikes! All the water, soda, and malts left the tray with great speed and crashed all over the front and back seat carpet, girls, etc. Judy came back to the car seeing all of us out of the car and said, "What happened?" She had no idea of the disaster she caused.

All movie plans were cancelled and the dining experience was over. We could not let my dad know what we had done to his beautiful car. We went to J. C. Penny's and got cleaning supplies and towels to totally restore the beauty of the orange carpet, seats, girls dresses, and even the ceiling of the car. It was unbelievable the havoc and total mess that six drinks could cause.

I was worried that if traces of coke and malts were left in the car, it would be a very cold day in hell before my dad would let me use his car again, so the world-class restoration by the six of us spent hours restoring the interior and left no trace of the disaster we had caused. In truth, we were all such good friends and had such a great party cleaning the car, it was much more fun than any stinking movie would have been anyway.

While on the car subject, another story comes to mind. Roger Goessling was the oldest of our group of friends, and the only one that had his own car. Whenever we went anywhere, Roger drove. We would all chip in for gas, which, believe it or not, was around 20¢ a gallon.

"OK, guys, let's pay up," so we would all chip in a quarter or dime, so Roger could keep driving. I remember seeing a sign saying "Gas War. Carl Bolch regular .18 per gallon." Those really were the days. Roger's dad was some sort of muckety-muck with Railway Express Co. (a predecessor to UPS), and on one Saturday, Roger was going to work with his dad, leaving his car available for our cleaning the interior and washing the exterior as kind of a payback for his driving any time the group went somewhere. It was a great Saturday project.

Don Flaskamper, Ronnie Thoene, Dave Twist, and I thought it would be a great idea to go above and beyond Roger's expectations and cover the interior seats with a new cover, so we went to J. C. Penny's in Hampton Village to see what material was available. There before us on a rack was probably the most hideous leopard skin fabric we had ever seen. All the other fabrics seemed humdrum and unworthy for Roger's car. He just wanted us to clean his car, not reupholster it, but this seemed like a really fun and devilish prank to play on him, so we purchased what we felt would be a sufficient amount of cloth. It was on sale (I guess it had been there so long with no one wanting it), and I think we spent $8.00 at the most. This was not even a classy fabric (if leopard skin could ever be so), it really looked as cheap as it was.

So, we drove Roger's car back to his house and commenced working on his surprise. We covered the front and back seats tightly using a staple's gun Dave's dad had, and it really looked just as hideous as we anticipated. We had plenty of material left, so we covered the overhead, the side armrests, and everywhere we could think of. There was a cover on the horn in the center of the steering wheel, and we popped off the metal casing and covered the horn button with leopard skin. We even covered the sun visors on both sides with that hideous material. Roger's '47 Chevy coupe looked totally ridiculous with all of those spots leaping out at you as soon as you opened the door. We finished the project and hung around, waiting for Roger to scream when he saw what we had done to his car. Roger's dad brought him home around 5:00, and we couldn't wait for his reaction.

However . . .

He loved it! He proudly possessed the silliest looking car on the planet, and I guess that our prank had an even happier ending. He kept it that way until the car let out its last roar and finally collapsed to big cat country.

Baseball

I was sitting in the Busch Stadium office of my best friend, Marty Hendin, Cardinals vice president, after a baseball game one night when Walt Jocketty, general manager of the Cardinals, opened Marty's door and said that the Memphis Redbirds just won the Paci c Coast League title on a home run by a player name Poo Jols.

Marty and I both said, "Who is that?"

Walt Jocketty said he had just been with the team for three games and didn't know much about him at all.

As I did for many years, I went to spring training with Marty Hendin, and in 2001, I was in the booth with Jack Buck and Mike Shannon when this kid, Poo Jols, was at bat.

I said to Jack, "What about this kid, Pujols? He is hitting around .450 in spring training."

Jack Buck said, "Forget about him. He needs another season or two in the minors, then we will see. He has no experience against Triple-A ball at all."

Maybe so, I thought, but he has faced some pretty good pitchers this spring and handled them very well. Several games later, I was with Marty Hendin in the stands when Albert came to bat again, still hovering around the .400 mark. I said to Marty that this Pujols kid seemed pretty good, could he make the roster up north?

Marty said without any hesitation, "Forget about him. He needs a couple years in the minors."

I was disappointed, but I thought Jack Buck and Marty Hendin certainly knew much more than me. I was just a fan, hungry for offense production, and Albert certainly showed that he was capable of producing many hits and RBIs. Well, as the team was heading north, Bobby Bonilla got hurt and so Albert Pujols came up with the team, never to get his proper seasoning in Memphis. Dagnabbit.

There are several other spring training moments that come immediately to mind. I have loved baseball since I was eight years old. I guess my brother and dad indoctrinated me to the point that I really had no choice but to love it. I think it is the perfect game, so different from all the other major sports. More about that later. At any rate, the point I am making is that I was into my sixties and probably didn't miss many games either in person, on the radio, or on television. at comes close to ten thousand games that I experienced from the time I was eight years old. I thought I knew baseball very well. There was an unoccupied booth on the press level at Roger Dean Stadium in Jupiter, Florida, where I chose to sit and watch one of the spring training games. Marty Hendin and Red Schoendienst came in, sat on either side of me, and started talking about the game. Lucky me, I was sitting with the intelligentsia of baseball flanking me on both sides. Being the watcher of almost ten thousand games, it felt I belonged and was one of the guys.

Red Schoendienst said to Marty, "That kid in left field will never make it."

Marty said, "You are right, never a chance."

What in the hell were they talking about? For all of the games that I had experienced, I never noticed one little nuance, yet a very important little nuance. All of the fielders are kind of moving around, some not, but most of them not very intent on the actions of the pitcher. That is until the pitcher is set at rest before throwing the ball. When the pitcher is set, all of the fielders get set also and lean forward just a little bit on their toes, so to speak, in readiness for the pitch. Red and Marty pointed out that it was almost like a ballet as every fielder gets ready to react to the next pitch. This guy in the left field stood flat-footed and wasn't prepared for the next pitch. I never noticed that one of the more beautiful moments in baseball takes place even before the ball is thrown. I guess I didn't really understand the game.

Back to Red Schoendienst for just a moment. I had gotten to know Red from all of the times I spent in the broadcast booth, just as an observer, due to my friendship with Jack Buck, John Rooney, and Mike Shannon. Several months after my wife of forty-two years, Susan, died, I started seeing a much younger and also very beautiful lady named Marina.

John Rooney and Mike Shannon were talking about my new relationship with this lady to Red, and he came into the booth I was occupying and said, "All right kid, tell me about this new 'very young' lady you are seeing." I showed him her photo on my cell phone. He looked at her, then looked at me, then her again, and said very emphatically, "You're out of your league, kid." I then showed him Susan's photo on my phone. He looked at her, then looked at me, then her again, and said, "You were out of your league then too, kid."

I said, "Gee, thanks, Red. Let's watch the ballgame."

I will speak for a moment to the greatness of the game of baseball as I see it. In every other game, the puck goes into the net, the ball goes through the hoop, the ball crosses the goal line, etc. In baseball, it is the man, not the ball that scores. No score occurs without "the man" crossing the plate. In every other sport, in the last moments of a game, you have the last few minutes to put out a major effort to score. In hockey, for instance, you can get the puck to your best shooter or leave an empty net pulling your goalie and have an extra man on the ice to score. In basketball, you can get the ball to your best three-point scorer. In football, you can pass to your best receiver. In baseball, you can't do that. You just have to wait until the best guy's turn comes up. You just can't insert him at will, so there is so much more strategy in the game. For instance, when Mark McGwire was chasing the home-run record, it seemed like everybody cared about baseball. Those who didn't know how many outs in an inning were hoping that Mark McGwire could come up to bat and hit another home run. is kind of reminded me of the forties in St. Louis. The first question about a game was, "What did Musial do?" and then the next question would be, "Who won?" Simply stated, that was the case with Mark McGwire. What he did was far more important than the game itself. Before any game starts, the lineup is given to the umpires and must be followed throughout the game. In every other major sport, you can take a guy out, give him a rest, then bring him back at will. In football, for God's sake, you even have two separate teams, one for the offense and one for the defense. Not so in baseball. Each player must eld his position as well as come to the plate to take his turn at bat. at "at bat" is one of the beauties of baseball. Everyone gets a "one-on-one" with the pitcher. Also, once you take a man out of the game, he is dead meat. You can't put him back in. Also, and probably the greatest difference, there is no clock! In the immortal words of Yogi Berra, "It ain't over 'til it's over."

Hotdogs are also better at a baseball game than anywhere else.

Marty Hendin became a friend when I had an idea to photographically depict the breaking of the home-run record of Roger Maris, who broke Babe Ruth's record of sixty home runs by hitting sixty-one in 1960. at record stood for thirty-seven years, much longer than Ruth's record of sixty home runs in 1927. There were only thirty-four years before it was broken. My idea was to crush sixty-two baseballs depicting the breaking of that record, putting them in a pile, and photographing them. I called Marty Hendin, who was the Cardinals vice president in charge of community relations, and told him that I wanted sixty-two baseballs for a photo.

He said, "That is an interesting number, Mr. Marquess. How long will you need them?"

I said, "Mr. Hendin, you won't want them back when I'm through with them."

He said that sounded interesting and he would get back with me. Two days later, I received six dozen brand-new baseballs from Rawlings, the official supplier of baseballs to the major leagues. I was ecstatic. I have almost ruined a four-hundred-dollar suit trying to catch one of those balls at a game and all of a sudden I had seventy-two of them. Marty suggested that as a "thank you," I should give them a print when I completed the photograph. My idea of crushing them went on the back burner as I started to open the boxes. Truly, I was like a kid on Christmas morning. They were gorgeous. It was getting late in the day and the light was warm and wonderful. I drove to a golf course and started to lay them out in a pile, and as I did, I thought these are the "Balls of Summer." e light was perfect, and my Zeiss 60 macro lens was just the perfect way to capture them on Fuji Velvia lm. I was right, the transparencies came back looking just as beautifully as I anticipated. My mind just started racing with ideas for treating the baseball itself as the star of the photos, not a player or a team, just the baseball itself. I went to a fabric store, purchased several yards of different colored silks, and started photographing these gorgeous baseballs. My mind was racing with so many ideas that I couldn't stop. I even went to

Molly Brown's reworks store and purchased several smoke bombs. I picked five of my photos, "The Balls of Summer," "The Patriot," "Old Glory," "Smokin'," and "Pastime," and had the lab make thirty-by-forty-inch Cibachrome prints, framed them, and hung them in my gallery in Plaza Frontenac. The next day, Mark McGwire came in, saw the prints and bought one. The next day, Gary Gaetti, Todd Stottlemeyer, and a couple of other players came in and bought my photos. Marty Hendin called and said that I was creating quite a stir in the Cardinals clubhouse and could he come out and look. I told him that we opened at 9 a.m., but he said that he would be at work by then. Was it possible to open earlier for him, like around 8 a.m.?

I said, "Certainly," and asked my gallery director, Darlene Parks, if she could come in early.

Marty arrived at 8 a.m. and in ten minutes mapped out my next ten years of photographic sales for me.

I was selling my Cibachrome print for $450 each, and he said, "Mr. Marquess, you will soon run out of ball payers that can pop for $450 per print. You need to produce something you can sell for $30 or so." He then said that he would contact the Hall of Fame in Cooperstown, New York. He then said that the Cardinals Hall of Fame would bene t from having my prints on the walls there. He said that boxes of note cards should be produced and would sell well.

All that in ten minutes or so. Marty Hendin had the greatest promotional mind that I had ever experienced.

When he left, Darlene, the gallery director, was in tears, saying, "Oh Don, this is it. He loves it."

Marty and I became close friends and shared lunch at least once a week for over ten years.

At that point, my original idea of crushing sixty-two baseballs was placed on the back burner.

The Acolyte Aspirant

St. Joan of Arc church had finally completed constructing the elementary school that was only a block and a half from my home. It was a brand-new school and I was excited to attend. I was only a half year from being able to serve mass. At that time, most good Catholic boys heading for fourth grade aspired for that occasion, as it was a major step in getting to be a grown-up. This was very similar to a Jewish boy's bar mitzvah. It was entering into the "Big Time!" I was confirmed at St. Gabriel's church by my savior from my left-handed persecution, Monsignor Steck. I was ready to enter the new school and eligible for serving mass, so finally I would get to wear the grown-up cassock and surplice. Big time! I was very religious at that time and seriously thought about becoming a priest later in life. That is until I learned about that celibacy thing.

I have been fortunate to have a very good and accurate memory. Sister Dolorene the third, fourth, fifth, and sixth grade teacher (she taught third and fourth grades, so I had her for two years; then she taught fifth and sixth grades, so two more years of Sister Dolorene). Sister Dolorene learned of my memory talent very quickly and used me for whatever benefit she determined. At the start of fourth grade, she presented me with the acolyte's manual, and I gobbled it up and had it memorized very quickly. She was impressed with my speed, pronunciation, and accuracy, and had me tutor the other eligible students in learning the responses to the priest during mass.

The procedures of the mass rituals were taught to us by the new parish priest, Father Rider. All of the mass proceedings were done in the church by the altar. We learned how to accompany Father when he was delivering the Holy Communion and, very importantly, how to present the cruets of the water and wine during the service. (Father Rider always consumed a complete vessel of the wine and just a dewdrop of water to make it truly holy).

Father Rider also had a great sense of humor and very little hair on his head, and told his future servers, "I have thirteen hairs on my balding head, I part them down the middle, and a major decision I have every morning is which side of my skull to put the odd one."

In the Roman Catholic mass, the acolyte gives the responses to the priest, which at that time were all in Latin. The mass was spoken in Latin, and for me, that made the church attendance a very special and sacred experience. Mass at that time was certainly different from ordinary life, and it made church attendance a very special occasion, even though we didn't know what in the hell the priest was saying. When the Catholic Church decided to change the Latin Mass to English and have the priest turn and face the congregation, it took away much of the mystique and splendor of the mass for me. I considered the priest a very special man and not just one of the congregation's buddies. I think that in order to draw more church members, they destroyed the special mystique of the Catholic mass. Nevertheless, at that time, the priest spoke in Latin, and the acolytes responses were in Latin as well. My responsibility was to assist the aspirants to learn the responses and prepare for mass assistance.

My first mass was being served at the 5:30 a.m. hour, a generally lightly attended service, and for rookie acolytes, usually their first mass. I, however, was no rookie. I had the responses in the palm of my hand. I was the acolyte tutor.

The performers (Father Rider and I) were in place and ready to start Holy Mass. The newbies first mass was usually at a very early time, so my debut was at the 5:30 a.m. mass. Father Rider and I exited the sacristy and took our respectful positions to start the Holy Mass, Father stood facing the altar, held his hands high toward the heavens and said, "In nomine Patris, et Filii, et Spiritus Sancti," and I was off and running for my assisting role.

I started by saying, "Ad deum qui laetificat, juventutem meam." I then said "quoniam ad hoc, blabber labber." I slightly paused again and said "mumble mumble deus something," all while the priest's hands were still extended heavenly.

He continued in that position and ready to speak while I continued my memorized responses. It appeared that every so often, his hand position took a momentary slight surge, as if to say something, but I kept giving my responses, flawlessly and with great speed. With his hands still extended, he lowered his head and quietly said to me, "Please wait for me." Egad, I was about a third of the way through the Mass when he was still on the opening salvo.

Fortunately, for the subsequent mass servings, I was much more gracious in allowing the priest to direct the proceedings.

An Unforgettable Evening at Busch Stadium

I was at a gas station filling my tank when Susan called on my cell phone.

This was September 16, 1997 early in the afternoon, and she said that at 2 p.m., there was to be an important announcement from the Cardinals in a press conference. I immediately turned to KMOX to hear Bill DeWitt announce the signing of Mark McGwire to a three-year contract. Incredible! Mark McGwire was traded to the Cardinals at the July 31 deadline, and many St. Louis fans assumed that he was just a "rent-a-player" and at the end of the year, he would opt for free agency and sign for the top dollar in MLB. is announcement was indeed one of the more pleasant surprises in my forty-five-plus years of Cardinals mania.

Then Mark McGwire took the podium and said many things that I wanted to hear from players for years.

He said, "First of all, I love St. Louis and the Cardinals fans. Many friends told me that I would love playing here, and they were absolutely right. I love coming to the stadium each day to play the game I love, and I'm in front of packed houses for every game at Busch Stadium." What a perfect opening statement. Then he said, "Many of my player friends thought that I should go to free agency and go to the highest bidder. Well, let me tell you, I know a lot of guys that did that, and they aren't very happy. I can tell you now, I am very happy here. It blows my mind how much money we players are paid to play this game. My new contract is worth a lot of money, and I am very happy with that amount. How much money does anyone need anyway?" (His contract was for three years and $28.5 million dollars. He was right, that is a lot of money.) Next, he said, "I am also donating one million per year for sexually and physically abused children." Another good deed! Mark McGwire said everything that an appreciative and honorable gentleman would say, and I loved it.

I called Susan to see if she wanted to go to the game that night, and she said, "Definitely."

I had given away our season tickets for that game, but we planned on buying a couple of tickets from a scalper on the street that evening. We couldn't wait for the game as we were so excited. We bought the tickets and got into the stadium. The usher in our section knew us well enough and found a couple of empty seats close to our season seats. We looked around and saw several people that had season seats close to ours sitting in different seats than usual. We were not the only ones that came to the game due to Mark McGwire's press conference. This was a meaningless game late in September when both the Dodgers and the Cardinals were out of contention for postseason play. Under normal conditions, such a meaningless game (if there really could be a meaningless Cardinals game) would have maybe fourteen thousand fans or so. There must have been close to thirty thousand people in the stands!

Mark McGwire was the third to bat in the first inning. He came up to the plate, and thirty thousand fans stood and cheered. Usually when that happens, after the first pitch, everyone sits down . . . not so this time. Fans stood and cheered through the first four pitches, and on the fifth pitch that Ramon Martinez threw, Mark McGwire hit the longest home run ever hit in Busch Stadium that traveled 517 feet to left center eld and dotted the "I" in his name on the batter's sign. (He later eclipsed that by hitting one to dead center eld 545 feet, which may be the longest home run ever recorded in MLB.)

People were high fiveing people next to them and everyone had watery eyes! What an unforgettable night at Busch. e Cardinals lost to the Dodgers 7–6, but no matter.

Sister Bee and the Special Chorus

At Bishop DuBourg High School, there were close to two thousand students, and it was the brand-new flagship school in the archdiocese. With so many students, there were many with outstanding voices. I was not possessed with an outstanding voice, although it was good enough for an elitist choral group called the Special Chorus. We performed in all of the school's productions, "Showboat," "Daddy Long Legs," "Song of Norway," and "Brigadoon." Great times were had.

The chorus director was a delightful nun named Sister Beatrice Marie, better known by all choral members as Sister Bee. Unlike most nuns, she was really attuned to the happenings of the day and was considered to be really with it. (As an example of the other nuns who weren't "with it," Elvis Presley was the biggest thing on the planet, and in the first day of second year Latin class, Sister Verona had us all write our names on a paper that was passed to her so she could learn who was who in our class. She would read the name on the sheet and ask that person to say a few words for identification. Someone [me] wrote the name Elvis Presley, and she read the name and said, "Elvis, Elvis, where are you?") Sister Bee wasn't like that at all, she knew all about Elvis, and also all the lyrics to Harry Belafonte's "Jamaica Farewell," and just about every new hit song. We were one big happy family. Our chorus was chosen to visit the other schools and perform, mostly due to several gifted sopranos, some very talented tenors, and one terrific bass who could very comfortably hit a low D and belt it out like Thurl Ravenscroft, (Mr. Grinch).

Sister Bee who was very up with current real-life happenings always had some special thing for us to do together after rehearsals. She created a very close-knit group, and cemented lifelong relationships for years to come.

On Ash Wednesday, the first day of the forty-six days before Easter, Catholics are reminded of "Ashes to ashes and dust to dust" with a black cross of ashes on the forehead given by the priest at Mass, and all good

Catholics are expected to do some sort of penance by "giving up for Lent" something. It always seemed to me that people sacrificed by giving up something they were trying to give up anyway, like smoking, eating fattening foods (trying to lose weight), or something more self-serving for improvement. At that time, meat on Friday during Lent was a definite nono. Now it seems like the only time to forego meat is the actual Ash Wednesday.

On the morning of Ash Wednesday at the 7:00 a.m. Special Chorus rehearsal, Sister Bee asked several chorus members what they were giving up for Lent.

"Betty Bohr, what are you giving up for Lent?"

"Sister, I am giving up chocolate until Easter."

"Beverly Shea, what are you giving up?"

"I'm giving up ice cream, Sister, and I really love ice cream,"

"Audrey Georger, what are you giving up?"

"I'm giving up soda, Sister"

And so on, then she came to me. Sister Bee always called me by my last name and said, "Marquess, what are you giving up for Lent?'

I said, "Sister, I always felt that a true sacrifice was giving up something dearly loved, so for Lent, I am giving up the Catholic Church!" Sudden dead silence fell upon the room. Sister Bee just looked at me with no expression whatsoever, then her right foot started tapping slowly, and that great twinkle in her eye gave her away, and she started laughing, gathered herself together, and said "Say two Hail Mary's, One Our Father, take two aspirins, and call me in the morning." That was Sister Bee, very hard to have one on her!

John Rooney, The Pro

Through my friend, Marty Hendin, I met John Rooney, the newly hired broadcaster for the Cardinals in 2006 who was stolen from the White Sox after eighteen years or so as their broadcaster. John is the only baseball announcer to broadcast World Series winners back-to-back for two different teams: the Chicago White Sox in 2005 and the St. Louis Cardinals in 2006. John and I met on a Cardinals Cruise and became immediate friends. John has a quick and unfailing wit and keeps me laughing. He invited me for five spring trainings to stay with him in his rented condo in Jupiter. After each trip, my sides ached for several days from laughing so hard. If baseball ever comes to an end, John could make a great living doing voice-overs for Saturday morning cartoons. John has a terrific ear for voices and does a Harry Caray better than Harry himself, a wonderful Vin Scully, Tom Brokaw, Pat Buttram, and countless others.

I asked John why he didn't use those voices on the broadcasts, and he said, "Because it is about the game, not about me!"

I will never forget that he said that and that he meant it. Fans are hearing exactly what is happening in the game as described excellently by John Rooney, but they have no inkling of his wit and ability to entertain with the many voices he possesses. Truly, John Rooney is the consummate professional.

One morning in Jupiter for spring training, there was a day off with no game, and John was sleeping in. He was going to wake up around 10 a.m. and we were going to have a fun day in beautiful sunny Southern Florida. We were going to stop at the ballpark (Roger Dean Stadium), then head down to Ft Lauderdale to the Seminole Hard Rock Casino to play a little blackjack, then head to his favorite restaurant for the best pasta fagioli soup on the planet. It was to be a great day!

Not so . . . the lawn guys started mowing and trimming the condo lawn at 7 a.m., waking John and depriving him of three more hours of desired slumber. He tossed and turned for an hour or so, finally gave up, and came out of his room. Then we headed for the ballpark about twenty or so miles away. We got about two miles from the park when John realized that he had forgotten what he needed to take to it, so we turned around and headed back to the condo. John has a terrific sense of humor; however, it was not very apparent at this time. On the way back to the condo, John wanted to stop at Starbucks for a cappuccino and a scone. The store was packed and the drive up was six cars deep, and then it started raining. We finally got the breakfast items, made it back to the condo, John got his stuff, we dropped it off at the stadium, and headed for Fort Lauderdale. e traffic was horrible, all the construction was in full swing, the rain was now a deluge, and things were generally stinky. Finally, we made it to the Hard Rock, parked the car, and walked in looking for the blackjack tables. No luck! No blackjack at the Hard Rock. They gave some flimsy excuse for no tables, but it didn't make us feel any better. We played slots and a little roulette until it came time for dinner. John lost in slots (big surprise), but John said that we were just about fifteen minutes away from this great restaurant with the fabulous pasta fagioli soup, so everything would be great. e rain stopped and the temperature was around ninety humid degrees and completely overcast. We headed for the restaurant, and when we got there, it was closed! Monday, it was closed. John was ruined. I said to John that a restaurant Tony La Russa liked named Nick's Tomato Pie had a great pasta fagioli soup, and if he could wait, so could I. It was about seventy- five miles away and about ten miles north of Jupiter, but why not, we both could wait. e journey back was worse than the trip down, and all the drivers were idiots. John, on several occasions, yelled at the idiot driver ahead of us and other times just yelled at no one in particular. It started raining again, this time like a monsoon.

We finally made it to Nick's Tomato Pie, and the lot was packed. John asked me to get out and get a table, and he would park the car and come in.

There was one table left, so I procured it immediately and asked for the waitress.

She arrived, and I said to her, "There is a man coming in to join me. He is going to ask for pasta fagioli soup, and you are going to tell him that you are out of that soup. Please do that."

She said she would, and as we looked up, a soaking wet John Rooney was headed for our table. John was exhausted, crabby, and wet.

He asked for pasta fagioli soup, and she said, "Sorry, sir, we are out of that soup."

John exploded and said that he was going to the drive-through at McDonald's. She immediately laid the blame on me and told him that they had plenty.

John looked at me and said, "I am not going to the drive-through at McDonald's, and you can walk home." Then he laughed, although I don't think he enjoyed that little prank as much as I did.

The Incredibly Powerful 1957 Mercury

My dad had an orange and white 1956 Ford Victoria that had orange carpeting, an orange padded dash, an orange steering wheel, and even orange sun visors. It was a very remarkable piece of machinery. It was time for my mom to get a new car, and she opted for a 1957 Mercury. She liked the orange and white of my dad's car and found an orange and white one on Trigg Mercury's showroom floor (Trigg will give you the shirt off his back). However, this one had very special package, which included a 290-horsepower engine. Why my mom wanted that car was a puzzlement to me because she rarely drove over thirty-five miles per hour. Cars behind were always honking at her to drive faster. It truly was much more of a car that she needed, but she liked it and it was hers. One weekend in 1958, she let me take it to Columbia, Missouri, where Roger Goessling and I were roommates at Missouri University. What an absolute thrill for me. That car had been deprived of a real workout and rarely hit 40mph.

From St. Louis on Highway 40 (now I-70), we headed to Columbia. There are several steep hills and I was just itching to see what that car could really do. So, coming down one of those steep hills, I floored it. We were picking up speed very quickly, and that incredibly powerful engine was putting out all it was worth. The speedometer kept climbing, and hit 110 miles per hour. I became scared to death, so I slowed down as fast as I could. As we peaked the top of the hill, there was a highway patrol car with lights flashing, and the man with the pointed hat signaled me to pull over.

My roommate said, "You are toast, pal."

I started to pull over and was still at a faster speed than I should have been, and the highway patrol officer had to jump out of my way to avoid being knocked into the ditch. I knew I was doomed.

He approached the window and said to me as I was shivering and scared to death, "Do you know how fast you were going? Son, you were clocked at eighty-seven miles per hour."

I nervously said while the sweat began to pour, "Oh, thank God. This is my mom's car, we are just heading back to college for the weekend, and I wanted to see what this car with its mighty big engine would do, but when it hit 110, I got scared and slowed down."

My roommate let out some sound that resembled the cry of a banshee, while the officer just stared at me in disbelief. I think that I was just so nervous I couldn't think clearly, and the officer just continued to stare at me and started to laugh. I had presented my license, and he noticed that I was only seventeen (I probably looked like I was eight years old and got caught with my hand in the cookie jar) as he continued to stare at me while still laughing.

He said to me "Son, that is a new one for me, and this is my eighteenth year on the force, I never heard anyone say they were going faster than they were clocked, so slow down and enjoy the rest of the day."

I said "Thank you, officer, I will!" I rolled up the window as the adrenaline kicked in and I started really shaking! I didn't even receive a written warning, much less a speeding ticket. In that incident, honesty was indeed, the best policy!

The Honeymoon
(Almost)

In 1968, Susan and I were married on September 20. We took a major trip together that previous summer. I was planning a trip to Phoenix to see a friend and then stop in Las Vegas. Susan wanted to visit her sister in San Francisco and would ride with me to Las Vegas, where then she would catch a bus to San Francisco. However, it was great that after several days on the road, her sister's visit was no longer a goal. To use Susan's own words, we were "goofy in love" and just decided to complete wherever I was headed, to head there together.

On my favorite driving trip across the Great Southwest through Oklahoma and the Texas Panhandle, there's a stop at the Big Texan restaurant where its free seventy-two-ounce steak is served. It's free only if you can finish it along with a salad, shrimp cocktail, and baked potato in an hour. If you don't finish it, the cost was, as I remember, $42. Somewhat hefty, even for 1968. We stopped and had two small steaks, which neither one of us finished.

New Mexico was beautiful as always, where the stars at night are big and bright, deep in the heart of New Mexico. I know it doesn't have the same poetic ow as deep in the heart of Texas, but I defy anyone to find a larger cluster of brightly twinkling stars anywhere on this planet than in New

Mexico. We continued my favorite trip (especially now with Susan as my companion) and turned north at Flagstaff and reached the south rim of LeGrande Canyon. Susan had never seen it, and as I looked at it once again with Susan standing on the edge, it was never more beautiful. We stayed the night at the El Tovar Lodge, saw the sunrise over the canyon, and then headed south toward Phoenix to visit an old "Group" friend, Ronnie Thoene, where we would play an assassin's game of Monopoly. Of course, I wiped everybody out. I tried to talk Ronnie into meeting us in Las Vegas, but he declined. We then drove north to old Route 66, then west to Kingman, Arizona (the home of Andy Devine), and turned right to head north to Las Vegas . . . maybe my favorite place on earth.

We arrived in Las Vegas, and the Castaways called to me. (The Castaways casino was eventually torn down for the building of the Mirage with its fiery water spewing from the man-made volcano.) e Castaways had a Polynesian theme, and it was just a storybook location. I was there with the most beautiful lady in the world and was very ready to win some "big bucks." I was well prepared as I had $200 in my wallet and had hidden another $200 in my suitcase that I didn't tell me about. You know, just in case things turned very sour. Around 8 p.m. or so, I approached a $3 table and started working on my fortune. I took $50 from my wallet and bought in. Beautiful Susan, in her white lace dress with a touch of turquoise piping around the neck and sleeves, stood behind me and watched. I was very lucky getting cards and betting them properly. Betting $3 a hand eventually caused my "buy-in stake" to reach $100. During the evening, I never went back in my pocket for another $50. Susan was very impressed, which really set the tone for our next forty-two years together and her very positive belief in my blackjack playing. Susan didn't gamble at all, so she walked around the casino a lot.

Around 10:30 p.m. or so, she stopped back at the table and said, "Don, I'm really sleepy. I'm going to the room. Wake me up when you come to bed." e dealer looked at me as if I were a fool to turn down such an invitation, but I continued playing anyway. is also set a precedent for many years to come. If I turned down her invitation in Las Vegas, she knew I couldn't be tempted to leave the table by those Vegas bimbos.

Night went on and on, and in the morning, I was still at the same table (a definite no-no from inveterate gamblers) when Susan tapped me on the shoulder and said, "Good morning, sailor, how are you?"

I had been extraordinarily lucky and had built up quite a stake. I still had not gone back in my pocket for another $50. She was standing behind me when I was dealt a pair of sevens to the dealer's six showing. My wagers had grown to $20 per hand, so I split and put up another $20. The first seven was hit with a four, so I doubled down on that and put up another $20. Now I have $60 on one hand of blackjack. The next seven was hit with another seven, so I split again . . . there goes another $20. The first seven was hit with a three, so I doubled down with another $20. At this point, I was trying desperately to remain very calm and professional; however, my right leg started vibrating. e next seven (four total) was hit with a ten, so I stayed. The dealer flipped his cards, and just as I hoped, he had a ten in the hole. Sixteen total, he had to hit. It was another seven! Bust! I won $120 on that one hand, however complex, of blackjack. Susan was so impressed that I felt that cloud nine had just passed by and we hopped on. I won over $1,300 with that evening's play. The pit boss came over and offered to buy breakfast for us. After breakfast, we went to check out of our room and pay the bill. The hotel desk clerk said, "No charge, sir. The Castaways has paid for your room." at one evening cemented my love for Las Vegas that continues to this day.

We then loaded the car with our luggage and my winnings and headed toward the Mexican border. Susan spoke fluent Spanish. I had three years of Latin, but very few people spoke conversational Latin, so I was relying totally on her as my interpreter. We crossed the border just south of Tucson and entered through Nogales. What seemed like a thundering hoard of eight-year-old Mexican waifs surrounded me upon arriving in Nogales, asking for money to watch my car. I became very nervous, but Susan came to my rescue and said something to those kids, and they skedaddled.

I learned several very important phrases such as "Dos Pepsis, por favor," "Donde esta el banyo?", as well as my breakfast order, "Buenos dias, senorita. Quisiero tener daysauna? Dos huevos con jamon e café negro, por favor." Every time I visited Mexico since, those simple phrases came in very handily.

We continued due south to Hermosillo, a thriving (?) town in northern Sonoma. It appeared to be around 110 degrees but felt like 180 or so, so we stopped at the first hotel/motel that had a swimming pool and checked in immediately. We had a great time in the pool as long as we were submerged. Afterwards, we went to our room, changed for dinner, and entered the restaurant, which had a band playing. There were maybe fifty or so people at tables, and when we walked in, the bandleader tapped his baton on the podium. The band stopped playing, then the band started playing a different song. Everyone stood and applauded toward us. To this day, I don't know for sure who they thought we were, but I have speculated with many possibilities. Susan closely resembled Cher, Barbara Feldon (99 in Get Smart), and Marlo Thomas. She also bore a strong resemblance to Jane Fonda. It is possible that the hotel could have mistaken her for a celebrity. Another thought that occurred to me was, perhaps it was my name that confused them. Marquess is a British title, just below a Duke, so maybe that confused them. We were happy with the standing ovation anyway.

After a luscious dinner with pineapple pie for dessert, we made it back to the room. We entered the room, and the temperature and humidity were just like outside. Steamy!

We put on our pajamas and soon realized that sleep was impossible. It was unbearably hot and humid.

I called the front desk and the clerk kept saying, "Mucho color, mucho color."

Susan helped by saying we wanted "mucho frio". He didn't seem to care. So just dressed in our pajamas and morning clothes, we left that hotel with our luggage and drove to a nearby hotel/motel that had neon icicles flashing on and off. Before signing the book, we had asked to enter the room . . . it was ice-cold. Bingo!

We had a beautiful evening sleep in the air-conditioned room. We found out later that "air-cooled" from the first motel basically meant a fan blowing over a pan of water. The next morning, upon awakening, Susan had heard many great things about Guymos, a vacation village directly on the Sea of Cortez that was due south of Hermosillo, and she thought it would make a nice day trip. So, without checking out of the second hotel (we had also not checked out of the first hotel), we headed for Guymos. We liked it so much that we checked into a resort to spend the night.

This was a night that we paid for three hotel rooms in Mexico, and as I recall, the total amount of all three hotels was $34. Total! Our premarriage honeymoon could not have been any better.

What a magnificent trip.

Berkshire Hathaway

In 1955, my brother's wife, Millie, worked for a stockbroker named John Heslop who was with a firm named Reinholt and Gardner. She was his administrative assistant and heard about many stocks, which she told my mom about. My mom and dad mostly invested in mutual funds, investments that had low risk and small profit potential, but were pretty safe investments. My mom had $1,000 to invest one day and Millie told her that Mr. Heslop liked two stocks, Berkshire Fine Spinning and Peabody Coal, which was a solid company established in 1883, the year my maternal grandfather was born. So, my mom spent her $1,000 between those two companies. She bought ten shares of Berkshire and forty shares of Peabody. She told me at the time the Berkshire company made Hathaway shirts, and she bought that stock for me. I didn't think about it again until my breakfast buddy, Peter Marcus, a fine artist and professor at Washington University, told me about a conversation he had with friends the night before at dinner.

Peter said that the conversation had turned to stock investments and a stock named Berkshire Hathaway was $1,700 per share. What? Who ever heard of a stock priced that high? I wondered if that had any connection to the Berkshire Fine Spinning stock my mom bought way back in the fifties. So, the next day I called her and asked.

"That is the worst stock we have ever owned! It never paid a dividend, and it never split, it is a useless stock." (My parents only bought stocks for the interest and dividends.)

"But Mom, it is $1,700 a share!"

"I don't care, it never pays anything to its shareholders! You can have it, I bought it for you."

My, my, that sounded great to me. I said "Swell mom, do it."

By the time it was transferred weeks later, the stock hit around $2,600 per share. It was like the heavens opened and showered me with money. Whoever heard of a stock being $2,600 per share? The transfer was made, and I had those shares in my grubby paws! I got reports from the company for a while, and the stock hovered around $2,500 per share. My son Donny was invited to the National Music Camp in Interlochen, Michigan, and my son Danny was going to Camp Taum Sauk that summer. Piffle. I had the bucks if I cashed in my "useless" Berkshire stock. So, I sold it for $2,500 per share—big bucks a share. I sat back and admired myself for my incredible brilliance!

Not so fast, Dumbo! That stock today as of this writing closed at $442,000 per share! I could buy Cleveland with that money (not really, but it would be a lot of cash).

As a realistic remark, I know for certain that I would not still have that stock today. I would have sold it long before it came anywhere close to a measly $300,000 per share.

As a side note, I had that stock being held in my account with A. G. Edwards in St. Louis, where I had also purchased a stock named Marinduque Mining at .01 per share. My stockbroker, Alan Hartman, said that I was not his largest customer, but certainly his most diverse!

Burt Reynolds - Peachtree Plaza

It was early in 1981 when the Ceramic Tile Distributors Convention was held at the Peachtree Plaza Hotel in Atlanta. While I was standing in line checking in at the hotel, my good friend, Bill Haslett, the district manager for a German tile manufacturer, saw me in line and came up to speak with me. The usual "How are you, what's new, etc." were exchanged, and then the really important subject of where we would dine that evening was discussed. There was a sign next to the registration desk advertising

Nikolai's Restaurant, which boasted five stars and wonderful French/Russian cuisine. Bill and I both thought that sounded just fine for dinner that evening, and so we asked about a reservation. The lady at the desk said that they were booked five months in advance and dinner for us that evening was a pipe dream, so we decided to look elsewhere. Other acquaintances saw us and started conversing, so we tabled our dinner venue discussions.

Later that afternoon, the owner of Epro Tile, Suzi Stillson, a tile manufacturer that I represented in St. Louis, called and invited me to dinner that evening at Nikolai's. Stupe ed, I asked how she managed to get the reservation when they were booked five months in advance. She said that she called a friend in Pittsburgh who made the reservation. Not asking any further questions about that, I asked if I could bring my friend, Bill Haslett. She said, of course, she knew Bill and he was always a welcome guest. She had a table for six and there was room for Bill. It was dinner at 7:30 p.m., and Bill and I were pleasantly surprised and definitely up for it.

Nikolai's Restaurant was an elite white tablecloth and tuxedoed waiter's restaurant and one of the most elegant dining rooms I had experienced. The host escorted all six of us to the table, and the table next to us was occupied by Burt Reynolds, Brian Keith, and a few others. They were there for the filming of Sharky's Machine. All six of us were greatly impressed. I can't remember who the other three guests at our table were, nor who the other three or four at Burt Reynolds' table. I feel certain that if one of them was either Sally Field or Loni Anderson, I would remember, so apparently neither was at the table.

The entire event, dining at a restaurant that had a five-month wait, and a table next to Burt Reynolds put all of us in a very giddy mood. It was an evening where everything was funny, and we laughed at just about anything continuously until the waiter came to take our orders. The waiter informed us that a specialty of the house for dessert was their Grand Marnier soufflé. And since it would take a long time to prepare, we needed to order it when we ordered our meals. at sounded just great to all of us, so we ordered three soufflés. I remember clearly that I ordered an entrée of a venison stew, which was delicious. My chair was to the back of the Burt Reynolds table, so I couldn't see him during dinner. Everybody else could, though, and it was hard to make eye contact with the other diners at our table. Everything that was said at our table caused a giddy response from us, and I began to think we were making a scene. The dining highlight, the Grand Marnier soufflé, was being placed directly in front of Bill and I. The waiter then scooped a long cylinder of frozen whipped cream and laid it on the center of the oblong soufflé bowl. As the steaming soufflé began to melt the frozen cream, the cylinder started to turn vertical and sink. Saying nothing, I saluted as if it were a sinking ship. Bill noticed this first and broke up in laughter. Everyone else at the table also saw me saluting and laughed uproariously. We were definitely making a scene and somewhat out of place in this very elegant room.

After the check came, which was paid by Suzi (great news), we all got up to leave. I turned to the table of Burt Reynolds, who was wearing a tan corduroy jacket with blue jeans, and said to him, "I know this has been driving you crazy all evening, but I am Don Marquess!" He exploded with laughter as did the rest of his table.

Dr. Dick

Richard London was my best friend as I was growing up (an achievement still in progress), and we both felt that the world was our play toy. We had much fun together and the world was our oyster.

We lived a block away from each other. One day, Dick and I were talking on the phone together, and Dick asked me to hold on a moment. A few minutes later, there was a knock at my back door while I was holding the phone waiting for Dick to come back on the line. I ran to the back door saw Dick there and said "Come in, I am on the phone," then I realized how dumb that was.

Months later, we were walking next to a phone booth at Hampton Village when the phone in the booth was ringing, I went to answer it, and there was no one on the phone. I pretended to talk for a moment and called out to Dick, "It's for you!" Dick walked to the booth, picked up the phone and realized that I got him back.

One very delightful evening, driving with all of the windows open in the car, we pulled up to a stop light and to our right was a car with two great looking girls with their windows open as well. I heard Dick yell at the top of his lungs something very obscene regarding those girls and how deliciously attractive they were. I turned and saw Dick scrunched on the floor below the window, and the only one visible to those girls was me. I received a glare from them thinking I was the person that said that horrible thing regarding them. Dick was hiding out of sight on the floor, laughing his vulgar head off! I was so embarrassed that those girls would think I said those really bad things. Even way back then, four-letter words were not part of my vocabulary. Dick knew it, and he loved embarrassing me so.

One of our favorite things to do when we entered Howard Johnson's or Steak and Shake, we would choose a booth next to a couple of really old ladies (probably fifty or so), and we would sit and start talking nonsense loud enough for them to eavesdrop and try to follow our conversation. The rules for our conversation were this: Neither one of us could say anything that had to do with what the other one of us was saying. Our conversations typically would be like this:

DICK: Is she feeling better now after the attack?

DON: I can't make it Saturday. Let's try for Sunday.

DICK: I have eaten there before and got really sick on that fish.

DON: I think political science or Asian tropical diseases.

DICK: It is now showing at the Esquire Theater. I would love to see it.

DON: Yes, that is right. She should never wear that again. Those colors just don't work together.

DICK: I've got $12 dollars, maybe that is enough

DON: I think he has some burr or something in his right front paw.

And so on and on.

We felt it was so much fun putting them in a situation of trying to figure what the hell we were talking about.

We also created a vocabulary of great words that to date have no meaning. Wonderful sounding words that have no definition. We created these great words that eventually will certainly be given meaning, they are just too wonderful to have no assignation.

Words: Snargel, Zorch, Twimbel, Thobblewakky, and the finest word ever, Urbrumpoo!

We felt then, as I do now, those words are just too wonderful to have no meaning. Dr. Dick and I are still hoping!

Dick continued on with his life and became a noted psychologist in helping patients overcome their summer crazies. (Totally disregarding his own as well as mine.)

Karen – Busch Stadium Attendant

My brother and his wife, Millie, didn't visit very often since they lived about five hundred miles away in Shreveport, Louisiana. But when they did visit, it was always an enjoyable meeting. At the end of one particular visit, we were all in my driveway saying "goodbye," "have a safe trip home," etc., when Millie asked Susan about Natalie, Susan's sister in Sonoma, California. Sadly, that answer was not a short one. After about ten minutes of Natalie talk, Susan made the blunder of asking Millie about one of her thirteen brothers and sisters. Millie talked for about eleven minutes (she just had to outdo Susan) talking about her sisters Linda and Ann. Okay, that should have been it . . . "Goodbye, have a great trip home." But no, Susan asked Millie about Bruce and Steve, her sons. Egad, that went on for another fifteen minutes or so. I was getting very restless because now it was 12:30 p.m. and the Cardinals game was starting at 1:15 p.m. I lived and died with my beloved Cardinals (One year, I attended seventy- five of their eighty-one home games), and our house was about twenty minutes from the stadium. So, say goodbye again for God's sake and make it take this time!

No luck. More questions and very lengthy answers. Finally, after about fifteen minutes, they got in the car and backed out of our driveway. I kissed and hugged beautiful Susan, and got in my car thirty minutes before the first pitch to the visiting Los Angeles Dodgers. Hoping there were no radar police vehicles on I-44, I raced to the ballpark.

I always parked at the same lot directly across the street from Busch, and Karen, the parking lot attendant, always placed an orange cone in my parking spot. I made the mistake of tipping her $20 the first game of the year (opening day) and I became her lifetime friend, and she always had that cone in my spot. e game was starting in eight minutes when I arrived. She moved the cone, and I parked in my spot right next to the street, so all I would have to do is park, exit, and trot across the street to the entrance just around the stadium to my entrance gate and I wouldn't miss the first pitch. Not today. Karen heard Jack Buck mention my name on the Cardinals broadcast regarding one of my photographs during the game before on Saturday and she wanted to talk about it. Good grief, doesn't anyone understand the importance of the first pitch? Well, I had to be polite and chat a little. I didn't want to be rude to the lady that held my spot on the lot, so I chatted for a few minutes before I got out of the car into the ninety-plus-degree weather to get to the game. I almost ran into the entrance, stopped at my favorite refreshment counter, purchased my jumbo dog with mustard, relish, and jalapenos, my bag of peanuts, my large Diet Coke, and just made it to my seat in time for the first pitch. Whew, I actually made it despite all of the chattery delays. However, when I reached in my pocket for my money clip, I didn't feel my car keys. Maybe I put them in my other pocket. No time to think about that now, the game was starting. I took one big bite of my dog, slurped on my Diet Coke, and opened my scorecard for a glorious day of baseball. Clear blue skies, slight balmy breezes, and a ninety-plus-degree temperature, I would get my keys out of my other pocket at the end of the game. is game was tied in the bottom of the ninth 3–3 and went into extra innings. e game ended with the Cardinals beating the "Dodgahs" 5–3 in the bottom of the twelfth inning. As usual, two-and-a-quarter-hour game was pushing four hours, but I was very happy (baseball games can't last too long for me, especially with a Cardinals victory), so I started to head for the parking lot to fetch my new Lexus (only three months old).

I exited the stadium and reached in my right pocket for my keys. Oh, oh, no keys. I searched my left pocket once again . . . no keys. My other pockets had the same result. Now, as I was about to round the stadium, I thought I may have dropped them outside of the car. Oh boy, a new Lexus with keys on the concrete parking lot floor just inviting someone to take my car and drive it away. I thought my car would be gone. However, as I rounded the stadium, I saw my car standing alone in my perfect parking spot. It was the only car left on the lot as many people left early due to the extra inning game. As I got to my car, I started looking around the front door of the car hoping I would see the keys . . . No luck, no keys! I thought maybe they dropped on the floor of the car, so I hoped I hadn't locked it. I reached the door handle, opened the door, . . . and . . . a . . . freezing blast of cold air hit me in the face! I had left the car running for almost four hours right in front of Busch Stadium where forty thousand-plus fans saw the game. Probably ten thousand people or more walked past my car.

That says many things. e engine of my Lexus was super quiet, and Cardinals fans are honest upstanding citizens (who apparently didn't hear the engine running).

Naja Karamaru

There was a burlesque theater in St. Louis called the Grand, where they had old burlesque comedians and skits plus four or five exotic dancers (strippers), including a top star. Our group saw that a headliner named Naja Karamaru was going to appear. We knew nothing about Naja, but the teaser photo in the Post-Dispatch looked like she was gorgeous. The four of us, Roger Goessling, 6'5"; Gary Duecker, 6'7"; Larry Giesing, 6'2"; and me, 6'1", thought it would be fun for us to attend the show. In truth, none of us had been there before. We had a smart-ass plan, which was for us to purchase several newspapers, sit in the front row, watch the comedians, and laugh at their age-old and tired jokes and skits. Then when the strippers came out, we would ignore them and read the papers until their act was over, put the newspapers down, watch the comedians, then continue reading the newspapers when the next stripper came out. It was just a plan made by smart alec teenagers, but we thought it would be really funny (at least to us).

I know that was a dumb and insulting thing for us to do to the dancers (strippers); however, this prank was not my idea. Nevertheless, all of us were very willing to participate and thought it would be great fun. It was a devilish prank, and the four of us, being well over six feet and taking up four seats directly in the front row, were certainly obvious to the others in the theater. We may have been the only ones enjoying our prank, but we certainly thought it was funny.

Then the emcee announced the headline exotic dancer (stripper), Naja Karamaru. Wow! She came on stage, and one by one, we slowly dropped our newspapers and just stared and lusted after Naja. She was built like she was drawn by Al Capp (Lil' Abner's Daisy Mae, or Moonbeam McSwine) and possessed a drop-dead gorgeous smile, and she kept looking directly at us. She was also a great dancer and extremely adept with classic and very beautiful movements. As her act continued and her clothes dropped, she proved that she was indeed an incredible feminine specimen. This was 1958, and we had never seen such a beautiful lady. It didn't matter to us that at the end of her act, she still was a lady and remained partially clothed. We fell in love anyway. Her act ended too soon, but we all were very happy that we saw her. Burlesque was not what we thought.

There was a hotel directly connected to the Grand called the York Hotel, and we assumed that it was where the dancers were being housed. We really wanted to meet Naja. It was decided that I would be a Brazilian who spoke no English but was a close friend of Naja's, and I was just visiting St. Louis and saw that she was appearing there. So, the four of us entered the hotel lobby and walked up to the front desk. I said some gibberish to my friends that I felt sounded Spanish, and Gary Duecker interpreted to the desk clerk that I spoke no English and was a very close friend of my aunt Naja. I continued blabbering in Spanglish with no meaning to any of my created words when the desk clerk turned to me and, in perfect Spanish, started speaking to me. I was at a total loss as what to say, and he continued speaking directly to me in Spanish (at least it certainly sounded like real Spanish, but it may have just been a higher form of gibberish), so I looked at my three friends, said my gibberish, turned, and headed for the door. They followed with great speed and the jig was up. However, it was a fun afternoon no less!

What time is it?

When I was seventeen, I started my first year at Missouri University. I had never been away to live before, and my mom's baby (me) was leaving home. She was very worried that I would oversleep and miss my morning classes, so she bought an alarm clock for me. This was no ordinary alarm clock, although it looked like many I had seen before, with a planger of some sort resting between two round-shaped bells. The bells could cause severe hearing loss if you didn't turn it off in time. However, that was not what made it so horribly treacherous. It didn't just ticktock, it TICKTOCKED! e sound was deafening. My roommate, Roger, thought it was the most obnoxious sound he had ever heard. Finally, after trying many parts of our dorm room that would somewhat soften the unrelenting tick tock, tick tock, we decided to put it in the closet with the door closed tightly. Still, with the lights out and in our respective beds, we could still hear, just like Poe's Pendulum . . . tick tock tick tock tick tock!

I need to tell you that our dorm was brand-spanking-new and was just constructed in the middle of a eld on the campus. There were four structures that were basically monuments to mediocrity, just simple concrete block structures with the distinct and very imaginative names of C, D, E, and F. We were in Hall F. (Apparently, someone named Hyde had made a donation of some sort, so our half of the building was named Hyde House in Hall F.) Our building was just a cow pasture away from Crowder Hall, the feeding trough for freshmen.

One morning at breakfast, the occupants of the room directly below us were talking about the obnoxious noises they were hearing from the eld as they were trying to go to sleep at night . . . cows mooing, dogs barking, and probably a few mountain lions roaring. Hyde House, Hall F had no air conditioning, so all of the room windows were kept open. My roommate and I never heard these feral sounds, as they were all shielded from our ears by the incessant tictacking of the monster clock.

Later that evening as nighty-night time had arrived and while listening to the killer clock's never-ending tick tock tick tock, I said to my roommate, Roger, "With all of the weird sounds our dorm mates are hearing, what would they think of hearing our (my) clock outside their window?" I was thinking that it would really make them wonder what would come next. We rigged up a sling of sorts with two belts, attached the killer clock, and slowly started lowering it to what we felt would be their window. e ticking was deafening. We held tight to our suspending strap waiting to hear them being awakened by yet another strange sound when suddenly, the sling went limp. I knew that our makeshift strapping had given away and the monster clock had fallen to its death in a crashing blow to the ground beneath. I, while in my pajamas, left the room, went down the stairs, and around the back of Hall F. I had no ash light and it was a cloudy night, so I had no assistance of moonlight. My roommate, Roger, was at our window waiting to hear the damage report. He called to me asking if I had found it, and I said, "No, dang it," thinking it must have bounced somewhere close to the building.

Our neighbors, the victims of our caper, apparently were awakened by my roommate and me talking about the loss, and one of them called through their window and asked, "What are you doing outside waking us up when it is so late?"

I said, "I lost something and can't find it."

They said, "What did you lose?"

I said, "My alarm clock."

They said, "Your alarm clock? How could you lose an alarm clock outside of the building?"

I replied, "That's a story for another time, but in the meantime, where in the hell did it land? I think I should be able to find a piece of it or something."

"How can you lose an alarm clock? Wait until morning, then you will find it," they both said.

My roommate, Roger, just said, "Come back. I'll help you when it is light in the morning."

So, I went back upstairs, turned out the light, and got into bed . . . still worried about my alarm clock. Then I heard . .

. tick tock . . . tick tock . . . tick tock coming from under my bed. It was the killer clock!

Then my roommate and the downstairs neighbors, who were hiding outside our door, started laughing uproariously. e ticking of the clock did indeed awaken them, and they looked out their window and saw my clock dangling. They retrieved it and just let me search for it. A big haha!

April McIntire

During my photography career, I purchased my film and photographic paper supplies from either Schiller's Camera (the one most professional photographers frequented) and Creve Coeur Camera, which catered to both hopeful amateurs and pros. Joe Crabtree was the sales person that I usually dealt with. One day, I came in and next to Joe at the counter was a very attractive lady. She was tall and cleverly constructed with long brunette hair, beautiful brown eyes, and a delightful smile. I just had to meet her. I was very happily married to my beautiful wife, Susan, and never strayed, and had no intention of doing so; however, I just had to have Joe's new assistant wait on me. Joe could tell that I (like every red-blooded male in the store) wanted to meet her. Her name was April McIntire.

I picked up a package of professional photo wipes, brought it up to the counter and asked her if she could help me.

"Good morning, ma'am, I am frustrated. All I can find are these professional photo wipes, where are your amateur photo wipes?"

She looked very puzzled. Joe Crabtree standing behind her was silently laughing, and she said to me, "I don't think there is such a thing as amateur photo wipe. What is wrong with these?"

"Well," I replied, "I am not a professional and really shouldn't try to use these . . . I don't know how, I would probably make many mistakes."

Joe interrupted the exchange and said, "April, meet Don Marquess, he is just pulling your leg." (Didn't I wish.)

April had a very delightful sense of humor in addition to being a very attractive lady, so she became my sales person whenever I went to Creve Coeur Camera. April was a photographer as well and offered to mount my portfolio prints, as she was quite good at doing so. I used April as the hostess for several of my gallery shows, and people seemed to like her as much as my photos. (Later I referred to my photos as "images" rather than "photos." My good friend Lewis Portnoy, Hall of Fame photographer, told me I could charge more if I called them images.) April and I became good friends, and she mounted the prints I made for five or six of my portfolios.

We had a very fun working relationship. Susan met her and thought she was a delight.

One afternoon, as I approached her at the counter, she met me with a great smile and said, "Don, I finished my portfolio, would you like to see it?"

April was a very beautiful lady who was an aspiring photographer, so I welcomed the opportunity and was anxious to see her work. She reached under the counter and brought out a very nice black portfolio album, opened it to the first black and white photo, and there standing next to a tree in a heavily wooded area was April . . . totally naked! Yikes! I was speechless and totally dumbfounded. I had wondered for a long, long time just what was hidden under her clothes, and here in beautiful black and white was her naked body with those beautiful brown eyes looking directly at the camera. I couldn't believe it. I had no Idea what to say. I probably said nothing while trying to keep from stuttering.

I had a very good friend, an architect, Bob Entzeroth, who was a Fellow in the AIA, and when we were having lunch one afternoon at his St. Louis Club, I related my April McIntire story. I said, "Bob, I thought about her great body for years, and I guess like every guy I knew, I desired to see it unclothed. When it was there staring at me in glorious black and white, I became embarrassed and didn't know what to say."

Bob just looked at me with his devilish eyes and said, "There was only one thing to say . . . nice tits, babe!" (That was Bob, always knowing just the right thing to say at just the right time.)

The Most Incredible Day

We, the Missouri Brick Company, were supplying a new slip-resistant floor tile to a facility in Branson, Missouri, named White Water, a fantastic water park the likes of which neither of us, Bill Haslett nor I, had ever seen. Bill Haslett was the U.S. representative for the German manufacturer of the tile we furnished for that water park. White Water was around 250 miles away, so we left around 5:30 in the morning for our 10 a.m. meeting. e tile was a brand-new product manufactured in Giessen, West Germany, named "Grip Glaze." It had a very high coefficient of friction and was pure white resembling a slightly puffy cotton ball. Just an explanation regarding "coefficient of friction," that meant that bare feet, leather, and rubber would not slide nor slip easily on its surface. The only problem with it was White Water was having a difficult time cleaning it, and the mops they were using were leaving fabric traces on the floor. Bill and I went to a hardware store and purchased a proper sponge mop and the problem was solved. We felt very heroic and we left them very happy.

When we left around dawn to travel to Branson, Missouri, we had four hours or so of conversation, which was great because we were good friends and enjoyed each other's company. After our meeting in Branson, we decided that if we had time, we would stop in Union, Missouri (sort of on the way back), and meet with a fabricator on a sizable federal project. Our discussions also included big fun because later there was to be a Cardinals/Cubs game at Busch Stadium in St. Louis and maybe we could make it back in time for that. Also, Bill Haslett was a big fan of horse racing, and just across the Mississippi from St. Louis was Fairmont Park, the local horse racetrack. Wow, what grandiose plans for one day. I also told Bill that if we had time to make it to the racetrack, I would bet the trifecta, and if I won, I would give him 10% of my winnings.

Well, well, everything worked out perfectly, all visits turned out positively, and all of our meetings were very productive, and they were over soon enough to give us enough time to pick up my son, Donny, and make it to Busch just before the first pitch. e game was over quickly (Cards won and beat those stinking Cubs), so we had enough time to make it to Fairmont Park for the last couple of races. I picked a horse in the eighth race that won and paid $4.80. So, for my $10 wager, I won $24. e next race was better. I picked the winner and won the exacta and my win wager... ka-ching, and another $182.75. Things were going very well. Then the tenth race with the trifecta race was coming up. I placed my usual bet of $6 on the trifecta, $10 on the exacta, and $10 to win. My evening was going very well. e long shot I picked as the third horse finished first, so sadly, I lost my win bet and my exacta bet. However, the trifecta paid $1,850. What an incredible day. When we walked out to pick up my car from the valet, it was already waiting for us.

I counted out $185 to give to Bill for his promised percentage, and he received it very graciously . . . at least for a little while.

Then he said, "You know, I am really mad. is morning on our way to Branson, you knew you were going to win the trifecta. You knew! If you didn't know you were going to win, you would have given me half instead of this lousy $185!"

What an incredible day.

The True Definition of Art

The Saturday morning breakfast group that I was invited to join in 1982 still exists today, although there has been many changes in members in the last forty-one years. Some moved, some passed away, and new breakfasters joining. When it started, it was with a group of professional photographers. Lew Portnoy (Hockey Hall of Fame: Photographer's Wing), Chuck Dresner

(St. Louis Zoo's official photographer), Bob Bishop (Stanford University, Ansel Adams Workshops, and Purina Cat Calendar), Neil Sauer (Anheuser Busch photographer, top photo studio in the Midwest), and Herb Wightman (director of photographic services at Washington University and St. Louis Football Cardinals's photographer)—a prestigious group indeed. I was invited because of my Great Forest Park Balloon Race art photos and the recent success I had with those photos. The breakfasts were a great relief to business and deep and serious personal issues were definitely verboten. In later years, we invited the noted psychiatrist, David Berland, to keep us on the straight and narrow. Recently we invited the retired exhibits director for the St. Louis Art Museum and an excellent landscape photographer, Dan Esarey.

Herb Wightman, Lou Portnoy, and I attended a two-day seminar at Missouri Botanical Gardens by noted photographer, Ernst Haas, a world-famous photographer who excelled in black and white as well as color photography. A rarity in the photographic world to excel in both. The seminar was indeed educational and greatly enjoyable, as Ernst had a highly sophisticated sense of humor as well as a very insightful approach to photography.

After the second seminar, Ernst was approached by Herb Wightman, who had a photo to show Ernst and get his opinion. He showed the photo to Ernst, who looked at it and passed it back to Herb. Herb passed it back to Ernst, wanting him to look at it deeper, and immediately passed it back to Herb.

He said to Herb, "This photo is photojournalism, not art. It carried a message. I got it, and that is all I need to know. Art is determined by how long you want to look at it. I got the message, and that is all. You made your statement, and I got it, but it is not art." (If Ernst would have said that to me, I would have jumped out the window and sobbed while being pelted by the freezing rain.)

That statement of "Art is determined by how long you want to look at it" is the most descriptive statement possible that there could be regarding art. It applies to photos, paintings, drawings, music (how long you want to listen to it) automobiles, and beautiful women. If something about that piece of art compels you to look at it again and again, or to listen to it over and over, it is truly art. It applies to all classic pieces of anything that has endured the test of time!

Trip to Shreveport

As mentioned previously, Susan would not get on an airplane for any reason, so our travels together were always auto or train. I had planned to visit my brother in Shreveport, and Susan thought that a train trip would be just swell. I have no aversion to train travel. As a matter of fact, all of my trips to Europe have been with Eurail Pass—the only way to travel in Europe. Amtrak rail travel is significantly different in the USA. they use the same tracks as the freight trains (which gives great stress to the tracks, so the ride is not quite as smooth as the European trains). Also in the Midwest, freight rules, so the passenger trains do not receive the same priority.

Nevertheless, I was game for our train adventure to Shreveport. However, at that time there was no direct travel from St. Louis to Shreveport, so my brother would have to pick us up in Texarkana, Arkansas, and we would be traveling on the train for over fourteen hours. What a wonderful time for togetherness . . . hmm. Train travel in Europe consists of individual compartments that seat two or three on each side facing each other. My experience traveling during the day was that most compartments were empty and stretching out was great in the empty compartment. Not so in the USA. The train cars were more like bus or airplane seats. Susan and I went to the last section of the rail car where two seats were facing each other. These seats were available only at either end of the car.

When Susan was in college, she worked during the summer at a bank in Woodbury, New Jersey. She did this for several summers and really enjoyed it. The Bank of Woodbury (I think) was also a bank that offered employment to handicapped high school and college students during the summer recess. One of the students was hearing-challenged and used sign language. is student taught Susan the sign language alphabet, which Susan then taught me. Herein the story develops.

It had gotten late and many of the passengers in our car, I assumed, were sleeping, or at least trying to, so I didn't want to disturb them with my booming voice. I got Susan's attention and signed "Hi." She picked up on that and signed "Hi" back to me.

I then signed, "What is cooking, babe?" (I should point out that my expertise in signing was not with continuous and fluid motions. I had to think about each letter and form them, so she could understand, but being the fast learner, I thought I was becoming better with each word.)

Susan said to me with those beautiful hands of hers: "Hey, sailor, what are you doing later tonight?" She was warming up to this whole idea.

Then I said, "Did you hear about the traveling salesman who stopped at a farmhouse?" I was getting more and more dramatic with my hand motions and was actually creating a stir in the rail car with the other passengers. I couldn't see this because I was facing Susan, who was in the last seat in the car. She started laughing. is encouraged me to continue (showbiz), you know. Then I, very dramatically, started to sing to her with my hand signals (I was on a roll): "Old man ribber, that old man ribber . . .," Getting more animated with each line. Susan lost control and started laughing really, really hard. I was still not realizing that I had caused a curiosity with the rest of the car, and everyone was watching my wild gesticulations.

Just then, a man across the aisle reached over, tapped me on the shoulder, and spoke very loudly and distinctly, pronouncing every word, saying,

"What . . . time . . . is . . . it?"

This was my moment of truth. I had to make a decision, one way or the other. I said nothing but reached my hand across the aisle and showed him my watch. I had done it. I made a commitment to be deaf and able to speak in sign language only for the rest of our trip. I just couldn't let the man know, so I had to remain speechless. Susan, who had a remarkable sense of humor, realized the situation in which I had placed myself, gained her composure, and accepted the fact that I had to be totally nonverbal. From that point on, we could only converse in sign language. After several hours, we left that car and went to the next car.

As soon as the door closed, we both said, "Let's talk!"

Liar's Poker

The Saturday morning Breakfast Club originally consisted of many very successful photographers. Most photographers, or anyone in the public eye, have an ego. Actors, artists, vocalists, musicians, anyone who puts his talent on display has an ego for sure. The great Spencer Tracy said, "Acting is a great profession, but don't let anyone catch you doing it!" The appearance of humility, whether feeling it or not, is a necessity in life. One of our breakfast members had an ego off the charts, and exhibited it with remarkable regularity. He was a great golf photographer, and did extensive photographic assignments for major Fortune 500 companies. He always made a big point of letting us know of his "greatness." Out of respect for the photographic profession and my fear of being sued, he will remain nameless.

One Saturday morning when the breakfast check arrived, on one of the very rare times that I had a hundred-dollar bill in my possession (which remains true today). I stated with a very boastful way as I produced my hundred-dollar bill, "This is the smallest I have, does anyone have change?"

I thought that was very funny, as did the other breakfast guys, except one. The egotist pulled out a hundred-dollar bill and said, "Do you want to play Liar's Poker with our hundreds?"

I thought he was joking and said, "Sure. How do you play Liar's Poker?"

He explained that it is played with the serial numbers on the bill. Without showing the bill, you state how many matching serial numbers are on the bill. Two 2s is a pair, consecutive 5 numbers are a straight, three of anything is three of a kind, three of one number and two of another is a full house, and etc. My serial number had four 4s.

I said, "One pair." He believed me.

He said, "Two pairs." I believed him.

I said, "Three of a kind." He didn't believe me. I showed him my bill with four 4s and gleefully took his hundred. That dirty, lousy bum pulled out his money clip and fanned out twelve-hundred-dollar bills, just to show me how pitiful and insignificant my lousy one-hundred-dollar bill was.

So, I invited two of my friends and their wives, along with Susan, to go to dinner with me at the China Garden. After dinner, we all got in the car and called Mr. Egotist, and thanked him in unison for the fine meal he provided!

Ducks on Parade

My brother lived and practiced in Shreveport, Louisiana, and he was also my CPA, a damn good one I might add. I had a lot of "splainin'" to do with my income and expenditures, so it seemed like a trip to visit him was in order. This was in the spring as the Cardinals were heading north for the regular season. They were making stops in Louisville (Redbirds) and Memphis (Chicks) along their trip to St. Louis. My plan was to see both games on our way to Shreveport. They were playing a game in Memphis, which was the home of the very famous Peabody Hotel. It was the first trip in a while for the two of us, and I made a reservation for us on an executive (very exclusive as well as very expensive) floor. The Peabody Hotel is well known for a very unusual tradition of marching ducks. I told Susan about this phenomenon, and she couldn't wait to see it. I had stayed at the Peabody Hotel in Orlando, Florida, where the same tradition continued.

Every morning at around 11 a.m. or so, the elevator opens on the lobby floor and a man wearing a top hat and a tuxedo with tails, and who is holding a long baton, not unlike a drum major at a college football game, emerges followed by a dozen or so ducks. These beautiful, brown, multicolored, and highly disciplined English call ducks march in line to the King Cotton march and jump into the fountain lobby pool. They stay and frolic in the pool all day until five o'clock or so until the elevator opens again and the same tuxedoed and top-hatted leader comes to the pond, the marching music starts again and the ducks jump out of the pool and march in line to the elevator. It is truly a wonder to behold. They must be very smart ducks.

Susan was really looking forward to seeing it. There is a coffee shop/restaurant very close to where the ducks do their marching, so we decided to go down early and have a pre-"duck watch" snack. I had been very busy with my work, so Susan and I didn't have many opportunities to just sit and talk. She was telling a story about what I don't remember, but I was enraptured. The Peabody has been in existence since 1869 and probably the dishes and glassware that were used at the restaurant were the originals from that time. The reason I am mentioning this is that their glasses are not just glasses—they are very heavy sculpted red glasses. I am an ice chewer, and after drinking water, the ice cubes are a delicacy for an ice chewer. After chewing several cubes, that last one must be swirled and loosened so the last cube can slip down and be consumed. Well, as Susan was still finishing her story, unknown to me, the waitress had filled my glass again with water. I turned to get that last ice morsel, not noticing the difference in weight, swirled the glass, and threw the entire glass of water in my face. It was an absolutely ridiculous thing to do. I was dumbstruck, and Susan was astonished and laughing hysterically. I looked around and half the restaurant was looking at me and laughing. I was blank-faced. Now, further unfortunately, I was wearing khakis, and with the water explosion, my pants looked like I had a major bladder accident. I could not get up and reveal the huge wet area of my pants, but duck time was fast approaching. We sat, hoping my pants would dry somewhat and I could walk to the lobby. I loaded my lap with towels that the laughing waitress delivered trying to speed-dry my pants, but it still looked ridiculous. Then we heard the ducks' marching music.

Susan said, "I don't care how you look, we are going to see those damn ducks. Follow me."

So, like two dogs doing the nasty, I walked behind Susan, and with the march blaring, we made it to the lobby. Unfortunately, the crowd was about five deep and all we saw was the ring master's top hat as the elevator door was closing. We had a very silent road trip from Memphis to Shreveport.

Really Good . . . Then Really Bad

My entertainment career spanned for five to six years or so, and the original professional career included a trio in which a talented guitarist, John James, who had a beautiful tenor voice, but a total inability to harmonize, was the lead vocal. The building could fall down around the trio, and we knew that John's unfailing melody would survive. Years later, after my many involvements in other vocal ensembles, John was performing as a solo at a Ramada Inn in north St. Louis County. Susan and I went to hear him. His voice was still a beautiful unwavering tenor, and as a solo performer, he had no harmonizing challenges. After his first set, he came to our table to chat.

After the usual pleasantries were exchanged, he said, "I bought a gun today, and I am going home to murder my wife!" What?

Susan and I thought he was kidding, but after a few moments, we realized that he was dead (sorry) serious. He said that he found a letter from a visitor to his neighbor's house the week before, thanking his wife, Evelyn, in detail for the great sex he had with her the week before. John said he was going to go home, wake his daughter, confront his wife, and then kill her after letting his daughter know how bad her mom had been. He was serious!

I said, "John, for god's sake, don't do it, you will spend the rest of your life in prison or, worst, get the electric chair. Listen to me and do it this way. First of all, get rid of the gun. Take it back, or throw it in the bushes somewhere. Now, go home, discover the letter, and after reading it, become enraged. Go to the kitchen, grab a sharp knife, and stab your wife many times, drop the knife, and stand there stupefied for a few moments, then go to the phone and call the police and say—now this is very important John. Use these exact words and say to the police— 'I think I just killed my wife.' Temporary insanity, John, that is your defense."

Both John and my wife, Susan stared at me slack-jawed. John looked at me and finally laughed and said, "Wow . . . you are just as crazy as I am!" After his second set, Susan and I headed home, and she praised me for my brilliance in painting such a ridiculous picture for John so he would realize his stupidity. She said "Don, that was perfect, you knew just what to say to jar his mind. The two of you have been friends for so long that he realized how dumb his murderous plan was and you beautifully pointed it out to him. Bravo."

Then when we were halfway home, Susan said, "What if he does it just the way you told him?"

Yikes! We had a very uncomfortable silence for several moments after that. Then the glee and glorious praise for my suggestion turned quickly to trepidatious fright. What if he does it? Those words kept repeating over and over in my mind. The rest of the ride home was greatly horrific, wondering if he really would do it. It plagued our thoughts all night, and most of the next day.

I picked up Susan after work, and we both felt that just a casual drop by to John's house was in order. We drove over. Before knocking on the door, we looked through the back window at the kitchen and saw a dozen or so long-stemmed roses thrown on the floor, and the huge refrigerator face down on the kitchen floor. We knocked on the door, and John's wife, Evelyn, opened the door for us. Her eyes were puffy red, as she had obviously been crying for a while, and said to us "The marriage is over, and John just can't accept it."

John then came into the kitchen and said to us, "Thanks for checking on us, I am OK now."

John's next several marriages were not quite as colorful.

The Crushing of the Balls

In 1998, there were several possibilities of players who had the ability to beat Roger Maris's record of sixty-one home runs in a single season. Andres Gallaraga who hit forty-one home runs for the Rockies in 1997, Ken Griffey Jr. who hit fifty-six for the Mariners the year before, and our player,

Mark McGwire, who hit a total of fifty-eight in 1997 between the Oakland A's and the St. Louis Cardinals, and Sammy Sosa who hit thirty-six with the stinkin' Cubs in 1997. My hopes were on McGwire to break the sixty-one home-run record.

My grandfather started a machine company in 1917 and had many types of machines that I felt were capable of assisting me in achieving my goal depicting the breaking of the record. I contacted my uncle, Virgil, and told him what I wanted to achieve—the crushing of one side of the baseballs as if they had been struck on one side by a baseball bat. My uncle then had a stainless-steel mold made by some company in Tennessee that the ball could rest in as well as a stainless-steel rod that has the diameter of the sweet spot on a bat. They had a thirty-thousand-pound hydraulic press and fitted it with the ball support and the "bat." I brought the sixty-two balls to his company, Multiple Boring Machine Company, and the process commenced. I stood by, cutting the seams of some so it would appear that they were hit so hard that the seams split.

The balls looked like they had truly been hit by a bat, and I had achieved my goal.

That year, 1998, Mark McGwire didn't just beat the record of sixty-one home runs, but he crushed it, hitting seventy home runs. I took just one of the crushed balls and two uncrushed balls and put them in a simple composition titled The Babe, Roger, and Mark, with Mark McGwire's the only one in color and the rest of the balls in the photo are in sepia. We sold out in two weeks.

My original idea of just showing sixty-two crushed baseballs was put on hold once again.

We Hit the Big Time

In the early sixties, folk music was really a big thing with the Kingston Trio, the Limeliters, Peter, Paul, and Mary, and about four million other folk groups forming everywhere. I was in a trio of two very fine musicians, of which I was not one. I was a French horn and trumpet player, not a guitarist. Fortunately, it wasn't required because the other two guys in the group were accomplished musicians on the guitar and banjo. I handled the microphone introductions and hopefully the humor in the group. Many people said that I sounded just like Bob Shane in the Kingston Trio. I readily admit it was a conscious effort, but I guess I did sound like him.

Gaslight Square in St. Louis was an entertainment center much like Bourbon Street in New Orleans, and on any given night in the summer, there were very large crowds walking the street and entering one of the thirty-plus clubs and restaurants on this three-block section of St. Louis at the juncture of Boyle and Olive. We played at many of the clubs, including the Laughing Buddha coffee club, the Tiger's Den, and the Crystal Palace. The Smother's Brothers, Barbara Streisand (at the beginning of her career), Miles Davis, Woody Allen, and others performed at the Crystal Palace periodically.

We ended up at Jack's or Better for the better part of three years. Every club was packed each night, and Jack's was no exception. Jack was a brilliant club owner. Our first nightly show was at 9:00 p.m. There would be a crowd waiting to get in. Jack had all of the lights on high and charged a cover charge of five bucks a head with a two-drink minimum. He would fill the club, turn down the lights, and introduce the Town Criers (us). We would do a twenty-five-minute show, then leave the stage with the customers clapping.

Jack would say, "Let's bring 'em back." We came back, as preprogrammed, and did a twenty-minute or so encore, and then we would leave the stage. Jack would then turn the bright lights on again and clear the house for the next group waiting to come in. He would say as the house was clearing, "The Town Criers will be back at 9:00 p.m. tomorrow night." He would then let the next group in, and we would do another twenty-five-minute show, and Jack would play the same game, fill the house, and take their money. He would then graciously invite them back for the next night's performance. He didn't want any stragglers hanging around for the next show. He wanted those new cover charges.

Our last show was at midnight and there was always another throng waiting to get in. We were not great, but we were good enough, and everyone seemed to leave satisfyingly entertained. For all of the money that Jack turned six nights a week, on Saturday night, he paid us $360 to split with the three of us. Jack took in twice that amount with just one of our three nightly sets. But we were happy to receive the money for having a hell of a lot of fun and feeling like big stars.

Darlene Theusch (Née Gardner)

I opened my gallery in Plaza Frontenac Mall in 1995. Due to the hours required by the mall owners, I needed it to be open seventy-two hours per week. My son, Daniel, covered forty of those hours, but additional help was needed. Lucky for me, a recent art and photography major from Southwest Missouri State stopped by and applied for a job. She was hired immediately due to the fact that she was knowledgeable about art, quite personable, and very attractive. Darlene had all of the necessary attributes to promote and handle sales at the gallery. Plus, she was devoted to making the gallery all that it could be. We were moving to a larger space in the mall, and she asked if she could come in extra early to prepare things for the move. at was very meaningful to me.

I have another business in St. Louis that was started by my father in 1960. It was a brick distributorship aimed at the architectural community for large commercial projects. I needed sales help there and Darlene was the perfect candidate, so I read her from my gallery and hired her for Missouri Brick Company. She very quickly developed a strong following from the architectural community.

There are two very delightful anecdotes regarding Darlene.

We were driving in my car looking at a building to match the brick when Darlene asked about a large project that I was chasing for the brick selection. The project was the new St. Louis Cardinals Stadium. I wanted to furnish it with every fiber of my being. Darlene asked me how many brick would be needed for the new stadium.

I responded, "You want a ballpark estimate?"

Ignoring that ultra-clever remark, she said, "Yes, how many brick will be needed?"

Once again, I asked, "You want a ballpark estimate?"

She said once again, "Yes, I do."

So, I almost screamed, "A ballpark estimate?"

It finally dawned on her how clever a question that was. She made a gesture with her hand right over her head and said, "How could I have missed that?"

By the way, we received the order for the project and furnished 2.14 million brick for the construction of Busch Stadium III.

Another wonderful moment with Darlene is as follows. She was a great fan of my photography, and after viewing a couple of my latest images (Lew Portnoy taught me that if I called them images, I could charge more), she stated, "I don't understand why you aren't rich and famous. Your work is so great."

I said, "You know, Mozart died penniless!"

She said, "Yes, I know, but look how well he is doing now!"

The Presidential Suite

With the enormous success of folk music in the sixties, and our years on Gaslight Square, the largest hotel in St. Louis, the Chase Park Plaza wanted to cash in on the Folk Fad, so we were stolen from our Gaslight Square home of Jack's or Better and lured with a $650 a week salary. We jumped at the opportunity for fame and double fortune and went west to the big time Chase Hotel. That venue was highly respected by the press and a full-page article by Dickson Terry was written in the Post-Dispatch. All systems were ready for us to perform in the Steeplechase room. We were having lots and lots of fun singing in the top hotel in St. Louis, and with the press influence of the Chase, our reviews were terrific.

I have been a major Cardinals fan since I was eight years old and loved the Cardinals with every fiber of my being. In September of 1963, the Dodgers were playing a series in St. Louis and staying at the Chase. They all came to the Steeplechase room that evening where we were performing, and I was somewhat rude to them. The Cardinals were in a pennant race, and the Dodgers were strong contenders as well. That day, the Dodgers beat the Cardinals in a day game, and I was not happy with their arrival. Being such a huge fan, I was suffering from that loss and just couldn't contain my emotion, although the friendly jabs back and forth made for a very exciting performance. I feel it was our best show ever.

There was a late-night open cafe in the Chase named the Tack Room, and we all had a late-night snack together and they were very friendly and gracious to our trio. Sandy Koufax and Don Drysdale were especially nice to us. Leo Durocher not so much, but it was a fun late-night event for us anyway. Afterward, at 2:30 a.m. or so, we went to the dressing room to collect our coats, store our instruments, and head home.

Not so fast. Our key didn't open the dressing room. This was not good at all since our car keys, and other possessions were locked in the room. We went to the front desk, and the night manager said that earlier someone had broken in the room and took several of the items that the Mary Kaye Trio, who were performing in the big room, the Chase Club, so they had the locks changed. The manager said that we were supposed to have been delivered the new key, but apparently, we didn't notice the delivery, so we went back to the Steeplechase room. No envelope and no key! We were at a major loss and couldn't even get into our cars to head home. It was after 3:00 a.m., and we had no place to go. The hotel was sold out, no rooms, except one.

The night manager said, "How would you, guys, like a nice treat? The Presidential Suite is unoccupied for this evening, and you gentlemen can have it!"

We didn't have to think very long and jumped at the offer.

We entered the suite, and ye gods, what a suite! It had three bedrooms, a living room, a dining room, four bathrooms, and a two-story window with a great view of the city. We called our wives and woke them up to explain that we were spending the night in very plush accommodations. If my memory serves correctly, we didn't sleep at all, and just worked on some new songs and had a great time doing so. The acoustics were just great. Around 9:00 a.m., we went downstairs to get the new key from housekeeping and had a very difficult time deciding to return the Presidential Suite key, but reluctantly gave it back. I requested another dressing room lock change so we could spent the next night there, but the morning clerk said that room was available again for that night if we wished to pay $925. We declined the offer, but that suite alone was enough of an incentive to run for president. None of us did, however.

Garfield, The Wonder Goose

There was a wonderful restaurant in Clayton, Missouri, named the Leather Bottle, which had delightful lunch fare. It was an ideal place to take an architect to lunch, as they had a room that was filled with my hot-air balloon photos. I always felt somewhat special going there as they treated me very well. And no matter how crowded they were, they always seemed to find a table for me and my guests. e restaurant was owned by the Bland brothers, Kenny and Dick. They were both very bright, with Kenny being a world-class bridge player. e other brother, Dick, had a great sense of humor and loved pranks. One Christmas Eve, Dick and an architect friend of mine came to my house and brought me an unusual gift for Christmas.

I came home several hours later, and as I pulled in my driveway, my sons, Donny and Danny, came to greet me, saying, "Daddy, Daddy, you won't believe what we have."

Susan followed closely behind and said, "Don, we have a serious problem."

She led me to the basement door where down those steps to the basement was my workshop and my photographic darkroom. I walked into the workshop, and there tied to my radial arm saw was a large snow-white goose. I stepped into the workroom and skidded on my newly very slick floor. e goose relieved himself and started honking at me with an evil look in his eyes. This was Christmas Eve, and they brought it to me for Christmas dinner. Susan had already named the damn thing "Gar eld." How could we cook and eat something with a name? We had a walkway on the side of the garage that led to the back yard. There was a gate at the front, but no gate at the back, so I had to run to O. K. Hatchery to get some chicken wire to jerry-rig a goose pen. Just the thing I wanted to do on Christmas Eve. Big joke . . . thanks, guys.

Christmas came and went, and the goose became part of the family, apparently fairly comfortable in his runway on the side of our garage. Early one morning, a few days after Christmas, our phone rang, and it was our neighbor, Karen, who had a newborn, just a couple months old.

She said to me with total exasperation in her voice, breathing deeply between each word, and said, "Don, I haven't slept in days . . . the goose honks . . . the baby wakes and cries . . . the goose honks . . . the baby cries... the goose honks . . . you have got to do something."

I apologized and made another trip later that day to construct a goose pen in our backyard surrounding a fort that I built years earlier for the boys to play in. It was a fairly easy modification for this doggone goose. Gar eld and I hated each other, and every time I came close, he would honk at me and I would honk back at him even louder.

We purchased an historic home that was built in 1850 in Old Kirkwood. One of my first tasks was back to O. K.

Hatchery to purchase more chicken wire and supports for yet another goose pen. Each time I had to build another pen, I grew to despise that goose more and more. Susan, however, loved Gar eld, and became known as the goose lady of our neighborhood. She cared for that goose daily, and the two of them, Susan and Gar eld, became close friends. Gar eld became our "guard goose." Anyone that came within fifty feet of our property was greeted with an eardrum-cracking honk honk honk. He probably scared off many bad guys, but probably many good guys as well. I always felt that when Ed McMahon came to our sidewalk to present me with my ten million dollars, he was driven away by the killer goose. I learned that snow geese live to around fifteen years or so, and midway of Gar eld's sixteenth year, he sadly passed away. Susan asked me to take Gar eld to Clark Animal Hospital to have his body cremated.

Ten days or so later, the phone rang, and it was Dr. Clark from his animal clinic telling me that Gar eld was ready to be picked up. This opportunity only comes once in someone's life, so I placed my hand over the phone, called to Susan, and said, "Susan, your goose is cooked." I thought that was much funnier than she did.

Susan's Delightful Grandmother

Susan and I had been married for several years, and I had met her parents, her aunt, and her uncle; but I never met her grandmother, Mary Miller. Mary Miller came to St. Louis to visit for a week or so, and she and I got along very well. I gave her a day-long tour of my beloved St. Louis and impressed her greatly. I am very proud of this city and love to show people how great it is. Susan's grandmother lived in Woodbury, New Jersey, just North of Philadelphia and very close to New York City, so impressing her with the wonders of St. Louis was indeed a challenge. Mission accomplished. The tour ended with a concrete at Ted Drewes Frozen Custard (try to match that NYC).

We arrived at Susan's Uncle Burr's house after the tour, where we had a very scrumptious meal prepared by Burr's wife, Carolyn. It was a terrific day. After dinner, Susan's grandmother, Mary Miller, proceeded to relate her family history. She had an ancestry that was traced all the way back to the 1200s. She delighted in telling me how this man from Ireland married this lady from England, and how this Scotsman married this Londoner and so on. It seemed to be an endless story that delighted her in telling. I was very interested, but kept getting confused as to who married whom and when, and all of the names bombarded.

After this long dissertation, she looked at me with her sparkling and proudly dancing eyes and said, "And not one Catholic in the bunch!"

Well, well . . . I was baptized Catholic, had sixteen years of Catholic education, and actually considered becoming a priest at one time in my life. I certainly ruined the legacy and purity of her waspishness. I considered momentarily telling her, "Whoops, I just tainted your legacy."

I just couldn't let her know how I fouled up her entire family. So, I just said, "Gee, that is wonderful!" She seemed to agree, and we continued our friendly relationship as I drove her to the airport for departure.

When I told Susan about her grandma's boasting, she told me that she was so glad that I didn't reveal my Catholicism as Susan would have been ostracized for messing up the family purity.

The Deutschland Experience

In 1982, I had an invitation to visit Gail Tile's manufacturing plant in Giessen, West Germany, and to attend the massive "Constructa Fair" in Hanover. I jumped at the opportunity for many reasons. e least of which was the fact that I had never been to Europe and a trip overseas was very enticing. I couldn't wait. Susan, who in her former life was a travel agent for a company in Denver specializing in European travel, mapped out a fabulous trip for me after my business part of the travel. She booked the nicest hotels for me in all of the key cities I would be visiting and said that I needed at least three weeks to see all the sights. My mom had always wanted to go to Europe, but my father had zero interest in leaving the United States. So, I invited her to meet me in Nice and we would travel together. In principle, this was a terrific idea, but my mom snored with infinite decibels. So, after one night of sleeping on the bathroom floor, two rooms were a necessity. The itinerary that Susan had mapped out for me was terrific. After the Germany meeting, Susan had arranged for a Eurail Pass, which was a first-class pass for all of the European railroads which was designed to encourage international travel. It had to be purchased in the USA. With Susan's travel arrangements, this was to be my trip of a lifetime. My stops included Heidelberg, Zurich in Switzerland, Milan in Italy, Nice in France (where I was meeting my mom at the airport), Venice, Florence, Geneva, Paris, and London before our flight back to St. Louis. More about this post-trip later.

Leaving Lambert Airport in St. Louis and waiting on the tarmac, there was a slight mist in the air, and the sky was very gray and gloomy at two o'clock in the afternoon. The flight was around eleven hours to Frankfurt, and thanks to my close friend, Dr. David Berland, as I was on the plane, I entered the time of the arrival city on my watch. Then, when that time dictated my normal sleep hour, I took a Halcion sleeping pill to force me to sleep on the destination city's time. It worked beautifully. I landed in Frankfurt well rested. Arnold Schneider (head of international business, who was fluent in five languages) met me at the airport, and we drove to Giessen. It was a short thirty-three-mile drive to the Steinsgarten Hotel where we met with the other invitees, Bud Morris from Portland, Oregon, Harry Atherton from Richmond, Virginia, Bob Klinges from Pittsburgh, Pennsylvania, and Arnold Mozes from Boston, Massachusetts (I think). Since we were all together, we went to the front desk and found a pile of room keys awaiting us. We all grabbed a key and squeezed into the teenytiny elevator to our respective rooms. I was very well rested (I thought) but fell asleep very quickly, only to be awakened by a phone call from my beautiful wife, Susan, who asked how the flight was and how rested I was. She then informed me that St. Louis had the largest snowfall in thirty years and was totally immobilized in twenty-two inches of snow. We spoke for a while, and then I went back to sleep. e next morning in the breakfast room, several of the Gail Tile travelers asked if my wife had gotten in touch with me last night. The hotel operator didn't know who grabbed which room key, so several rooms were contacted before Susan found me. They all remarked about the big snowfall and how nice my wife sounded. I then worried about that international phone call bill.

The Gail people treated us like royalty, and wined and dined us in the top restaurants in the area. One night we were hosted at a very old castle named Staufenberg's Castle in Durbach, Germany. We were ushered in and given the bill of fare on a parchment scroll. The meal was decided for us and it looked fabulous. The first course was garlic soup, which arrived at our table in a large bowl containing the blackest soup I had ever seen. It was incredibly delicious; however, with the principal ingredient being garlic, it was greatly odorific. For days, intense scrubbing in the shower failed to remove the pungent aroma emanating from our pores. Personal distancing ruled for several days thereafter.

Every night, we dined in a different first-class restaurant, mostly white tablecloth tables and served by tuxedoed waiters. The food was outstanding.

Bill Klinges, who was of a fairly surly nature and had never been to Germany, kept saying that all he heard about German food was sauerkraut. How come he hadn't seen any sauerkraut? I felt this was a great insult to our German hosts who were treating us to absolutely delicious gourmet meals. I became aware that our Gail hosts considered "sauerkraut" a peasant food. It was some sort of an insult to the hosts who were treating us to very elegant Germanic cuisine.

We attended the Constructa Fair, which was an unforgettable experience with seven huge buildings devoted to construction materials. One building was entirely tile-related. e building trade fairs in the USA at that time were contained in one building, with small booths for vendors of various building materials to show their products. The U.S. shows generally were two to three days at most, which required exhibitors to display their wares in very quickly assembled displays that could be easily disassembled and packed away for the next trade show. Not so in Germany. The trade fairs last for two weeks or so, plus one entire week for preparation and construction, which allows for massive and very elaborate displays to be constructed. I was totally overwhelmed. Also, in the U.S. trade shows, that is exactly what occurs, a "show." There are lookers, but no business transacted. In the European shows, at least in Germany, business is actually transacted. Arnold Schneider said that as a rule, several million dollars of Gail Tile sales actually occurred during these shows. Quite different from our USA trade shows.

After our trade-show visit, we were then again returned to Giessen, where we were regaled with several wonderful dinners, but no sauerkraut! Bill Klinges continually complained. I considered it to be very rude to our hosts. Apparently, so did they.

On our last night in Giessen, we were taken to a very old, probably several hundred years old, heavily wooden paneled restaurant. We were seated at a long table, given menus, and placed our orders. Bill Klinges was seated at the head of one end of our table. All our food was delivered except for Bill Klinges's food. After several minutes, a very large silver platter with a large hog's head with wide open eyes resting on a large pile of sauerkraut was placed in front of Bill Klinges.

Arnold Schneider, our host for the trip, walked to the head of the table and at the top of his lungs shouted, "Here, Herr Klinges, is your Goddamn sauerkraut!"

Ten Las Vegas Casinos in One Afternoon

    Susan and I had been married for just a few months and were "goofy in love" (Susan's terminology, but I agreed), and we were dining at a sidewalk café in the Central West End of St. Louis. Susan likened that area to Greenwich Village in New York. It was a beautiful early spring day with cerulean blue skies and an unseasonably warm breeze. We were awaiting our lunch sandwiches and just enjoying each other's company. Susan was telling me something about her sister in San Francisco when a very attractive young lady was passing by on the sidewalk next to our table. She had a beautiful face and a very delightful and somewhat bouncy walk directly in front of our table. She captured my eye, and I stopped paying attention to what Susan was saying.

Susan noticed my admiring eyes, stopped the sister story, and said, "You think she is pretty good looking, don't you?"

Yikes, I was caught! In a very fortunate moment of quick thinking, I replied, "Susan, if I didn't like beautiful women, I never would have married you."

There was a very long silence as Susan just stared at me, and stared at me a little longer, then said "Oh . . . you are really good!"

I think that must have been the most fortunate statement of our marriage because she became my spotter of beautiful women and always pointed out one of special note, knowing that I knew that she herself, in my eyes, was the most attractive of all.

Two weeks later, we left for a trip to Las Vegas, one of the greatest cities on the planet. No other place has a totally different resemblance to anything in real life like Las Vegas. You will never find a clock in Las Vegas. Three or four days in Las Vegas is truly like being on a different earth, and it is an extreme departure from the daily existence in any other city in the US. We checked into the Castaways Resort and Casino, which was directly across Las Vegas Boulevard from the Sands. Both casinos are gone now and replaced by the Mirage and the Venetian. Susan loved the swimming pool at the Castaways; however, she forgot her swimming suit, which was just fine with me. She felt it was a necessity for sunning the poolside. I remembered seeing an ad or a movie short of a shop called Fredericks of Hollywood located in Las Vegas, so I suggested that we take a cab and head there. (I guess at that time, the only thing separating me from being a dirty old man was age. I have finally caught up.) Susan, in addition to being a strikingly beautiful lady, was very cleverly constructed, and it was very enjoyable seeing her modeling the various swimsuits and bikinis. She finally chose the least revealing and most tasteful swim attire in the store, but still whoop-de-doo as far as I was concerned. We headed back to the Castaways for her afternoon by the pool. I had a time-killing and fun expedition in mind.

I do not play slot machines as a general rule and feel that the term one arm bandit is aptly named. I think that most people who play slot machines go for the big money jackpots and usually play until all of the money is gone in their quest for jackpots. My mission was to prove that at one point in playing the slots, there would be a profit of some sort that was usually ignored with the quest for greater rewards. So, my journey while Susan was sunning her beautiful self-poolside began my slot adventure.

I decided to visit ten casinos and prove, at least to me, that my theory was correct. I would visit each of the ten casinos, go to the cashier, and purchase $10 in nickels. That was two hundred pulls on the one arm bandit. I wouldn't touch the nickels that made that hollow tin sound landing in the bucket, and would just play until the two hundred nickels were gone. I would then empty the trough, take the nickels to the cashier, and collect my total. It was a very fun way to spend an afternoon. I walked out of eight of those casinos with a profit ranging from $1.35 in one casino to a profit of $32.05 in a different one, with the other six being somewhere in between, resulting in an afternoon gain of just under $100. Neither casino of the two losing one's lost more than $5.00. My theory was proven, to me at least. Apparently, all of the casinos in the world learned of my proven theory, so now no more clang of nickels, dimes, and quarters echoing in the tin bowl. It is all paper now. No buckets, no blackened fingers, and no paper rolls of coins. Such a sad passing.

I returned to poolside to find my freshly roasted Susan napping in the recliner, wearing her sunglasses with a paperback book resting on her exposed tummy. I awakened her to brag about my proven theory, and she said "Great! Just don't let the casinos know, they will alter the payouts!"

We dined that evening at my favorite restaurant, the Ah, So Steak House, and for weeks later, the corner of the book imprint remained on her beautiful middle torso.

Saturday Morning Breakfast

My friend, Lewis Portnoy, who was a great sports photographer and a longtime friend, was having breakfast every Saturday morning with a group of very successful photographers who worked for Anheuser-Busch, NBC Sports, Ralston Purina, PGA, Southwestern Bell, Post-Dispatch, and Globe Democrat newspapers. I recently had success with my hot-air balloon graphics and was doing all of the photographs in the program for the Great Forest Park Balloon Race, so I had the credentials and was invited to join this elite group. at was in 1982, and believe it or not, that breakfast is still a Saturday morning event that had been going on for thirty-eight years. Members have come and gone, died, moved away, etc., but the event lives on.

Drew Karandjeff is one of the longer-tenured members and is a true perfectionist. Drew always has the best of whatever there is and will eagerly tell you why it is so perfect. He has several hotsy-totsy automobiles now, and in the past, had a Testarossa, an NSX, and several others of world-class quality. One morning, he told us that he had found the perfect detailer to work on cleaning his car and making it absolutely perfecto. All of us at breakfast were greatly impressed as usual. He informed us that this detailer was weeks behind, but he was fortunate to have found him as this detailer was the absolute best. As always, we saw it later after Drew's car of the moment was impeccably detailed, and indeed, Drew was right, the guy was very, very good.

I owned my first Lexus, which I referred to as being a childhood version, the Lexus ES, which stood for Economy Sedan. This car was a fabulous vehicle with a white exterior and beige leather interior. It was right at the top of vehicles that I had ever owned in my life. However, this was 1995, and my 1992 ES had 104,000 miles on it. It was time for a new one. There was no visible difference between the 1992 and the 1995, so I ordered the exact color combination as the 1992 since I loved it so. The new vehicle would be in in three to four weeks after I placed the order.

The next week at the Saturday morning breakfast, I informed the table, especially Drew, that I had found the absolute best detailer in the world and I made an appointment with him in about four weeks. Drew left early that morning, and I told everybody else that it was a prank and I had ordered a new car.

The dealer, Plaza Motors, informed me that my car had arrived and I could pick it up Friday evening, just in time for the Saturday morning breakfast. When I arrived, I ate breakfast and then announced to the table that my detailer had finished with my car and he did an incredible job. Drew couldn't wait to see it after breakfast. We all went to the parking lot to view my "detailed" car, and everyone just kept remarking how perfect a job it was. Drew kept looking at all sides, and even the tires had gloss on them.

I popped the trunk, and he said, "Wow, this guy is really great." I opened the driver's door and that brand-new car aroma hit us all in the face. He said, "Good grief, the carpet looks perfect and the leather seats have been totally refurbished. I can't believe how good this guy is." Then, my friend, Lew Portnoy said, "Look, he even rolled back the odometer." It showed thirty-six miles on it. The jig was up, but what a great moment!

Susan thought for years that the only reason that I got exactly the same car was for that very moment when I got Drew.

She may have been right.

Pardon Me, What Did You Just Say?

For years, it was a very welcome treat for a Cardinals game to be televised. Every game was broadcast on KMOX radio in St. Louis with 147 radio affiliates throughout the country. Before the Dodgers left Brooklyn in 1957, the St. Louis Cardinals were the furthest west baseball team and the furthest south baseball team. Most southern and western states considered the Cardinals to be their team of choice, so the Cardinals Baseball Network was one of the largest in the country. It remains the largest radio network in the MLB to this day. However, in 1981, games were telecast selectively, not every game was telecast. It was a fine event when a game was televised, with maybe a game per series being aired.

The games were, at one time, being televised on the NBC affiliate, KSDK with various personalities at the mike. On a particular game in 1982, Ron Jacober and Jay Randolph were handling color and play-by-play in a game against the Cincinnati Reds. In the fourth inning, the Cardinals were losing 4-0, and the Reds had runners on first and second with only one out.

Jay Randolph said on the air, "Doug Bair is throwing up in the bull pen."

After a long pause, Ron Jacober says, "Doug Bair is doing what in the bullpen?"

Jay Randolph, while laughing, says, "Doug Bair is throwing . . . up in the bull pen."

Ron Jacober said, "That didn't fix it, Jay."

Jay Randolph, who was a fine announcer for golf, and a superb gentleman that knew baseball very well, was still laughing when he rephrased his guffaw by saying, "Doug Bair is up and throwing in the bull pen."

To which Ron Jacober replied, "OK, Jay, I'll accept that!"

There is a very famous outrageous blunder with Harry Caray and Jack Buck during a Cubs game at Wrigley Field that I wrote about in the first "Quickies" book that I advise you to read. Well, I guess that is an unfair plug for my first book, so I will just tell it again in this one.

It was a teen night event at Wrigley with a band to be playing after the game for dancing in the aisles and on the field. During the broadcast, both Harry and Jack noticed a teen couple paying far more attention to each other than the game, with hugging and kissing overshadowing their attention to game on the field. Jack and Harry mentioned this on the air several times.

After a while during the game Harry Caray says to Jack Buck, "Jack, I have been watching that teen couple in the stands, and he kisses her on the strikes, and she kisses him on the balls."

Jack just looked at Harry in total disbelief as to what Harry just said. Harry then realized his blunder and was laughing so hard. He pointed to Jack as if to say "save me." Jack then pointed back to Harry because he was laughing so hard he couldn't take over the mike. They broke in the middle of the inning for a commercial, then came back to the broadcast, but neither could speak again while still breaking up over the outrageous guffaw.

They broke again for a commercial, and after missing an entire inning, Jack took the mike and said to Harry "Let's just talk about the game being played on the field."

Harry's response was "Deal"

My Mother, The Brilliant Lady

My mother was a very well-educated and very well-read lady. She loved crossword puzzles and had the remarkable ability to work the New York Times crossword puzzle in record time. She always used words in her everyday language that should have been left in books. I constantly had to ask her the meaning of a particular word that she was using for some everyday object. However, as an avid reader, she read Valley of the Dolls by Jacqueline Susan and said that it was the filthiest book she ever read.

She said, "There were so many dirty words in it. I didn't even know the meaning of most of them."

I said, "If you didn't know their meaning, how did you know they were dirty?"

She said, "Well, you could just tell."

My mom was indeed a brilliant lady who was always deep in thought. However, it was rarely about what she was doing at the time. If she were a professor, she could have been termed "absentminded." However, being just a schoolteacher, I would term her "scatterbrained."

We always had the latest newfangled items (my dad was a real sucker for those) and we were the first ones in the neighborhood to have that new thing called television. It was so exciting that our neighbors wanted to come over and see it. Word spread to people in the neighborhood that we had never met before, and soon our living room became an every-night venue for lots and lots of people, many of whom we had never met. My mom brought all the kitchen and dining room chairs for people to sit and watch our TV. After several weeks of this, one evening, my dad, on his way back to the TV room, had to step over a couple of people who were sitting on the floor and who we really didn't know at all.

My dad stood up and said, "Everybody, out!"

We also had, I think, one of the first dishwashers. At that time in the forties, there were no built-in dishwashers as far as I knew. Our dishwasher was a freestanding unit that was a round top loading white porcelain item on rollers that was hooked up to the kitchen-sink pipes by hoses. At some point, our dishwasher lost one of its castor rollers and was slightly tilted forward. On this particular evening, my brother, dad, and I were sitting at the kitchen table talking baseball (actually, they were talking and I was listening). Then, sometime after dinner, my mom asked if we wanted some ice cream. Of course, we did. Mom had already placed the dinner dishes in the dishwasher, and it had just finished its cycle. e top of the washer was still very hot. Years ago, ice cream quarts came in "bricks," which were long rectangular boxes that you would open and slice the ice cream into squares for serving. My mom placed a serving platter on the slightly-askew dishwasher and started slicing the ice cream. My dad, after talking about one of Stan

Musial's hits that day, looked over at the dishwasher and saw a slice of ice cream on the floor. He glanced up and saw another slice balancing on the edge of the platter. He saw it drop to the floor and land on top of the slice on the floor. He got our attention, and my brother and I looked up and saw another slice slowly, with the speed of a snail, make its way to the edge of the platter, teeter a moment, and then plop to the floor. We, my dad especially, always watched things develop with my mom without interrupting the occurrence, just to see how it would develop. My mom was happily slicing the brick when she glanced at the platter and saw just melted ice cream liquid. She looked down, saw the slices in a pile on the floor, and started laughing so hard that she had to excuse herself to change her dress.

Another time that my mother was deep in thought about something other than what she was doing at the time, was one day when my dad came home for lunch. My mom had cooked a couple of pork chops and placed one on a plate directly from the frying pan on the stove. She turned, and the pork chop slipped off the plate, skittered across the floor, and stopped just at the door to the basement. She then placed the plate on the table, not noticing that the pork chop was gone and with just a little grease remaining from the launched pork chop. She set it down in front my dad at the table and then turned back to the stove. My dad looked at the plate that had just a little grease and nothing else. Of course, he said nothing, wondering what would happen next. My mom turned and saw my dad's empty plate, thinking he was ready for another and not wondering how he ate the chop, bone and all. She picked up his plate, returned to the stove, and placed another pork chop on his plate. Now with the grease from two pork chops, the plate was even more slippery, and when she turned, the second pork chop slipped off the plate and slid within a couple of inches of the first one.

My dad said, "Aha, that's what happened."

My mom saw it and once again laughed so hard. It was time to change her dress again.

That is Not Exactly What I Meant, Ted

I am a readily admitted Ice Cream addict. I love it! Over the years, I have developed a somewhat snobbish attitude toward the richness in ice cream, the greater content of butterfat, the better for me. Just as a sort of tutorial regarding butterfat content, ice cream does not deserve the "ice cream" name until the butterfat content is 10 percent or greater. But that is not the entire story.

Air plays a big part in the final product. There is a devil called Over Run. Let's say that you start off with 100 oz. of your ice cream mix that is 10 percent butterfat, and you whip it up to give you 200 oz. of product, that is termed 100 percent overrun. So, what you are tasting is 50 percent air. That makes the ice cream not taste nearly as great to me. I want the real stuff, not mostly air! It is a simple fact that air is free, and the more you can put in ice cream, the greater the yield. So, in my ice cream, I always buy the more costly product. I don't like buying air. Haagen Dazs ice cream seems to have the least airy product and contains 16 percent to 18 percent butterfat, which is to my liking.

Another type of ice cream is Frozen Custard, which in addition to cream, milk, and sugar, it also contains egg yolks, making it smoother and more like the French variety of ice cream. It is served soft and smooth and delicious. There is a frozen custard stand in St. Louis called Ted Drewes Frozen Custard, which several years ago was termed the best ice cream in the world, an award that was given by a company in Ireland. Ted himself was given that trophy that is now proudly on display in his ice cream stand in St. Louis. Ted Drewes primary ingredients are cream, honey and eggs, which makes a delightfully delicious concoction that is hard for me to resist. His frozen custard has very little overrun, which makes an unbelievable and very smooth product that delights my pallet with the creamy deliciousness I love.

Ted Senior opened his first custard in Florida in 1929. The following year, he opened his first stand in St. Louis.

In 1941, he opened his stand on Chippewa Street, very close to my boyhood home, the year after I was born. In the later forties, I used to ride my bike to his stand to get a cone of that delicious ice cream. Ted Junior has carried on the tradition of creating that scrumptious ice cream with very few improvements since I traveled there in my childhood. Ted and I became friends since I was such a loyal and continual customer.

As an aside to this story, I remember that in the early fifties with Dairy Queen's national expansion that made a very different product (masquerading as ice cream) with the "curl on top," Ted's father was encouraged to try his hand in offering a similar product that had only 5 percent butterfat and mostly air like Dairy Queen's. He was his own worst enemy with that product that he named (if I remember correctly) Freezo. When a customer came to the window, he would say, "Do you want the real custard or that junk over there?" Freezo was very short lived.

Ted Drewes frozen custard became so popular that in 1985, he expanded his custard stand from five windows to twelve. Nowadays, if you pass his stand during his open hours, the lines leading to the street are about twelve people deep with most of the windows serving the customers so quickly that your wait for the creamy product may be no more than ten minutes or so. Ted is a major Cardinals fan, and since my closest friend for years was Marty Hendin, vice president of the Cardinals, Ted would always come out to talk baseball with me and to see if I had any inside information to impart.

On one particular June night, when all of the windows were packed and customers lined all the way out to the street, while talking to Ted, I said, "Ted, this is the first time I have ever seen a manual cash register overheat. I bet the only problem you have now is counting your money."

Ted said, "You know, you are right, wait here and I will show you something."

I waited and shortly Ted returned with a hand full of quarters. He lined them up in his hand, counted them by fours and in a flash said. "There. Ten dollars! People used to pay with quarters. They are easy and quick to count. Now people pay with dollar bills and higher, we have to flatten them all out, sort the $5s, $10s, and $20s, turn them the right way and band them in stacks for the bank. We stay an extra hour every night just counting the money!"

I almost said, "Ted, your story truly touched my heart," but I didn't.

Instead, I said "That is not exactly what I meant, but I see the problem!"

My Brother, Robert Marquess

Robert K. Marquess, whose middle initial stood for Kingsland, a forever kept name in our heritage, was called King by our family. My father's name was Robert Lee Marquess, so not to be confused with two Roberts in the family, my brother became King. (I learned much later in life that he hated that name and told everyone that his name was Bob.)

My brother was one of the smartest people I have ever known, but also the most frugal (cheapest) person I have ever met. He was also ten years older than me and considerably taller—he was almost 6 foot 5 inches. My brother's frugality caused him to never pay to park his car anywhere. He would prefer to find a spot on the street somewhere and walk the hundred or so blocks to whatever destination chosen. Needless to say, he would never valet his car because he would not consider giving the attendant a tip. As a matter of fact, I don't think he ever gave anyone a tip in his entire eighty-six years of life.

This may seem like a fabrication regarding my brother, but it is an absolute fact. He kept a book with him every day, recorded every penny spent during the day, and balanced before going to bed each night. He would purchase an occasional candy bar or jawbreaker for me, but never neglected to write it in his little book (jawbreaker,

Don, 1 cent). I have very vivid memories of lying in bed as a three-to-four-year-old and hearing my father calling to my brother, "King, go to bed," with my brother responding, "I can't, I'm a nickel out."

My father would then say in louder more definite terms, "Go to bed, I'll give you the nickel."

My brother would respond, "I can't. If I'm a nickel out, I could be a dollar out."

My father would then say, "Go to bed . . . . I will give you the nickel!"

To further iterate my brother's frugality and brilliant reasoning abilities, I was probably three or four, with my brother being thirteen or fourteen, when we were all in the living room listening to the Baby Snooks radio show (Maybe not, but that was one of my favorites) when my mom and dad decided that chocolate malts would be a great thing for all of us to enjoy. My parents gave my brother the money and sent him to Ted Drewes Frozen Custard for four chocolate melts. My brother jumped on his bicycle and went to fetch. Sometime later, my brother came home to the backdoor in tears and said that something terrible had happened.

My mom and dad said, "What happened?"

My brother sobbingly said, "When I turned the corner on Mardel, Don's malt flew out of the basket and smashed into the gutter."

My mom said, "How did you know it was Don's chocolate malt? Did it have his name on it?"

My brother said, "No, it didn't, but you and Daddy paid for it. I went and got it . . . it just had to be Don's."

I remember that vividly. However, I didn't realize the humor in it until several years later. If I remember correctly, my mom got four glasses and made four malts from the three.

My brother became a prominent CPA in Shreveport, Louisiana, and married a lovely (and very understanding) lady named Millie. My brother still balanced his pocket money with daily expenditures before going to bed each night and convinced Millie to do so also. As Millie explained it to me, one night she was out about $15 or $16 and she couldn't remember what happened to it.

My brother said, "All right, now, think. You woke up this morning, and where did you go? Then what did you do?"

Millie started to think, then threw up her hands and said, "I don't know, and I don't care. It is gone! I'm not doing this ever again!"

Surprisingly, my brother accepted this, and the marriage did not end in divorce. (Lawyers cost money.)

When our parents died, my brother's part of the estate was our parents' home, with the contents to be split equally between us. Susan and I invited my brother and Millie to join us for dinner at our home.

When they arrived, my brother said to me, "I have great news for you. at colored spotlight thing that Mom and Dad had, I sold for forty dollars. Here is your twenty."

He gave me a bill and entered the kitchen to say hello to Susan. I looked at the bill and it was a ten, not a twenty.

I called to my brother and said, "You gave me a ten, not a twenty."

He said, "No, I gave you a twenty."

I repeated, "You only gave me a ten."

He reached in his pocket, pulled out his notebook, did some calculations, then opened his wallet, counted his bills, and said, "You're right!", and then gave me another ten. He was seventy-two at that time, still keeping his little notebook.

I have always equated intelligence with a sense of humor, and my brother, whose IQ was in the 150 territories, had a terrific sense of humor. He could tell a joke with the best of them and laugh uproariously when he heard a doozie. He was drafted into the army and truly thought that it was a colossal waste of time. He was a very strong patriot, believed strongly in our armed forces, and served his country in the 5th Army's Finance Corp. He just never thought of it as a lifetime commitment. He was selected for OCS (officer candidate school) but respectively declined. He told me that one of the only things he learned in the army was when the drill sergeant was explaining the functioning of the M1 rifle.

The sergeant said, "These two things happen simultaneously . . . one right after the other."

A fellow draftee and lifetime friend of my brother told me that the drill sergeant at Fort Riley, Kansas, got nose to nose with my brother and said,

"Marquess, you are not a soldier now and you will never be one!" My brother replied, "Thank you very much!"

My Jaguar XKE

My very good friends, Lon Gilbert and Barry Oxenhandler, were two of the finest musicians I have ever met. We sang together for a couple of years, performing on the entertainment area called Gaslight Square in St. Louis, and we remained close friends thereafter. Barry, an incredible natural musician, became the chief pilot for Enterprise Leasing. Lon, a studied musician, continued in the music business, playing guitar for Jerry Gotler's (a Juliard grad) band called the Chasers. Jerry Gotler was an outstanding clarinetist. Lon's brother, George, was in the group as well, and other than music, we all shared a love for poker.

The Chasers were in town one weekend, so I invited them to our apartment for a poker game. Low stakes of course, and the most you could bet was one dollar. There were a lot of 25¢ chips being bet if two people had good hands. It was always dealer's choice, and when the deck got to me, I always dealt 5 card studs. One down, four up. I guess I always felt it was the best game. This was long before Texas hold 'em became so popular. Other games that we played were five cards draw and seven card studs. Never any cards wild, we thought wild card games were for kids or novices. We all understood the game and loved playing. Most of the time, when we played, the big winner of the night would win around $100 with the biggest loser losing maybe $30 or so. They were very fun games. However, evil lurked.

This night when the band came to my apartment, a silly game called guts came on the scene. It was more or less a complete gambling game with little or no skill involved. It was a game played against an imaginary player called the pot. Players got three cards face down and after looking at their cards, declare "in" or "out" as to whether they can beat the pot hand or not. Three dummy cards are placed in the center of the table face down, that becoming the hand to beat. If after looking at a player's hand, he declares "in," meaning that he thinks he can beat the pot hand. If other players declare "in," then the players that stay must beat the dummy hand. If they don't, they have to match the pot. All this action takes place before the "blind hand" is revealed. If one player beats the dummy cards in the pot, and the other players don't. Each player must match the pot and the winning player wins it all. However, if no one has a better hand than the dummy, each player who declared "in" must match the pot. A simple inexpensive poker game that can very quickly get out of control. That evening it got way out of control.

My friend Lon had to match the pot a couple of times and asked to borrow chips from me after he ran out of his own. The pot on this night grew to $80. Lon had to match the pot. and I loaned him $65 from my winning stack. That was lots of money to me. The pot grew with several more losing hands by several other players, and Lon again filled out an IOU to me for $630. Ridiculous for our little $1.00 limit poker game. Believe it or not, that pot continued to grow, and it was in the $1,000 range. Lon had to match and asked for another loan. I refused.

I said, "What do you have for collateral?"

He jokingly replied, "All I have tonight is my Jaguar XKE."

I said, "OK, I'll take it."

He gave me the keys to his XKE. I loaned the chips to match the pot to him. He matched the pot. This fun evening turned sour very quickly with this stupid game, but I had his Jaguar, and the evening continued. The pot got to be absolutely stupid, as it continued to grow beyond any sensible number. It got to a point where I had to match the pot, so I threw in Lon's keys to his Jaguar. My good friend Lon turned white as a sheet, and for a moment, I felt he would pass out. Something had to be done to stop this foolishness, so we all decided to end the game and split the pot equally. I grabbed Lon's keys and said, "I've got my share, you guys split the rest."

I was kidding of course, but for a couple of hours, I owned a Jaguar XKE. That was the last time we played guts. The rules for future poker games became No Guts Poker Nights!

World-Record Gambling Conversation

My son, Jeffrey K. Marquess, is an intelligent and well-educated individual with a degree in economics. However, he has a mental blockage when it comes to one certain thing—gambling!

We were in Florida on a business trip at the Peabody Hotel in Orlando when Jeffrey saw that the sport, JAI ALAI, was being played at a location not very far from our hotel. Jai alai is generally thought of as the fastest sport in the world, with the "pelota" (the ball) reaching speeds of 180 miles per hour. e ball is approximately three-fourth the size of a baseball and much harder. e center is made of hard Brazilian rubber and is handstitched very tightly with two layers of leather producing a ball so hard that after about twenty minutes or so of 180 mph pounding, it must be replaced by a new one. At any rate, the sole purpose of this sport is gambling, which made it very attractive to my son and, in all honestly, to me also.

Even in a sport totally unknown to either of us, Jeffrey instinctively knows who should win the game. He studies from the program, reads up on it, does his Jethro Clampett ciphering, and comes up with the best possible wager. Jeffrey always knows which player, horse, or dog should win. Sadly, that is not always who does win.

Without question, Jeffery is a most informed gambler. I, on the other hand, will pick a horse for its color or number, or the dog who appears to glance at me with a well-directed tail wag. I never intellectualize my wagers. Every so often my method works. I have a friend whose science at picking dog or horse possible winners is based solely on which animal relieves himself before the race. He feels that that makes the animal lighter and less stressful. Everyone has a system. Jeffrey's system is with pure intellectual logic as well as intense research. When his pick loses, evil lurks.

Our jai alai adventure went the wrong way for Jeffrey, and our (almost) never-ending discussion ensued.

I said, "Jeffrey, before you wager even a penny, you have to accept the possibility that there is a strong chance that you will not see that penny again. It is a fifty-fifty chance you are taking by risking that money."

"Dad, what do you mean fifty-fifty? What about the odds?"

"Jeffrey, either they keep that money or you get it back."

"Dad, have you ever had a class in statistics and probabilities? I have, and I think what you are saying de es the basic premise of probability."

"Jeff, you are denying the simple fact that you are risking the loss of whatever wager you make, and you have to accept that outcome before you place any bet on anything. You either get your wager back or they keep it."

"But Dad, there are the odds to consider. Don't you understand?"

"Jeffery, the odds are just the reward you receive for the likelihood of the occurrence. ink of it as a bonus you receive, but nevertheless, it is a fifty-fifty chance that you get your money back or they keep it."

"But Dad . . ., the odds are based on knowledge by the handicappers who make their living by studying past performances and wagering results in the past. Where do you come up with that stupid fifty-fifty statement? Do you think you know more than these great minds who make their living by creating the odds?"

I could see that this was a hopeless endeavor to get across my simple statement of you either get your money back or they keep it. It is a fifty- fifty chance. A bettor must accept the possibility of losing whatever he wagers. I felt maybe I could try another tack.

"Okay, Jeff, look at it this way, all bets are equal regardless of odds. And if an unlikely wager wins, think of the money you receive as a lagniappe that you receive for playing. The money you wager is the entertainment cost for the event. If you get it back, hooray. If you get it back with an award attached, a greater hooray is realized. Either way, it is a fifty-fifty chance of receiving your money back or they keep it."

"But Dad . . . smart bets usually win."

"Jeff, that is not the point at all. My point is that before you risk your money, you must accept the possibility of the loss. If you can't afford the risk, don't play. It is a fifty- fifty proposition."

At this point of our discussion, we had reached our hotel room, and I was ready for sleep time.

I turned off the lights and rolled over on my king-sized bed.

The lights came back on, and Jeffrey said, "But Dad, think about this..."

I said, "Jeff, you think about this... I no longer care. Goodnight!"

"But Dad ...."

I replied, "Zzzzzzzzzzzzzzz."

Really Fun Afternoon

In the early 1990s, the Board of Public Schools passed a very large bond issue that was matched by the federal government to pay for the addition of full-sized gymnasiums on all of the St. Louis schools, elementary as well as middle and high schools. The architectural department of the school system put out design parameters to equate the buildings that Architect William B.

Ittner created in the early 1900s. William B. Ittner was a nationally recognized architect for his beautiful school designs, and his use of brick in exquisite complex patterns and colors were magnificent examples of the capability of brick in creating elegant and very beautiful facades. The Board of Education architects were to find brick that would match what Ittner used in the early twentieth century. This goal was right up our alley.

We, as all the other brick suppliers in St. Louis, were given the challenge of matching the brick on those schools built sixty to seventy years previously. My father, the founder of Missouri Brick Co., said that when he moved to St. Louis in 1926, there were twenty-five brick manufacturers within the city. In 1990, there were none. So, matching the colors of those bricks used on those schools was indeed a challenge. There were close to fifty gymnasiums to be built, with quite a large amount of brick to be furnished, and we loved that challenge.

The school architects in charge of the additions, in order to be fair to all of the suppliers in the area would have what the lead architect, Scott Ritter, termed a "brick-off," where the brick suppliers in the area would gather at the site of the existing school and dry stack their best offering to match the brick in that particular building. These meeting times were generally around two o'clock in an afternoon on a day in mid-week. I was the brick matching specialist for my father's company, and fortunately of the first fifteen schools, we received the orders for thirteen of them. It was a difficult task, but we spent a great deal of time and effort in matching those old brick blends and colors.

Our main competitor was a company named Richard's Brick Co., and their sales person, Don Edris, put in a great effort to match the schools as well. We represented a brick manufacturer named Belden Brick Co. with their plants in Sugarcreek, Ohio, and their products more closely matched the old colors and textures that William B. Ittner used, so we were more successful in supplying the matching brick used on the schools. Don Edris really made a strong effort, but mostly failed. Don and I had never met in person; however, we were aware that we were strong opponents.

There was a brick-off at 2:00 p.m. on a school on South Broadway, very close to the Anheuser Busch world headquarters, which we also furnished using Belden Brick. I had arrived at noon and built what I felt was an almost perfect match. I was satisfied with the panel and left to grab a quick lunch before the meeting. I returned to the school at 1:30 to find another brick supplier with the trunk of his car loaded with brick, and he was constructing his mock-up to match the building. He had boxes of brick that said Richard's Brick Co., so I figured that the panel builder had to be Don Edris, my main opponent. Unlike most of the other brick peddlers in town, I always wore a suit or a sport coat with a white shirt and tie. I got out of my car and watched Don Edris constructing his panel for the 2:00 meeting.

After he finished his layup, he not knowing who I was, but I guess that I was looking sort of official in my suit and tie, he came up to me and said, "Which panel do you like?"

I replied, "They both look good, but I think the panel on the left is a better match, (mine) the panel on the right (his) needs a little more red." He went to his car trunk, tore down his panel, and rebuilt it with redder brick in his trunk while I continued expressionlessly watching him in the ninety plus degree weather putting the finishing touches on his "redder" panel. Satisfied with his new submittal he came back to me and very proudly said to me, "Well, what do you think now?"

I said "It is better, but I still prefer the panel on the left. The panel on the right needs more of those browner toned flashes."

Don, now sweating heavily, went back to his car again, tore down and reconstructed his panel adding more of those brown flashes. He finished it and said, "How about now?"

I said, "It is much improved, but I think the panel on the left nails it."

He looked at me with his sweaty and sagging shoulders and said, "I am Don Edris with Richard's Brick."

I replied, "Finally nice to meet you, sir, I'm Don Marquess."

His face went totally blank and his shoulders sagged even further and muttered a four-letter expletive.

The school architects arrived and looked at both panels, and unanimously selected the panel on the left. Don Edris, got in his car and dejectedly drove away, probably to Anheuser Busch just down the street.

Just as a postscript to this delightedly devilish story, through our efforts, we furnished forty-three of the fifty-plus school additions.

Twenty-Six? Why?

Good question, eh? Well, here is the reason: The number 26 is a significant number for me. I was born on the twenty-sixth, my mother was born on the twenty-sixth, my son was born on the twenty-sixth, and my grandmother was born on the twenty-sixth; therefore, it seems to me that the number 26 has a certain degree of importance in my life. Anything with twenty-six on it touches off a bell for me. I know that is silly, and I know it is truly meaningless; however, when I see the number 26 on anything my eyes light up and my ears perk up considerably.

Missouri Brick Co. was in the ceramic tile business as well as brick, and there was a ceramic tile distributor's convention in Reno, Nevada, at the MGM Grand in the early nineties. I was on the board of directors of that organization and was happy to attend the convention. It was a great event to see friends, establish some distributor guidelines, and perhaps snag a new line or two.

Three good friends of mine, Tom Brann from Chicago, Bill Haslett from Atlanta, and Suzy Stillson from Columbus, Ohio, were in attendance, and we met for lunch. It was a great lunch, and it was a pleasure to be with good friends again. At this lunch, we formed a limited partnership and the four of us contributed $30 each to invest in a slot machine that we would choose on the casino floor. The machine our LLC partnership chose was a typical bandit with the proper amount of bells and fire and smoke. It had an option of one or two coins. We had a board meeting to decide if it was a good time to pop for two coins or just stay with our twenty-five cents per spin investment. We were guessing correctly and doubled our corporate slot investment. Our initial buy in was $30 each ($120), and we now had over $250 for our newly formed corporation. One of our investors, Tom Brann, thought that we were pushing our luck, and we should unload our stash into one of those popcorn-like buckets and seek another machine for a while. This was such a fun adventure, and we initiated a search committee to find a new source of funding.

We all voted on several machines and finally agreed unanimously on a new bandit. Same thing as before, voting on one or two quarters, however not with the same profitable results. We lost a considerable amount of our profit, and with a motion before the board, we elected to return to the original machine, which we named Mom. We returned to Mom, and she continued bestowing us with great rewards. We loaded up and left Mom several more times, but always returned to Mom, and she was indeed very kind to the shareholders. Our $30 investment gave us over three hours of giggles and laughs, although we eventually went bankrupt (chapter 7), but what a fun-filled afternoon.

We agreed to gather back at Mom's for dinner at 5:00 p.m. So, I went strolling and found an empty roulette table. The dealer was a very friendly guy and seemed to be happy to have someone play his game of chance. I guess everyone that gambles have some sort of system for whatever bet they make, and I do as well. I rarely play roulette, but when I do, my system is as follows: I start off with $1 on number 26 and place $1 on each corner. The odds on one number are 35:1. The odds on each corner surrounding number 26 are 8:1. So if any number from 22–30 hits on the spin of the wheel, I win something. After each spin of the wheel, I add $1 to each corner along with my number 26. On the first spin, I hit a corner $3.00 profit. The second spin now has $2.00 on each of the corners, plus the number 26 in the center. The second spin got another corner—that yielded a profit of $11. The third spin (a total now wagered of $15) got two corners, which pays 17:1, so I got $105–$15 netting a profit of $90. The fourth spin missed me completely, so $20 lost. I still have a profit of $84. The next spin hit number 26 with $5 on each corner along with $5 on number 26. Whoopee! That yielded $175 for the number ($5 x 35) plus 8 x $5 = $40 for each of the corners a total of $335. When a win occurs, the dealer pays you directly and leaves the original bet on the table. So, as I am stacking my chips number 26 hits again. Good grief, another $335 with my cherished number 26 hitting twice in a row. I couldn't believe it, and you probably won't believe the rest of this story either, but it is very true.

I felt that I had pushed my luck just about as far as it could go, so I went to the cashier and cashed in $785. I got seven beautiful $100 bills and kept the $85 in chips. It was almost 5:00 p.m., time for me to meet the members of our LLC slot partnership, so I returned to our meeting place at the good mother slot machine, and met the three limited liability board members. I was so excited with my winnings that I led them to the roulette table of my great fortune, and as I walked up with my friends, the dealer said, "Well, here comes Mr. 26."

I told the complete story to my friends and took my $85 in chips, placed it on number 26, the dealer spun the wheel, and number 26 hit again— $2,975 win. I took that, plus the $85 wager, and cashed in $3060. This delightful bounty was added to those beautiful seven $100 bills, bringing my total catch for the day being $3,760. Deducting my $30 investment in the limited slot machine partnership, I still had a profit of $3,730. I bought dinner at the Asian restaurant in the hotel for the entire board (four people, including me) in our LLC slot corporation. My beloved number 26 hit three times in a row!

I didn't play roulette again for at least five years.

Bill Haslett And
The Las Vegas Caper

Most people are concerned with quality to a certain degree, but there are some people who are obsessed with quality to the utmost degree. My friend, Bill Haslett, is over the top in quality obsession. He cared greatly about the material used in shirts, jackets, and shoes, and in cars, it had to be a Lexus. Bill demanded perfection in most everything.

In 1990, there was a CTDA (Ceramic Tile Distributors of America) convention in Anaheim, California, that we both would be attending. Bill's office was in New Jersey, and mine was in St. Louis. With both of us loving Las Vegas and with the lure of the blackjack tables, we decided that it would be a great stop for a couple of days on our way to Anaheim. We had decided to meet in front of the white tiger's area at the Mirage Hotel shortly after our arrivals. Bill was staying at the Tropicana, while I had a luxurious (standard) room at the Mirage. Bill, the perfectionist, met me at exactly 2 p.m. as scheduled. After the usual greetings of how our individual flights were and our room accommodations, Bill showed me his new business card that was specially designed for him by a highly respected rm in Atlanta. He pointed out the special font that was used as well as the perfect deep red shade of burgundy on the ecru-colored card stock. He kept flipping the corner of the card, remarking about the thickness of the stock. We then walked through the casino seeking a blackjack table with the best-looking female dealer. We found a hot one at fifteen-dollars-minimum table and sat down to play. At that moment, the dealer was so great-looking that I don't think it mattered at the time to either of us whether we won or lost. Bill took out his card again and passed it over to me again to look at it again and asked me to comment on the quality of the card stock, font, selection, and color of the printing. He asked the dealer what she thought, then he asked me to pass it to the player next to me for his comment. Bill was over the top regarding his new card. At dinner that evening, he passed the card to me once again for inspection. He also asked our waitress what she thought about the card. No question, it was the "card of the century," but I had way too much of that business card and I didn't want to hear about it anymore.

    We played blackjack most of the next day and did not adversely affect the coffers of the Mirage. I checked out of my room while Bill and I hailed a cab and headed to Hertz to pick up the car I preordered. e temperature in Las Vegas was a toasty 112 degrees. People say you don't feel it as much because of the low humidity. Not so. It was scorching. As planned, we were to pick up the car, then go to the Tropicana, check Bill out of his room, then make the drive to Anaheim.

Everything was going to plan . . . until the counter person at Hertz said, "Sorry, Mr. Marquess, we don't have the car you reserved".

I said, "What? You can't be serious. I ordered and paid by credit card for a Cadillac."

I guess I shouldn't have made such a big deal about it, but a really nice car for the drive to Anaheim was a necessity. e clerk was being very nice, but I was being a real jerk. After a very heated and immature attitude on my part, I told him just where he could put the substitute car and stormed out of the office . . . directly into the stifling heat . . . and no cab to be seen anywhere. It was hotter than hell, and we had no way of getting anywhere.

Bill said, "Well, you showed them, didn't you?"

In 1990, the Hertz Car Rental was pretty far off the strip with no possibility of catching a cab. Considerably away, we saw an Alamo Car Rental across the road and past the bridge underpass, and we lugged (never before was the word luggage more appropriate) my suitcase, camera bag, and gear to the Alamo office. e temperature at this time was, I'm certain, around 180 degrees. e Alamo office was a stroke of luck in that they had a fairly new Lincoln that they wanted to go back to their Anaheim office. What an absolute stroke of luck! It was actually less costly than that stinking Cadillac at Hertz.

We then drove to the Tropicana to check Bill out of his room, I gave the valet $5 just to hold the car until we got back downstairs. In Bill's room, I saw his box of those world-class business cards. I picked up the box and concealed it in my hand behind a small airline carry-on bag of Bill's, and we went downstairs to get the car and start the drive to Anaheim. I secretly hid his business cards behind the passenger seat and said nothing to Bill. We started our four-hour drive to the CTDA convention in Anaheim. Bill and I were very good friends and enjoyed the ride.

The Alamo Anaheim office was closing at 6 p.m., and we arrived in plenty of time at 5:30 p.m. or so. e young lady at the counter was very nice and friendly and asked if the car was full of gas. I said no, it wasn't.

Then she said that they would charge $4.25 per gallon, and it would be best if we would drive a couple of miles up the road to fill up. She said that she had a barbecue to go to and would have to leave, but when we come back to leave the car at the gate, drop the key, and contract through the slot in the door, and she would call a cab for us to be waiting when we returned. How great was that! She was not only good-looking but greatly efficient and accommodating. We filled the tank and returned to the rental office, and there waiting for us was the promised cab. We loaded the luggage in the cab, but I totally forgot all about Bill's cards and told him what I had done. He was ashen. I promised to call them in the morning and pay for a courier to deliver the cards to our hotel. He felt better about it after I told him that I would x the prank, and I think he actually thought it was funny.

Waiting for them to open the next morning, my wife, Susan, called me and said that Alamo called and wanted to know my hotel and room number in Anaheim. She gave it and said that I should expect a call.

The call came! Alamo wanted to know why I didn't leave the car at the gate under the canopy. I said I did leave the car and all of the paperwork along with the key that was dropped through the slot in the door per instructions.

They thought I still had the car. I gave them Bill Haslett's room number to call for verification. Ten minutes later, I received a call from their home office wanting to hear my story again. A few minutes after that, I received another call from their insurance specialist asking for details. The car was stolen! And I was the primary suspect.

Bill called after realizing that if the car was stolen, so were his business cards. Whether I would be doing time for car theft didn't matter. His cards were all that mattered.

This story does have a happy ending, at least for me. The car apparently was stolen, but since I left the key in the envelope with the paperwork, I was no longer a suspect. Bill contacted his wife in New Jersey, and she FedExed the other box of his cards, which he received the next morning. Fortunately, Bill and I remained friends.

English Is Hard

In my years as architectural representative for my father's brick company, I met many brilliant architects and artists. One of them was both, an architectural designer as well as a very talented artist. His name was Ralph Broughton. He designed many banks and commercial structures as well as providing art for the buildings. Ralph became a very good friend and presented me with one of the paintings I loved titled Elaine, you had to look closely, but after a few moments, you realize that Elaine is naked with a couple of her attributes clearly drawn. We had it hanging in the room where den mother, Susan, my wife, had several of her Cub Scout den meetings in front of that beautiful painting. When the cubbies discovered Elaine's beautiful body parts, the meetings were then moved to a different room. Elaine was better left alone.

Ralph also traveled to Mexico on occasion and discovered the bronze statues of a sculptor named Hernando Guernica, bought five, and offered me my choice. Since Susan loved horses so much, I chose the horse. It is a beautiful bronze, which is still in our living room. It was a gift from Ralph, which is still enjoyed in our house. Ralph was indeed a very good and generous friend. Ralph for years pronounced his last name, Broughton, as in though. Then for some unknown reason, started pronouncing it broughton as in bought. He said that pronunciation was closer to the original English pronunciation. OK, I understood. But then I got to thinking, why stop there? There are other ways of pronouncing that grouping of letters (diphthongs?).

It brought a mindboggling litany of possibilities:

He could elect to be named Bruffton, as in tough.

He could say he was Ralph Brooton, as in through.

He could become Ralph Browton, as in thou.

He could become Ralph Broffton, as in cough.

He could also become Ralph Bruppton, as in hiccough (hiccup).

I give up!

An artist (architectural renderer) friend of mine, Don Webb, whenever the three of us were going to lunch, which was often, would refer to Ralph as Mr. Brooton, Broughton, Broffton, Browton, or Bruppton. Even Ralph thought that was funny.

The Brits have always been the worst. How in the hell do you pronounce Gloucester, Maine, as gloster? Totally disregarding syllables as they choose. How about Worcester sauce? This way of thinking is far too exhausting to continue.

I would despise trying to learn English and think that Chinese would be the only way to go!

(All last night, I dreamed I was a tail pipe. I woke up exhausted) Sorry about that one.

Linda Zorsch

Susan and I were living in what we considered a luxury apartment in General Grant Colonial Village in suburban St. Louis. It contained two bedrooms and a very large recreation room on the lower level. We felt we had hit the big time. Pat and Linda Zorsch, our new upstairs neighbors, had just moved in and seemed to want to make friends with us. Pat Zorsch, the husband, was a tall (six feet) slender CPA who was a friendly sort and he wanted to socialize with us. His wife, Linda, was a moderately attractive brunette who was a stay-at-home wife. Linda was of normal build, probably around five feet five inches and mostly slender with one major exception— she had the largest breasts that neither Susan nor I had ever seen before. We knew that her chest had to have set some sort of breastal record. When you stood face to face with Linda, you had to give an extra couple of feet or so distance so as not to brush up against those two whoppers.

Susan and I had several close friends that would come over with regularity for dinner and charades, clue, Monopoly, or some other enjoyable game. At some point in the evening, the subject of our upstairs neighbors would come up. Both of our guests (the guys especially) would find it an intriguing bit of information regarding Linda's breasts, and not completely believing our descriptions, would ask to meet her and her accountant husband. I would call upstairs and invite them down to meet our friends.

They would arrive, and we would all make small talk for a while. Then I would go to the kitchen to freshen drinks or get chips or something, and one of our friends would get up to assist.

As soon as we rounded the kitchen wall, a very animated, yet totally silent reaction as our guest mouthed, "My God, I can't believe it."

Exaggerated hand gestures extended as far as the arms can reach were given as the reaction to the enormity of Linda's chest. Husband Pat, the stereotypical CPA, was either unaware of our attitude or way too nerdish to think much about it. He assumed that we invited them as friends. I guess that sounds very cruel and heartless, but her breasts overshadowed all other considerations. Pat and Linda may have been an interesting couple, but thoughts beyond her breasts were nonexistent.

Like many apartment buildings, the tenants' mailboxes were clustered on the first-floor hallway close to the entrance to the building. One Saturday, Pat Zorsch and I were retrieving our mail at the same time and started a casual conversation regarding our summer plans. I told Pat that we were planning a trip to New England (Susan's birth area) and the usual day trips to interesting local attractions (Cardinals baseball mostly).

He started his litany of summer plans: "I'm going to summer camp in July, going to a CPA seminar in early August, then Linda is having her operation, then . . . ."

I interrupted him in midsentence, "Linda is having an operation? For what?"

He, with a very serious look, said to me, "You may have noticed that Linda has very large breasts . . . " (I was trying very hard to keep a straight face, although his "you may have noticed" statement was causing internal hemorrhaging of my explosive laughter.) Then he continued, " . . . and she is having terrible backaches (I guess!) due to the size of them, and it is causing her to bend over from the weight of carrying them. So, she is having 74 percent removed from her right breast and 60 percent from her left one."

Again, trying with great difficulty to be serious and quieting my giggle urge, I said, "What are they doing with the overage?", thinking that would cause a smile on his face or maybe even a chuckle.

He just looked at me for a moment and, in typical nerdlike fashion, said,

"I don't know, I never asked. I assume they are just throwing it away." at did it for me. I was about to explode. I turned to my apartment door, and as I was going in, I said, "Keep me abreast."

I told Susan as soon as I got in, and we both tried very hard to keep our laughter as quiet as possible. The ceiling was thin, and we didn't want them to hear us.

Incredible Trust

My father started his brick business in 1960, and he rented space from a concrete block manufacturer located on Page Avenue in St. Louis County. The block storage yard was huge and had a rail siding. All the bricks at that came in by rail and had to be palletized by hand, which was a very hard work as a tong full of ten bricks weighed 40 lbs. or so and stacking five hundred bricks on a pallet was heavy labor. Thirty thousand or so bricks came in a boxcar, and unloading it would take my friends and I a couple of days to unload one. During the summer vacation, my friends and I spent many labor-intensive days between semesters, palletizing bricks. My arms and shoulders became somewhat massive.

One very hot July day, a man named Millard Hauck came into the office and told my dad he wanted to purchase a large amount of brick and wanted go through our yard to see what we had available. Millard had his ten-year-old or so son with him, and my dad and I went to the brickyard to show him the availability of what we had in stock. As we all went to view the brick we had on the yard, he would ask the quantity of each stack and would say, "OK, this will be fine, I'll take these," or "this is not enough, but I can use them for trim," and as we walked from pile to pile of brick, he was making his selections and building up quite a tab. We were really enjoying this brick excursion. Millard said he had a contract to build quite a few post offices in rural areas in Missouri, and my dad's new company was his first stop to buy brick.

As he was selecting another batch of brick, his son, who was picking up brick and looking at them and screamed in pain. As he was setting a brick back in the pile, he set it down too hard, and a brick chip flew and imbedded itself in the boy's right eye. His father told the boy to be calm as he inspected his eye. Sure, enough in the white of his right eye was a very sharp chip of red brick. As his son was really hurting and in great pain, we went back up to the office, and the boy sat in the chair while really suffering.

His father said, "David, open your eye very wide and look to the ceiling." His son obeyed his father and did exactly what his father told him to do. His father reached into his pocket and pulled out a knife that my father termed a "frog sticker." It was a knife that had a 6" blade with a sharply pointed tip.

He said, "David, hold very still and don't move your eye at all." The father then put his hand on the cheek under his son's eye pulled it down while his son remained very still. Millard Hauck, using a very steady hand and with that sharply pointed knife, plucked the brick chip from his son's eye.

What incredible trust the son had in his father, and my dad and I were both amazed at the bond that existed between father and son. To this day, I tear up thinking about the total respect and trust that David had for his father, and the skill that his father had, and that he knew that his son would do exactly as instructed.

Afterward, Millard Hauck asked my dad for the total cost of the brick he selected. My dad did the calculation and the total was $15,850.

The man said, "Will you take $15,000 in cash?"

My dad said, "Sure!"

Millard went to his car and brought in a rather bulky brown Manila envelope and presented fifteen paper clipped sets containing ten $100 bills in each. He said he did his shopping for projects with $100,000 or so in cash because he always got the best deals paying in cash. How true!

My dad and I drove very carefully to the bank while feeling that every car we passed knew we had all that cash. When we got to the bank, we very nervously walked in and suspected that everyone knew we had it. We sat very close to the guard on duty. Once it was deposited, we drove back to the office fully relaxed.

Missouri Brick Co. has been in business for sixty-two years and has furnished brick to the most prestigious projects in the St. Louis area, Busch Stadium, huge hospital complexes, and countless schools and condominium projects. However, in all of those sixty-two years, no one paid as much as $15,000 in cold hard cash! Those two unforgettable moments happened on the same day way back in 1960.

Boarding House Audi

Susan, the gorgeous lady I was married to for forty-two years and who greatly resembled Joan Collins, was a great admirer of ne automobiles, especially the high-performance fast ones. She drove a Jeep Station Wagon but longed for a "real performance automobile," and she especially loved Audi's. We lived close to an Audi dealer in Kirkwood, so I went and checked out the available cars in stock. I can't remember the exact model I found, but there was a really nice one that was a deep green, maybe olive green, that had a powerful engine, leather upholstery, and a great sound system, all wrapped up in a "real performance machine." I loved Susan beyond sensibility, so I bought that car (much more than I could afford) for my beautiful Susan. She was ecstatic. We took delivery of the car Friday afternoon, and she drove it all around the neighborhood. I seem to remember hearing her singing some sort of vroom-vroom song from blocks away. She was totally enraptured. at evening, we had made reservations at a very popular restaurant called the Jefferson Avenue Boarding House, and our best friends, Pat and Barry Oxenhandler, were meeting us at our house and we were taking them in the "driving machine" to dinner with us. I need to tell you that Susan, my beautiful Susan who loved high-performance cars, never had and never would drive on any highway anywhere, anytime. She felt (probably rightfully so) that her depth perception would be a danger to herself and anyone else on the highway. However, that didn't prevent her from instructing me how to drive on any highway or any thoroughfare for that matter. The Jefferson Avenue Boarding House required about ten miles of highway driving, so I was our pilot.

We arrived at the restaurant and pulled up to the front door, and the valet came to park our car.

I gave him the keys and said, "Drive carefully . . . this is a performance car. Be very careful and very respectful."

Susan echoed my instructions. We went in and ordered our gourmet meals. I excused myself after ordering, purportedly to hit the bathroom and seek the manager. The manager, who was also the owner, had, in addition to magnificent cuisine, a rather delightful sense of humor.

I met with him out of sight of our table and said to him, "As we are finishing our desserts, I will ask the waiter to have the valet bring the car to the front door for us. He should look a little puzzled and go to find you. You will come to our table and say, 'Sir, I am very sorry, we don't have valet parking.'"

He thought that was a delightful prank for my wife's new Audi, so the plan was put in place. I went back to the table just before the appetizers arrived and then enjoyed our delicious meal. Susan had lamb cooked in some sort of mint sauce, and I will never forget the fabulous calf's liver "something or other" that I had. It was spectacular. We ordered desserts, and per plot, I requested the waiter to inform the valet to fetch our car. He looked puzzled (as planned) and went away.

Then the owner came up as planned, wearing a very sad puzzled look and said, "Sir, I'm very sorry, we don't have valet parking."

Susan's face went through many expressions. First surprise, then confusion, then anger, then absolute rage, saying, "My God . . . we just gave my new car away to some thief!" The owner knuckled under immediately, pointed at me, and said, "He made me say that . . . we do have valet parking, and your car is waiting at the front door!"

It is difficult to describe laughing rage, but Susan had it. She was so relieved knowing that it was my harmless prank and she really still had her "driving machine." The ride home at first was kind of quiet.

Then she said, "Just you wait, Henry Higgins, just you wait." Then she smiled and said that she knew why she loved me. (That fact had always puzzled me.)

Mount St. Helens

In most Cub Scout organizations, there are many events that are fundraising projects for the pack. The Cub Scout pack at Tillman Elementary and Henry Hough middle school had mini car races called the Pinewood Derby and various other competitions. My son Donny won the Pinewood Derby in a triumph with a cigar made from the block of wood complete with the cigar label, and he beat all competitors. They also had cake-baking competitions where the rules were No Mother Participation. Donny won two of those with a turkey cake that looked exactly like a roasted turkey complete with a clear baker's glaze that made it look just like it just came out of the oven. A follow-up to that was a turkey dinner cake with all the trimmings. These cakes were auctioned with parents and guests bidding with fine rewards for the Cub Scout pack.

On the Fourth of July, there was another cake bake competition, and Danny, the younger son, wanted to make a big firecracker. Great idea! However, it was going to be a really big firecracker. We baked six layers of cakes to build this firecracker. As we were stacking the layers, when we got to the fourth layer, the cake started to sag, so I got some masking tape to hold it together. The fifth layer caused it to tilt further, so I went to my workshop and cut some wooden dowel rods to further support the layers. The sixth layer was another disaster. As we placed the top layer, it was revealed that I had cut the dowel rods about a half inch too long. So, I went back down to my workshop to cut off about an inch from all four rods.

In the meantime, the cake had tilted much more, so more masking tape. The reinsertion of the dowel rods straightened the cake, and it looked ready for the shiny deep red icing. We iced the firecracker and stuck the six-inch piece of clothesline for the wick, and the cake was indeed a beautiful sight to behold. It was ready for the auction, and the den mother gave it a lot of hype and stated that it indeed would be a great value since it was six layers tall. One lucky bidder paid $16.50 for that firecracker. I felt that I needed to explain a few of the hidden supports to the buyer, so I revealed the masking tape and dowel rods that he was also getting as a bonus. As I was explaining these issues to him, I was laughing all the way; however, the purchaser had zero sense of humor, and the more I revealed, the more I laughed, but the sourer his expression became. This individual apparently didn't appreciate the hoodwinking we perpetrated, so I offered to reimburse him for his bad investment. That bum took it. We took the firecracker home and after disassembling all of the extras, the cake tasted rather good.

The next cake-baking contest was the summer of 1980, the year of the March twenty-seventh eruption of Mt. St. Helens. Danny decided that we should bake a volcano. Terrific idea for winning another prestigious award in his glorious history of competing in Cub Scout events. I had the brilliant idea of placing a little votive candle cup at the top of the volcano with several of those little black snakes inserted so that when the snakes were ignited, a spew erupted with black snake foam ashes that greatly resembled lava. It was certainly going to be another victory to be added to his stellar list of his Cub Scout awards. The evening of the competition with Mt. St. Helens on display and ready to be ignited when the judges came to view, Danny was telling several of his friends about the impending eruption and how his cake would again win the top prize. He lit the black snakes and the very acrid smoke started spewing as the snakes were erupting. The gymnasium became filled with this terrible smoke, and it had to be evacuated and all of the windows were opened in the hope of clearing the smoke from the hall. It was indeed a brilliant idea that wasn't thought completely through.

The volcano was just as hoped, but the outcome was not as desired.

The Killer Stalactite

The time on the "killer clock" with its sound-deafening tick tock showed 10:30 p.m. when a knock on our dorm-room door banged loud enough to almost out-volume the clock. So, I opened the door to find Ed Warnol, our down-the-hall neighbor, announcing that a trip to the Minute Inn for Matty's incredible chili was happening and did we want to ride along. Matty's chili was legendary, and any evening would be gleefully interrupted with a trip for her gourmet (?) red bean spicy beef chili containing garlic, red and yellow peppers, along with a semi lethal dose of cayenne pepper. Once tried, never refused. So, Ed Warnol, my roommate Roger, and me along with Tom Brooks from down the hall all got into Ed's car and headed toward the Minute Inn. is was late November, the day after a significant snowfall occurred, but the sky was crystal clear and appeared to have about eight billion or so brightly twinkling starts. The temperature was somewhat south of freezing, but Ed's car was nice and toasty. e sun during the day had caused the melting of the snow and created giant icicles hanging on the eaves of the houses, and most of them were quite impressive.

Matty's chili was indeed a bowl of wonder, and we all had at least two bowls. Then as we headed back to Hyde House Hall F, we passed by the most incredible icicle we had ever seen. It was hanging on the side of a garage with a top measurement approaching three feet. at sucker was over six feet from top to bottom and probably weighed sixty pounds or so. Ed Warnol's roommate was sort of a creepy individual who never said much and had a turtlelike appearance as he walked with his head tucked very closely to his shoulders. He wore thin-rimmed glasses halfway down his nose with his beady dark eyes peeking over the top of the glasses. His pastime was cave exploring. He was a spelunker. His name was Ed Bardett and he was very unsociable and appeared to have very little personality, if any at all. His favorite record was an album titled e Sounds of Sebring, which had nothing but the sounds of engines as they rounded the track. No Elvis, Johnny Cash, or Julie London. Being a spelunker, there was no doubt that this mammoth icicle was a stalactite that needed to be Ed's gift.

The four of us stopped the car, got out, and tried our best to remove the icicle from the roof's edge. at chunk of ice must have weighed fifty-plus pounds and was taken down with great care. The icicle was so big that it wouldn't fit in the car, so I in the front and Roger in the back seat carefully held the prize outside the car, as Ed Warnol drove very carefully back to our dorm. We parked the car and with great care carried the icicle up the stairs to our second-Floor hallway. Ed Warnol and I carried the stalactite down the hall to Ed's room. Ed opened the door, and his roommate was sound asleep in his bed. Roger came in and gently folded back the bed cover of Ed's bed. Ed Warnol and I very carefully set the icicle next to the sleeping Ed. We tiptoed out of the room, closed the door quietly, and waited for the scream. As discretely as possible, we knocked on most of the doors and told our dorm mates of our caper. Ten or so of the guys came out, and we all huddled around the door waiting to hear the spelunker screaming as he discovered his gift. We waited in gleeful anticipation. Nothing at first... then nothing at second. We kept waiting, nothing. Slowly, one by one, our dorm mates returned to their rooms giving up. Roger, Tom, Ed, and I would not give up. We still waited. After almost an hour, Roger and I gave up and went back to our room. Ed said goodnight and told us that we would probably hear the wild scream that would wake us up sometime in the middle of the night. Still nothing!

Probably the greatest prank of the year fell at. Very disappointing! e dorm had a gang shower and bathroom at the end of the hallway, and there in the shower the next morning was Ed Bardett soaping himself up as if nothing happened.

Egad. One of the dorm mates said to Ed, "How did you sleep last night, Ed?"

Ed replied, "Someone put a big chunk of ice in my bed last night. I woke up around three and put it in the shower."

Over the corner of the shower was the melting three-foot hunk of ice. There was no further emotion from the spelunker. Bummer!

So sad, so very, very sad.

1982 McDonnell Douglas Aero Classic

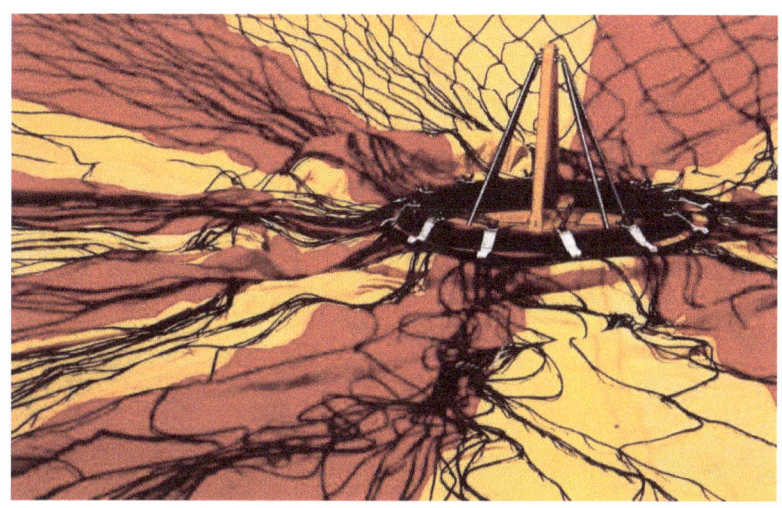

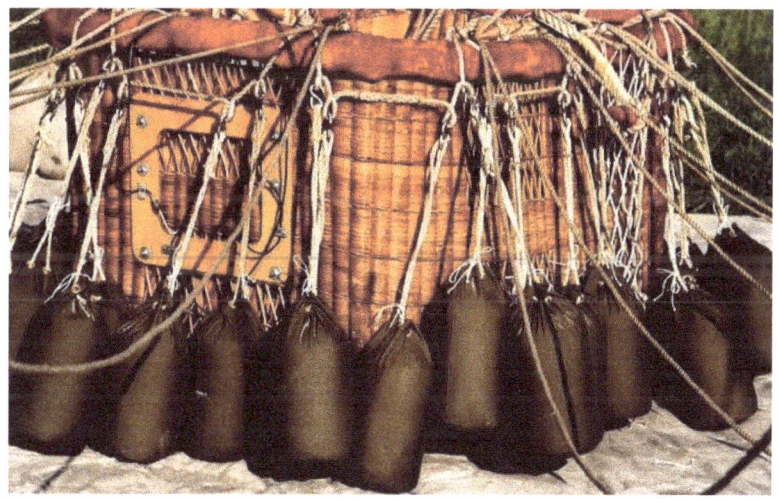

My photographs graced the pages of the program for the Great Forest Park Balloon Race for several years, and I was enjoying the experience to photograph that event. My photos were used exclusively in the official balloon race program. In actuality, whenever there was an unsold space in the program, one of my photos was inserted and I received photo credit. One year all spaces were sold, so none of my photos were used; nevertheless, I received credit for all photos in the program, when none were there.

Each year, there were seventy-five to eighty hot-air balloons in that event, and it was touted as the largest viewed balloon launching in the country. However, the balloons did fly over the St. Louis Metropolitan Area, consisting of almost 3 million people. I also had the opportunity to photograph the Big Balloon Event with over seven hundred balloons in Albuquerque, New Mexico. Albuquerque has what is referred to as the Albuquerque Box, which means that due to wind currents, a balloon may be launched to ascend to an altitude and be carried by the wind for a couple of miles or so, then descend to a lower altitude, catch a different wind current, and be transported back to the starting point.

It should be pointed out that balloons rule the skies. Since the only control that balloons have is altitudinal, they can only go up or down depending on the heat in the envelope (the big balloon itself), and they are at the mercy of wind currents. All aircraft must give precedence to balloons. A hot-air balloon is heated by propane tanks directly over the transport basket, the gondola, and the hot air in the envelope causes the balloon to rise. This usually takes a crew of three to four people laying the balloon out and preparing it to receive the hot air created by the heat from the propane burner. They usually volunteer in exchange for the hope of being offered a ride in the future. A balloon ride is indeed a wonderful pleasure, and I have been fortunate to ride in one five times. In fact, if I were offered a ride from one landing on my front lawn today, I would jump in and take an hour or so ride. It is an experience not to be missed. Gas balloons, however, are a completely different situation.

The inflation of a gas balloon is a totally different inflation process. A gas balloon is the type that can fly for hours, up to days, not hours. They fly at altitudes up to 18,000 ft. (three and a half miles), while a hot-air balloon only flies at three thousand feet max. The cost today for a hot-air balloon is thirty to forty thousand dollars. The cost for a gas balloon is $250,000 plus. Also, the time to fill a gas balloon with helium or hydrogen is $3,200 $5,000. A gas balloon takes a major financial commitment and usually has a corporate sponsor.

In 1982, there was a huge gas balloon event in St. Louis at Laclede's Landing close to the Mississippi River. There were eight giant gas balloons participating in the event being sponsored by McDonnell Douglas (now Boeing), with the projected target being the Washington Monument in our nation's capital for landing. The gas being supplied for the event was helium that cost over $25,000, about $3,000 per balloon, and was being paid for by McDonnell. Sandy McDonnell himself was on hand for the event. So was I, as the photographer.

The balloon guru in St. Louis was a fine lady named Nicki Caplan, who also instituted the Great Forest Park Balloon Race, and she had a gas balloon entered in the event. At this time, Nikki was giving hot-air balloon instructions to her student Flip Wilson who was also in town to view the launching. We had a pre-event screening of my hot air balloon photos, with accompanying music, at the St. Louis Planetarium. Flip Wilson, wearing his stark white Nehru jacket, kept us all entertained with his stories as the reverend of the "Church of What's Happening Now," and his Emmy winning character, Geraldine, famous for, as she explained to her husband, the church pastor, "The devil made me buy this dress . . . I didn't want to do it, but the devil made me buy this dress."

For you youngsters reading this book, Flip was at the top of his game with several Emmy's and Grammy's under his belt due to his unique approach to comedy. The balloonists and crews in the theater seemed to enjoy Flip's humor even more than my photos. This was a very important event that captured national attention in the ballooning world.

Filling a hot-air balloon takes around an hour with three to four assistants. Filling a gas balloon can take six hours plus and ten or so volunteers. Most of the volunteers usually have no experience with hot-air balloons, much less with gas balloons, and are quickly schooled with on-the-job training. With a gas balloon, there is a netting covering the envelope with ballast bags about the size of a quart size bottle of milk. These bags are filled with sand for holding the balloon on the earth during the filling of gas before going aloft. As the gas is sent to the balloon through the umbilical, the balloon envelope begins to inflate and rise slowly. The volunteers are surrounding the balloon, and as it begins rising, they are instructed to lower the sandbag ballast gently from netting square down to the next netting square while always keeping the bags hooked for holding the balloon securely on the ground.

A frightening and very costly occurrence happened as these volunteers started having fun dropping the sandbags from hooking spot to hooking spot as the envelope was rising. These kids seemed to enjoy dropping the bags instead of gently moving them down from netting square to netting square. When all of a sudden, I heard a snap, snap, snap, and a chain reaction occurred as all the bags dropped to the ground and Nikki Caplan's balloon took off with no pilot and no passenger. It was a complete disaster!

Sandy McDonnell quickly ran to his car and called his company to scramble and launch two phantom jets to chase and surround the balloon to inform other aircraft of the hazard in the sky. All other airborne craft had to be aware of that balloon with no pilot, rising in the sky. (I thought at the time; what absolute power he had to just make a phone call and launch two phantom jets.)

That balloon traveled to Iowa where it crash-landed, destroying the balloon and instruments totaling close to $100,000.

Nevertheless, master balloon pilot Nikki Caplan continued to rack up more and more awards and was given the Top Woman Balloonist in the World title and was enshrined in the National Balloonist Hall of Fame in Indianola, Iowa, on July 27, 2014. Nikki Caplin was like the unsinkable Molly Brown. She wouldn't let a little loss of a $100,000 balloon slow her up even a little bit!

Breeders' Cup Gambit

My son, Jeffrey, loved horse racing and the thrill of the wager. The simulcast of the 1985 Breeders' Cup was at Fairmount Park, which was just across the Mississippi from St. Louis, so we planned to attend. We made a reservation at the Black Stallion room, which had a very nice buffet and monitors galore. e one-mile race (I think there were seven or eight races in total) had a great-looking gray horse named Cozzene. It fit right in with my highly scientific method of horse selection for any race. Bet the gray horse! I guess the real reason is that as you look at all of the horses rounding the track, it is very easy to spot the gray horse and to see his position in the group. At racetracks, the betting windows have very creative in ways you can wager. There are at bets where you can pick a horse to finish first, second, or third. Then there's an option called the exacta, where you pick the horses that finish first and second. Then there's the most difficult wager of all, where you pick the three horses that finish first, second, and third.

The racetracks have devised many different ways that the bettor can structure his wager, many of which confuse me. However, one way I do understand is "boxing horses." It is possible in a trifecta race to "box" three horses for six dollars, which will result in half of the payout of the winning amount. This figure is generally a very big payout for the winning tickets due to the difficulty of picking three horses that finish first, second, and third. The higher the odds on the individual horses, the bigger the reward.

There is another method of betting the trifecta and that is to "box" four horses, and three of those four horses must finish 1st (win), 2nd (place), and 3rd (show); however, this wager costs $24. I wagered the $24 and picked and boxed four horses.

The race was off, and the easily seen gray horse, Cozzene was easy to spot on the monitor. It looked like my individual bet ($20) on him was going to win. A couple of the other horses of my four chosen looked like they were strong possibilities to finish in the top three. The race ended with the gray Cozzene winning, and one of the other horses I picked finished second. Sadly, the horse I selected to finish third finished fourth. There goes my $24 on that bet. But wait, there's more. An inquiry sign was flashing on the tote board involving the third and fourth finishers. It seemed like an eternity, but they eventually disqualified the third (show) horse and bumped up my horse for my winning trifecta. The payout for the trifecta showed $867.950. I thought that is terrific, I get $433.475 . . . wait a minute, that is three digits after the decimal point; there should be only two. The payout was actually $8,679.85. I was getting half. Incredible! I was paid in cash for $4,339.75. What a win! There were still two or three races to go.

The next race was fast approaching, and Jeffrey and I were in the line leading up to the betting window when

Jeffrey said to me, "Who are you betting in the next race, Dad?"

I responded, "I like the name Pebbles, I am betting her."

Jeffrey said, "How much are you betting on her, Dad?" I told him $20.

Then Jeffrey says in a very loud voice, "With all that money in your pocket! You are only betting $20?"

I could hear all of the eyeballs in the room snapping in my direction. At the time, I felt that everyone at Fairmount Park had a prison record and carried a knife. My life was probably over. I could have strangled Jeffrey. Anyway, Pebbles won, and I added another $400 to my winnings. I was heavily loaded with close to $5,000, and this was Saturday and the banks were closed. No ATMs. We had a dinner date that night with friends, and I was afraid to leave the money at home knowing that the house could burn down and my money would go up in flames, so I just kept it in my pocket for the evening. I truly had the feeling that everyone we saw in Union Station (it was very crowded) while we were walking to Dierdorf and Hart's restaurant could tell by looking at me that I had $5,000 in my pocket and they were plotting to take it from me. I charged our portion on my credit card because I didn't want to reveal the wad I was carrying.

I was first in line at the drive-up window at Bank of America Monday morning.

Susan, Donny, Danny, and I had a wonderful week at the Polynesian Hotel in Disney World with the special meal and hotel program that cost $2,800, which we paid in cash thanks to Cozzene and his fellow racers. The balance of my $5,000 win is still drawing interest.

OFB 2003

If you are a baseball fan, spring training is an experience not to be missed.

The stadiums are much smaller than the major league stadiums, (six to seven thousand compared to thirty-five to fifty thousand capacity), so almost every seat is closer to the action. There are very few two-tiered stadiums for spring training games, and the entire atmosphere is more laidback than major league stadiums. Every game is more relaxed than the intensity of a major league game. Granted, the games outcomes are meaningless since none of the games count in the regular season; however, many hopeful players are given an opportunity to showcase their talents in the hope of getting noticed and to be included on the major league rosters. A minor league player may make $15,000 to $35,000 a year, while the minimum salary for a major league player is $720,000. A major, major difference for a player to jump from the minors to the majors, so the pressure for a player is gigantic. Marty Hendin with the Cardinals told that the major league traveling meal money is more than a minor league makes in a month. While the experience is laid back for the fans, it is very intense for the young aspirants.

Just as an example, every high school in the country has a baseball team. That is an unbelievable amount of players hoping to be one of the eight hundred fortunate baseball players in the MLB. Showing the difficulty of hitting major league pitching, a player that fails seven out of ten times to hit a baseball, makes $20,000,000 per year. Failing seven out of ten times means that player hits three hundred, which is the definition of an elite player. That shows that hitting a baseball is the single most difficult thing to do in all major sports. My good friend, photographer Lewis Portnoy, who was chosen to be on the USA Olympic team of photographers for four Olympics, said that without question, hitting a baseball is a more difficult action than any other sport accomplishment. If a player has that talent to put the round bat on the round ball, heading to him at ninety miles per hour or more. The pot of gold awaits. Spring training is the time to show talents to those who make a thumbs up or thumbs down decision regarding those with talents hoping to make the big league team. Spring training is indeed a laidback and easy experience for the fans, but a much more intense situation for aspiring players.

Being a baseball art photographer for eleven spring trainings, I was invited to attend the games by the vice president of the Cardinals, Marty Hendin. Later years, that invitation was given to me by John Rooney, Cardinals broadcaster. My photos were being sold in the team store at Roger Dean Stadium in Jupiter, Florida. Seven of my prints were sold with the request that I sign them. Lou Brock and Bob Gibson were having a signing in a private room after a spring training game in 2003. Marty Hendin set it up that I would be signing my prints next to Brock and Gibson.

Lou Brock was signing his items, balls, cards, jerseys, etc. He was signing his name and below his name signing "HOF 1985," Bob Gibson was signing his name with "HOF 1981." HOF was the year of induction to baseball's Hall of Fame in Cooperstown, New York, a very exclusive honor, and since its inception only 269 players as of 2023 have been inducted.

I was sitting next to Lou Brock, who was including his HOF 1985 induction on each item he signed. I started signing mine Don P. Marquess, OFB 2003. Lou, in between his signings noticed that I was signing my prints with the OFB 2003 under my name and kept looking, trying to figure what the OFB stood for, and eventually asked, "Don, what does the OFB mean?"

I said "Old, Fat, and Broke 2003."

MY GRANDFATHER - THE INDESTRUCTIBLE

My maternal grandfather, Albert F. Froussard, was born in 1883 and died in 1984 at the age of 101. He was an inventor and received his thirtieth patent when he was eighty years old. He was a charter member of the Power Engineers' Association in St. Louis and sat on the review board for future applicants. When I was eight years old or so, my granddaddy was explaining some mechanical thing that he was working on and he was very impressed that I understood. I truly don't remember what it was or if I really understood what he was explaining, but from that moment on, he felt that I was the only one of his descendants that had any sense at all. My grandfather started his machine company named Multiple Boring Machine Company in 1917, and during the Second World War, he had sixty- five machinists working for him. My father, my mother (his daughter), my brother, and I all worked for my grandfather at one time or another. I was in charge of assembling the pages and binding them for his catalogues. I also was in charge of addressing and mailing his yearly calendars. I felt very privileged and important to have such a responsible position when I was ten years old or so during my summer vacations from school. I got paid also! Whenever the minimum wage requirement raised, I got a raise, always bringing my hourly wage up to the minimum. My granddad, in addition to being a brilliant inventor of machinery, was also very frugal. He always paid me the minimum wage. e catchphrase for my grandfather was, "He had all of his assets tied up in cash!"

Many people would come into Multiple Boring to see Albert F. Froussard, but the only way to meet with him was for the guest to go anywhere in his sixty-thousand-square-foot building, three-sectioned shop, stand there and wait, and in ten minutes or so my grandfather would pass by. He was always a hands-on boss who continuously checked on the jobs in process.

There is a story about him seeing one of his machinists in the shop and saying to him, "What are you doing?" The man replied, "I'm helping Shaefer."

My grandfather approached Shaefer and said to him, "What are you doing?"

Shaefer replied, "I'm not doing anything."

My grandfather then red "Shaefer's helper" saying, "Schaefer can do nothing without your help!"

Several visits with the machinists' union representative occurred shortly thereafter.

One of A. F. Froussard's many patented inventions was a portable boring bar that was used to remove the calcium deposits and suck them out of boilers on large ships. My grandfather would rent out these bars and a machinist to do the work while the ship was at sea. Prior to his invention, the ships would have to be in dry dock and immobilized for several weeks. His invention enabled the ships to keep sailing while the boiler was maintained.

My grandad rarely paid attention to allocation requirements during the Second World War. He somehow or another got just what he needed to complete whatever piece of machinery was necessary for his participation in the war effort. However, there were certain restrictions on many items that my grandfather just ignored. One day, a government man came to the shop with a letter stating that my grandfather had violated many of the material restrictions. My father at the time was my grandfather's accountant and was in the office working on the books. However, he had developed some allergic rash and had several facial splotches.

My grandfather yelled at the government inspector and said, "Look what you have done to my son-in-law, you have given him hives!"

He then picked up the inspector by the scruff of the neck and threw him physically out of the building and onto the sidewalk. My dad was certain that that was going to be the end of my grandfather's business. Two weeks later, a letter arrived that was very nicely written and appreciative for Albert F. Froussard's efforts during the war, however, with the cautionary request to pay more attention to allocation restrictions. at was all. Whew!

My grandfather's machinery company was highly respected in the industry and had the reputation of being a precision shop. My grandad was in his mid-eighties when a large bell-shaped iron casting was tooled and ready to be shipped to the customer. e truck was next to the machine that had finished the product. As always, my grandfather had his trusty micrometer with him and measured it only to discover that it was one thousandth of an inch off. He would never permit anything to leave from his shop that was not up to his standards. He told the machinist to rework it to make it perfect. The bell had been prepared and ready to ship, but it was disconnected from the machine. The machinist, who had been with my grandfather for over thirty years, got very nervous about his error and restarted the machine without refastening the item and making it secure.

The bell-shaped object slid off the machine and crushed my grandfather against the truck, doing serious damage to the truck as well as breaking many ribs and causing severe internal bleeding for my grandfather. He was rushed to the hospital, and when the family heard about it, we had all assumed that tragic accident would take his life. I was elected to spend the night with my grandmother at her home to be with her and comfort her through this tragedy. My grandad was in a coma for five days, and we all thought his life was over. The family members all took turns staying in his hospital room hoping he would recover. I was in the room when he awoke from the coma. His eyes uttered a little, and he saw me in the room.

He said, "Don, it is a damn good thing that happened to me because it would have killed anyone else!"

He probably was right. He lived for 101 years.

The Sparkling Hawaiian Rainbow

I was fortunate to travel to Germany twice in one year, as well as a trip or two to Phoenix in the same twelve-month period. TWA airlines, at that time, was headquartered in St. Louis, and announced a program that for traveling four international segments and four domestic segments within a calendar year would receive two first-class round trips to anywhere TWA flew. I was only two segments short. I found the cheapest round trip from St. Louis to anywhere, which was to Columbus, Ohio, for $122.00, so I booked it. There was a delay of two and a half hours before the return trip to St. Louis, so I jumped on board.

Two free first-class round trips to anywhere TWA flew was an offer not to be missed. All I had to do was convince my beautiful wife, Susan, to forget her fear of flying and accompany me on a trip anywhere she desired for free! A major convincing job was needed.

"Not now, dear, the boys are in school now, and I can't leave them now," "No, this is not a good time, let's plan on it later," "Not now, my sister wants to visit us this year, and I don't know when she can make it," "Who will feed the cat?"

Excuse after excuse. No matter what, it was apparent that she was not getting on a plane for any reason! In 1999, TWA said that all free flights must be taken before the end of 2001 or they would be lost forever. I checked with TWA who said that my two free tickets could be taken on two separate flights. I realized that my dream of Susan and I going together was a hopeless goal, so I knew that one of those trips would be to Hawaii. I had been to forty-eight states with the two missing states being the hardest to get to, and going to Hawaii would leave only Alaska in my quest for traveling to all fifty states. So, Hawaii, here I come. Ticket number 2 would be decided later. Trip number 2 was later chosen to be in October 2001 to Cairo, Egypt; however, after the 9/11/01 disaster, all trips to the Middle East were cancelled.

My first-class ticket to Hawaii included a stop in Los Angeles with about a two-hour-or-so wait before the flight to the big island of Hawaii. The gate area in the Los Angeles airport was a very large circular room with six or so other gates. My flight showed it would be on-time leaving at 2:35

p.m. My flight there landed at 12:30, so I had time for lunch and a little stroll. I kept passing by that gate showing 2:35 p.m. departure. but there were no attendants nor passengers lining up. So, I continued to walk around the area and entered a small bookstore (I am a bookworm) and surveyed the latest publications. No matter how hard I tried, or how many books I read, more books were published than I could read every year, so I made notes of what I would put in my reading queue. Then returning to the gate again at 2:20 and seeing no activity at the gate, I was getting worried that maybe the flight was cancelled. I walked around another few minutes then went directly to the gate, and there was a sign at the gate that the entry had been moved to down the hallway, not at the gate desk. I almost ran down the hallway just in time to see my plane take off. My luggage and everything were on the way to Hawaii, and my first-class seat was empty. I explained my error to the personnel at the makeshift gate, and thankfully they were sympathetic. Another flight was leaving the next day at the same time, and they made a reservation for me to have the same seat. They even made a TWA-paid reservation at a nearby Holiday Inn for the night.

I was at the airport the next day in plenty of time, and the same gate was there with attendants, so this time I actually got on the plane and sat in my first-class seat while hoping that my luggage of two suitcases would be located when I arrived. As I exited the plane at Kona airport on the big island of Hawaii, I saw my luggage being wheeled to the lost luggage area. I flagged down the attendant and captured my luggage. This airport was small and very open with no big closed-in building, and with the beautiful lei, now around my neck, I was well aware that I had indeed reached paradise. The temperature was a very comfortable eighty-five degrees, and I was thrilled to finally arrive.

I had rented a condo right on the beach a mile or so from the airport, and I was hoping it wasn't occupied by someone else; but then again, I already paid for it for eight days, so I assumed they didn't care if I ever showed up. The condo was directly on the ocean, and I could only see the beach if I leaned over the balcony (Lanai). I had purchased an island-hopper ticket before I left the mainland (which was the only way you could get one at that time) from Aloha Airlines that cost under $300, if I remember correctly. I think it was actually $299. It was a first-class ticket with unlimited travel between the islands. All I had to do was show up at the airport, show the pass, and get on the plane. I don't think that is still available, but what a great bargain. The big island, Hawaii, actually has just about everything Hawaii has to offer, a volcano, a coffee plantation, a rain forest, a pineapple plantation (I was surprised to see how short pineapple trees were), great hotels, and dining. I traveled around the island several times in the PT Cruiser that I had rented for the week. The weather was spectacular, and I did everything that I could squeeze in in one week's time. I rode in a submarine, went deep-sea fishing, rode in a helicopter around the big island, and dined very well at several Luau events. I had a wonderful dinner at the Orchid Resort and Spa. They set up a table for me right on the edge of the beach, I ordered dinner, and I saw a man in swimming shorts with a green leaf headband, run out to the edge of the rocks, and blow a long note on a conch shell signaling sunset. Immediately thereafter, I heard a guitar playing and turned to my right, and there was a gorgeous young lady in a grass skirt dancing in front of a Hawaiian guitarist. I looked around for someone to pinch me, as I felt that surely, I was dreaming. However, the highlight of this trip was yet to come . . .

My trip the next morning was to the Island of Kauai, which was another gorgeous island paradise. The Waimea Canyon on the island was breathtaking with lush trees and greenery and a spectacular waterfall. It was a photographer's dream, and I burned a generous amount of Fuji Velvia film.

As I was departing the canyon a rainstorm hit and somehow or another, it appeared from a clear blue sky. I guess I truly was dreaming. The rain stopped almost as quickly as it started, and in the distance ahead of me on the road was a beautiful rainbow. Rainbows always seem to get further away the closer you get, but not this time. The closer I got to the rainbow, the closer I got to the rainbow. The road was approaching a creek at the bottom of the hill, and the rainbow didn't disappear and remained straight ahead of me. As I got to the base of the hill crossing the creek the rainbow still remained, and as I drove through it, little dewdrops of multicolor were sparkling out the window on the passenger side of my car. It was incredible, and I was almost shaking. At the top of the hill, there was a pull off at the side of the road, and I stopped there to catch my breath. A white pickup truck pulled in next to me, and a man jumped out of the cab with eyes almost as large as billiard balls said to me, "Wow . . . Did you see that rainbow we both drove through?"

He said, "I moved here from the state of Oregon fifteen years ago, and I have never seen anything like that in my life." Needless to say, neither had I.

A year or so later, a lovely lady from Hawaii was in my gallery in St. Louis, and I told her my story of driving through that sparkling rainbow with the multicolored dew like drops. She looked astounded and said, "That is called the hoonimakkeewanie rainbow (or something like that), and it is an island legend. If you drive through it, you will have great luck for life." I have never found proof of that legend, but she may have been right. I am eighty-two years old and writing my second book, and have had an incredibly gifted life. However, I have yet to win the lottery. That will happen when I drive through the next rainbow. Hopefully before I am struck by a lightning bolt.

Beautiful Virginia Beach

I was thirteen years old in 1954, and my dad had a very luxurious 1949 Lincoln Cosmopolitan just itching for a highway driving vacation. is car was referred to by my friends as "a boat." at Lincoln was almost eighteen-and-a-half-feet long and had a very luxurious and very comfortable interior. Just great for sleeping in the back seat (at thirteen, I couldn't think of other backseat activities). My dad and mom loved driving vacations. My dad had a recommendation from a friend that Virginia Beach was beautiful, and his friend even suggested a great hotel named Ocean Terrace that was right on the beach. I had never been to the ocean and was eagerly stoked for the adventure. The trip took us through the Blue Ridge Mountains of Virginia (that really had a "blue ridge" of fog on the top), and my dad couldn't stop talking about the great power of that Lincoln and kept saying how it "just walked" up those mountain roads. I felt that we were truly special in that fancy-smanchy automobile.

We arrived at the Ocean Terrace Hotel, went to our "luxurious" room, jumped into our swimming suits, and headed for the beach, which was just a few steps from our hotel. The beach was crowded on this very sultry July afternoon, and the ocean was just at incredible for me to see. We found an open spot on the beach, laid out our towels, and headed for the surf. I have a very clear and embarrassing memory of my mom in her two-piece (just purchased for our trip) swimsuit that had a bright orange top. My mom was the first one in the ocean, and a giant wave hit her, knocked that orange top down, and revealed her naked breasts. Egad! She was greatly surprised and replaced it quickly. My dad didn't even see it.

I went into the ocean for the first time in my life and soon realized that swimming was a hopeless task until you went past the breaking waves. I was not a great swimmer, but an accomplished one, and managed to get past those breaking waves and take my first swim in the Atlantic Ocean. It was a totally different sensation than swimming in the close chlorinated swimming pool where my dad took me on many weekends, but I was loving the adventure. There were no sightings of sharks or stingrays, but I knew they were lurking for an attack. After an exciting fifteen minutes or so, I attempted to swim back to the beach, but a big wave caught me and just propelled me back to the sand. I felt that I had safely avoided those ocean predators that were planning on me for lunch.

I found our spot on the beach were my mom and dad were waiting and reclining on the towels. e sky was greatly overcast and the sun never made an appearance. What beautiful white skies of Virginia Beach! We got comfortable on our towels and coated ourselves with Coppertone oil. I will always remember that photo on the bottle of that partially covered little buttock showing that little child's tan line. We had been clouding ourselves on the beach for an hour or so when a lifeguard came up and said that we were out on the beach too long and we could get sunburned. How could that be possible with zero sun? I thought at the time the lifeguard was trying to sell us an umbrella or some sort of sun protection.

My dad saw the same ruse and said, "We are just fine, we have suntan lotion," and sent the lifeguard back to his canopied beach chair. Later, I realized that the suntan oil was just like basting the thanksgiving turkey in the oven.

After four hours or so on the overcast sunless beach, while still in our swimsuits (Mom actually was all in hers), we went to a drugstore across the street from our hotel to get some treats and postcards to send to the landlubbers back home. I saw my mom looking at a postcard spinning rack. I looked away for a moment, turned back, and my mom was not there. I saw a clerk rushing over to pick up a lady on the floor and it was my Mom! She passed out in the middle of the store. My dad and I rushed over as the clerk was helping my mom to her feet. She said she was okay and had just gotten very dizzy and must have passed out.

We helped her back to the room, and she kept saying, "I'm okay, I just got dizzy."

We got in the room and helped my mom onto the bed.

Then my dad said, "I feel very strange," and then he passed out.

He laid on the floor for what seemed like an eternity to me and then got up on his bed. My mom said that she was feeling better and was very hungry that she would love a tuna salad sandwich. She had seen a deli a block or so from our hotel. She gave me some money and sent me on my way to get several of them. I felt very energized, and at thirteen, I felt I could save my parents and fetch those chilled tuna salad sandwiches. I was also thinking way back in the recesses of my mind what happens if they don't fully recover. I exited the back of the hotel, ran across the lawn, hurtled a hedge . . . and passed out. I laid there for a while and then made it to the deli to get the sandwiches. I brought them up to the room and knocked on the door, and a man I had never seen before answered the door. He was a doctor. My dad had called the hotel desk, and they sent a doctor to the room. My parents had sunstrokes. e lobster red of their skin sent me to the bathroom mirror to look at my face, and yep, I looked the same. We all had sunstrokes, and what the doctor called "sun poisoning." An afternoon on the beach ruined our trip to beautiful Virginia Beach.

After eight days of recovery in our room, we packed our luggage, had the bellman take it to our car, and tried to get in the car with our blazing red bodies. We, during our week of rest and drinking gallons of fluids, went through countless jars of Noxzema cream. We learned that Noxzema relieved the pain for about three minutes, then it caked and veined, and had to be reapplied, but it was the only thing that helped even a little bit. We could not put our clothes on and remained in our swimsuits for the trip home. e tendons in our legs stiffened and tightened up, so we could barely walk. We looked like crippled homeless lobsters going into a restaurant. I always lagged behind. My parents explained to the diners that we weren't crippled, we were just sunburned.

My skin peeled about three layers, and I developed three fluid-filled blisters on my upper right thigh. For anyone who cares to look, I still have three scars from those blisters, and my legs became badly infected.

My father's remark telling the lifeguard that we would be okay because "we have suntan lotion" still rings in my ears!

The Remarkable Marty

Marty Hendin was the most incredible catalyst I ever met in my life.

Marty was always putting two people together to make things happen. "You need to speak with Melvin Schmidlap, who produces products that could utilize your gizmos." Marty always knew who did what and who could benefit from a mutual relationship. Marty introduced me to Jack Buck, the Hall of Fame broadcaster, who, in his later years, became a very fine and prolific poet. Marty told Jack that he should incorporate his poems on my photos, and we could produce posters that would enable fans to purchase prints that contained nice backgrounds for Jack's poems. We produced seven posters together that sold very well. Marty was a great catalyst indeed.

Marty Hendin was vice president of Community Relations for St. Louis Cardinals and the greatest ambassador for baseball ever, especially for Cardinals baseball. Marty and I had lunch once a week for over ten years. On the way to the restaurant, we talked about baseball. During lunch, we talked the about the Cardinals, and on the way back to his office, we talked about Cardinals baseball. Marty was always promoting the Cardinals and was on the board of at least ten charities, and constantly succeeding in raising funds for each of them.

Many times, when a person is approached for a charitable donation, the individual, if indeed donating, afterward would think to himself, Why in the hell did I just give my money away? However, it's not like that with Marty. He always made you feel important and very fortunate to donate.

"Boy was I lucky Marty asked me." Marty had that incredible talent to make people feel very fortunate in giving their money away. Marty also had that unique talent that never offended anyone nor made them feel that they were just fleeced. Marty was also very impressive in stature being 6'5" tall. Maybe deep down inside, people had a comfort in acquiescence.

Due to Marty's very friendly nature, and being the VP of community relations, anytime a celebrity came to a Cardinals game, Marty Hendin's office was a necessary stop. In Marty's office, I met innumerable celebrities. Marty's office was a very enjoyable stop after every Cardinals game.

I met Rob Reiner, Kenny Rogers, Bob Uecker, and Tony Orlando, among many others.

It was always after a game, and it just didn't seem right if I didn't stop at Marty's office. Usually there was a celebrity of some sort, or a great looking blonde, or some beautiful lady involved in a charitable endeavor. One day in the fifth inning of a Cards/Cubs game, Marty called me on my cell phone and said that I had to come to his office immediately. Well, I knew that it would be someone very famous, or at least some incredible looking babe, so I hotfooted to his office, anticipating a meeting with someone special. As I entered his office, there was just a nice-looking lady in her mid-thirties, wearing a blue tee shirt with the red and white big C of the Chicago Cubs logo. She was just a nice-appearing lady, but not a celebrity nor a bombshell. I wondered just why Marty said I had to meet her.

Marty said to her, "Please turn around so Don can see the back of your tee."

She turned around, and on the back of the shirt, it said, "Chicago Cubs... Heck, any team can have a bad century."

Marty had a love-hate relationship with the Cubbies. He loved them to come to St. Louis for the Cubs/Cards games, but he hated them to win, which fortunately was a rarity.

Every year for over ten years, Susan and I went on the Cardinals Cruise. There were always very interesting Ports of Call and the cruises were very much fun. One such cruise took us to the island of St. Thomas, which was probably the most beautiful island in the Caribbean. We took a cab to the top of a storybook mountain overlooking a gorgeous, deep, and very verdant valley. There was a wall with a railing at the end of a terrace outside the gift shop. The drop must have been close to one thousand feet or so. As we were standing and taking in the beauty of this wondrous valley, a young lady wearing a Chicago Cubs shirt walked between us and leaned against the railing while taking photographs of this beautiful sight. Marty looked at me, looked at her, and stared over the railing at the very long and very deep valley. Marty looked at me again, stared at the valley, and kind of nodded his head at the lady, then at the valley, then at me again. Then the lady walked away. Marty looked at me and said, "Mr. Marquess, we both missed a great opportunity to thin out an alien fan base!"

I went to spring training with Marty every spring for many years, and he always gave a ticket to the visiting celebrity next to me behind home plate. I sat with John Goodman, John Pizzarelli, George McGovern, and Leonard Slatkin. One of the guests was Bruce Adler who was a major Cardinals fan as well as an incredibly talented singer and actor. Bruce and I became very good friends and had lunch together on his visits to St. Louis. He was a very close friend of Marty's. One spring training he was starring in a one-man show at a theater in Ft. Lauderdale when he told this hysterically funny joke:

A man was visiting a loved one at a cemetery when he heard a man sobbing. He looked around and saw a man kneeling at a gravestone and crying very loudly while banging his fist on the grave and screaming, "Why did you have to die, oh why did you have to die?"

The man walked up to him and tried to comfort him. He said, "Oh, sir, I am so sorry for you."

The kneeling man continued sobbing and saying, "Why did you have to die . . . oh why did you have to die?"

The man was totally pitiful and just couldn't stop wailing and banging his fist on the grave. The man asked him who it was that died. The sobbing man said again while banging his fist on the grave, "Why did you have to die, oh why did you have to die?"

He then looked at the man who was trying to comfort him and said to him, "It was my wife's first husband!"

Prom Night, 1958

At Bishop DuBourg High School in 1958, prom night was a big deal, as I guess it was in every school in the country at that time. It certainly was a big deal in 1958. I loved my high school years and was madly in love (I guess back then it was more "in lust" than "in love") with a super intelligent girl named Joan Eichenseer (pronounced "I can see her," just imagine all of the high school comments regarding that name). We had been together (going steady) for two years, and this was the big deal, the senior prom! Our group of friends, I guess, were considered nerds because none of us drank alcohol, did drugs, or anything really wrong except we were all very strong on romantic intimacies. We always had to park the car in very remote places at night after dinner and a movie. Everyone in our group was constantly an honor roll participant; however, my Joan blew all the rest of us away. She never shied to the "B" roll, always "A."

As a further description of our social group, one night I had my daddy's beautiful, but garish, orange and white Ford Victoria, with Joan and I in the front and two other couples squeezed in the back seat. We had gone to a movie at the Fox and afterwards took the long way home through Forest Park, where there was a very secluded road behind the St. Louis Art Museum. I made a joke that the car was running strangely and said that I needed to stop. It was a very private and empty road.

I said, "Gee, what should we do now?", knowing full well that loving and kissing was on all of our minds.

Larry's date, Margie, then said, "I know. Let's say a rosary." That was the worst mood breaker I could ever remember. The car seemed to have no mechanical problems after that remark, so we headed home. is prom night was anticipated to be truly memorable since it was our graduation year, and it meant that after we all went off to college, an era was ending. Larry Giesing took his Beverly Shea, Jim Sullivan (1957 graduate) and Dolores Meyer, Jim Coombs and Margie Brandhorst, along with Joan and me. This was a big, big night. Just as a little insight to our group, for Christmas that school year, I gave Joan a cashmere sweater, Larry gave Beverly a bracelet, Rich gave Margie a necklace, and Jim gave Dolores . . . a subscription to Reader's Digest. Dolores was totally embarrassed to tell everyone what gift she received. Jim Sullivan, always the practical individual, defended his gifting by saying that every month she would be reminded of how much he loved her. at was Jim, ever so sensible. So, anyway, this night was the night of nights for us. Jim made reservations for the eight of us at a moderately expensive restaurant named Steiney's Inn situated on the banks of the Meramec River. He secured a table in a private room overlooking the "scenic" (?) Meramec River. It really made no sense because at midnight after the prom, it would be very dark and no "scenic" was to be seen.

We all arrived in two cars just after 11:30 p.m., and our white tablecloth table was ready for us. All of the guys were in rented tuxedos and the girls were beautifully adorned in their special prom dresses. As I recall, Joan's was a light lime green kind of taffeta thing that had the beautiful orchid corsage (set me back eight bucks). I don't recall the others except the beautiful white formal dress that Dolores was wearing. It was made of some sort of white satin along with white fluffy cheesecloth material. Her dress won the prize of the evening. She was wearing a very tasteful wrist corsage (I had never seen one of those before), and with her high heels, she was close to five feet eleven. Her long brunette hair made her a striking young lady for certain.

We all placed our orders, which were all steaks, as Steiney's was well known for steaks. is dinner was definitely setting me back, close to twenty- five bucks, but what the hell, it was prom night. e tuxedoed waiter delivered our steaks, and an incredible culinary experience was about to occur. e steaks looked fantastic. Dolores ordered a let mignon (the most costly on the menu). She took her knife out to cut it, but it caught the steak, and it slid it off the plate, on to her dress, and down to the floor. Jim didn't see it happen. He just looked at Dolores's plate and saw just a trace of grease but no steak!

He said to Dolores, "Where is your steak?"

Dolores, now completely mortified, said, "Jim, don't worry about it."

He said, "What do you mean don't worry about it? at steak cost $11.50. What happened to the steak?"

"Jim, just forget it."

"I won't forget it. What happened?"

"It slipped off my plate and fell to the floor."

Jim screamed, "What? It fell to the floor? . . . Are you serious?"

He proceeded to have her get up, yanked her chair away, and climbed under the table chasing that steak. It had rolled several feet and was almost still sizzling on the floor just at Beverly's feet.

He grabbed the steak with his bare hands, slammed it on Dolores's plate, and said, "There it is, now don't cry about it!" The rest of us at the table were laughing so hard at maniac Jim and feeling so bad for Dolores. What we all had for prom night dinner became forgettable.

I don't think Jim and Dolores dated again after prom night 1958.

Tornado Encounters

In our first house in Kirkwood we had a garden room on the south side of our Cape Cod style one and a half story home. That garden room was my favorite room in the house. It was a converted sunroom that had beautiful white handmade ceramic tile on the floor. During a snowfall or a rainstorm, it was a wonderful experience looking out of the three walls of windows while being warm and snug inside. One such evening in August, while enjoying the movie Elephant Walk with Elizabeth Taylor and Dana Andrews, there was a vicious rainstorm occurring outside. It got even heavier and then suddenly stopped, and the air in the house became very heavy. I felt incredible pressure and several doors in the house blew open. Then I heard a train. It actually did sound like a train, then a big thump on the house that shook the walls and all the lights went out. Yikes! Susan was in the kitchen, and we ran to each other, considerably frightened. Donny, the four-year-old, came finding his way down the stairs as I was going up the stairs to check on our one-year-old Danny. Danny was standing up in his crib with eyes as large as teacups, not looking frightened, just wondering what the dickens happened.

I picked him up, held him tight, and said that we just had a terrific storm. I carried him downstairs to be with Susan and Donny as we all just relaxed, took a deep breath, and tried to survey the damage.

I looked out the back of the porch to our backyard, and one of the twin oaks was gone. There were two before the storm. I looked further in our yard and found that giant oak lying across our neighbor's fence on the north side of our property. That mighty oak was no challenge to that strong wind. The rain picked up again, and the Kirkwood tornado sirens began blasting. (A little late for sure.) Then our front doorbell rang. I answered it to find a fireman in his rain-soaked yellow coat asking if we were all right. I told him, "Yes, but pretty much shaken up, and we were slowly calming down."

Until a tornado touches the ground, it is just a funnel cloud. Only when it touches the earth does it become a tornado. The taller one of our twin oaks in back was high enough for that funnel cloud to grab it and twist it out of the ground, bounce it off our roof, hit our power lines, then land across our neighbor's fence. The next morning, as I further inspected the damage, the stump from the oak tree was twisted in the ground. I then understood more fully the term "twister."

I had heard that many people say that a tornado sounds like a train. It truly does, and a mighty big train at that!

The other encounter is very unusual as well. We were headed to Interlochen, Michigan, to visit our son Donny who was performing piano concertos at the National Music Camp. We were in Illinois on Highway 52, heading north to Michigan. There were many layers of gray and dusty blue colored clouds in the sky, and two of those cloud layers had a connector of a white cylinder, like an umbilical cord, in the center of those two layers. This cloud formation was maybe five or six miles ahead of us, but Susan and I both felt that those clouds really looked mean. We kept driving while keeping our eyes on those two layers of clouds with that white umbilical between them. The distance between the clouds slowly separated as we were watching, and that white connector suddenly broke through the bottom cloud. I will always remember seeing the cotton candy-like swirl looking like white and gray spinning together. I immediately pulled to the side of the road, and the three of us jumped out of the car and laid together in a ditch as that twisting mass crossed the highway not more than five hundred feet ahead of us. Being a photographer, I had three cameras in the trunk, but not one in my hand to take a photo of the actual formation of that tornado that crossed the road directly in front of us. It kicked up a lot of dust and traveled East through Northern Illinois, tearing up land and vegetation.

I feel that we saw what meteorologists and storm chasers never get a chance to see—the actual formation of a tornado. Lucky us(?). We saw one form, although we never were transported to that wonderful Land of Oz.

Popcorn

I was born in late 1940. As I remember, from the time I was four years old or so, every movie theater would have double feature, a newsreel, and a cartoon, sometimes two cartoons, which was always great for me. After dinner many times, my mom and dad would take us to a movie. Usually, we would arrive when the middle of the second feature was being shown. Then we would find three or four seats depending if my ten-years-older brother would come with us. After disrupting the moviegoers in the chosen row, we would sit down and try to figure out the plot of the movie that was showing. Actually, I wouldn't have understood it anyway. I was just waiting for the cartoon. Anyway, we would sit through the portion of the second feature, wait for the main attraction, watch that in full, then wait 'til the second feature got to "this is where we came in," then we would get up and leave. Usually, I would fall asleep long before that happened. If I saw the cartoon, I felt fulfilled for the evening. e point of this digression is to further illustrate how moviegoing has changed. As I remember, no one ever cared when a movie started; you just went to a movie. The first time I remember the starting time of a movie being important was for Alfred Hitchcock's Psycho. e movie ads said that no one would be seated during the last twenty minutes of the feature. How strange was that?

There was a new beautiful and quite large movie theater named Des Peres Cinema. (The movie theaters were used to be called "movie theaters," but now they are "cinemas." I guess that makes them sound much more fashionable.) is chapter is not intended to be a parenthetical chapter, but I feel that a digression would there . . . later to be assigned to its proper location. is new, beautiful, and quite large "cinema" was showing a new movie with Robert Redford called e Great Waldo Pepper. This was mid1975 and it was the first time we had seen Susan Sarandon. She didn't last very long in the movie, but she made a positive impression. As usual, with our movie dates, Susan and I would enter the auditorium when all the lights were on and choose our seats, and then I would go to the lobby to get the popcorn and drinks (I would secretly add a box of Jujyfruits) and head back to our seats. For this particular showing, I got the popcorn and returned to our chosen location. The lights were still on, and I was holding this long tube-shaped tub of popcorn. For some reason that I have been unable to figure out, I felt the popcorn tub start slipping in my grasp. I squeezed it tighter to prevent losing it, but like a rocket launch, the popcorn box exploded from my hand, showering three or four rows with a cloudburst of popcorn. The rows of moviegoers were laughing uproariously. As a matter of fact, I think the whole theater was laughing, except Susan . . . she was pretending that she didn't know me. I was really embarrassed but laughing because I had no idea what large an area could be covered with one box of popcorn.

With a somewhat sheepish grin, I went back to the concession stand while holding my empty box that once contained popcorn. I said to the concession lady that I spilled my box of popcorn (resisting the urge to tell her how it exploded), and she very graciously took the box and filled it again for me.

As I entered the auditorium again with the box of popcorn, the lights were out and the movie started. I found our row and started apologizing for the disruption when once again I felt the popcorn slipping. Not wanting it to spill again, I increased the pressure of my grasp, and unbelievably, the popcorn container shot skyward and showered the three or four rows with another hail of popcorn.

From the back of the theater, I heard someone shout, "It's the same guy!" Susan hung her head in disbelief.

I forgot about getting another box, and I think we both missed the first half hour or so of the movie because we were attempting to be invisible.

Wonderful Pranks

In my career of being an architectural representative for my father's company, Missouri Brick Co., I was fortunate to meet many remarkable individuals. One such individual was Joe Drachnik. Joe was a graduate of Washington University and possessed two engineering degrees, electrical and architectural. Joe was a delight to be with, and we had lunch together on many occasions. Joe was a spec writer and associate with HOK architects (Helmuth, Obata, and Kassabaum), one of the top architectural firms in the world. It was at one of our luncheons he told me this outrageous prank.

One of Joe's good friends worked in the accounting department at McDonnell Douglas, the producer of fighter jets in St. Louis. The Phantom F4 was one of the most versatile jet aircrafts in the world, and they were produced in the St. Louis plant, which employed over ten thousand people. It was so large. It was like another city. Joe's friend said that one of the accountants had purchased a Volkswagen Beetle and continually bragged about the incredible gas mileage he was getting on his new car. With American cars getting eleven to thirteen miles per gallon, his new Beetle was getting over twenty miles per gallon. With his constantly talking about it to his fellow workers, they devised this wonderful prank.

At lunch several of his coworkers would bring cans of gas and secretly add gas to the Beetle. Being an accountant and excellent with calculations, the Beetle owner would continue regaling his office buddies about the remarkable gas mileage he was getting from his auto.

"You won't believe this guys, I am getting over thirty miles per gallon."

"Yeah, yeah," his coworkers responded, "we are getting tired of hearing that."

The office guys had so much fun with the prank, they intensified the adding of fuel. The Beetle owner, against the pleading of his coworkers, just couldn't stop bragging about his gas mileage.

"It is just flat unbelievable guys, I am getting over fifty-five miles per gallon!".

"Oh, come on. That is ridiculous, how can you be getting fifty-five miles per gallon?"

"Look, you guys, I know how to calculate mileage, and it is a fact!"

The office guys continued until over seventy miles per gallon was achieved. The owner lightened up on his wonderment and stopped his aggravating boasting.

The pranksters had so much fun doing that, they decided to do the opposite for a while and started siphoning gas from the Beetle. The owner stopped bragging about his gas mileage and didn't mention the incredible drop in miles per gallon. It must have dropped so low that he was probably getting under ten miles per gallon.

The owner took the car back to the dealer and said, "There is something drastically wrong with this vehicle, I was getting over seventy miles per gallon, and now I'm getting under ten."

The service manager just stared at him like he was a four-year-old.

When the owner told his coworkers about his dilemma, they revealed their delicious prank!

At the same lunch, while on the subject of remarkable happenings, Joe told me of this incredible money-grabbing situation. A man took an ad in several major publications, including the Wall Street Journal, stating the start of his new company. His company was an investment company not listed on any stock exchange whatsoever, and he was offering shares in his company for $25 per share. In the ad, he stated that "The US government guarantees that after ten years, you won't lose your investment." Joe Drachnik then said the man took the $25 per share in his company, and purchased a savings bond for $18.75 with maturity in ten years and sent it to the "investors" in his company, thereby pocketing the $6.25 for himself. According to Joe, this entrepreneur made over $430,000 in the shares he sold. He was stopped only because he couldn't use the federal government in advertising to further a private enterprise.

True or not, that was an incredible story.

Joe, also at that very lunch, posed this question: "What does an insomniac, dyslexic agnostic do?"

"He stays awake all night wondering if there really is a dog."

The World's Greatest Blackjack Dealer

I hadn't been to a casino for several years, but after Susan died, I brooded for several months and decided to see if I still remembered how to play blackjack. There is a casino in downtown St. Louis that is named Lumiere and is quite beautiful inside with lots of yellow and burnt orange walls and carpeting. It sort of reminds me of the old Wilbur Clark's Desert Inn, which was one of the few non-glitzy but very elegant casinos in Las Vegas. So, I went to Lumiere as some sort of diversion. Standing behind a blackjack table was a very beautiful and stately red-haired lady whose table was empty, so I approached and sat down to try my luck. is dealer was very personable, incredibly accurate, and the perfect diversion for me. Her name was Marina and she spoke English very well. But being originally from Azerbaijan, which was part of the U.S.S.R., she spoke Russian as her native language. We seemed to have a sort of connection other than the blackjack table, and she seemed to like me as I definitely liked her.

To my mind, it seems to be that the last thing to occur in learning a new language is the subtlety of humor. is very beautiful Marina Melikova, the best and most attractive dealer I had ever experienced, seemed to possess a very ne sense of humor. We made each other laugh from time to time. I am a very rm believer that humor heals many wounds, and she got me laughing on many occasions and certainly assisted in healing several of my wounds. Also, I must tell you, I was very lucky playing at her table and won a nice sum on that first session. I was also very lucky playing at her table the second time when I went back the next day. Then the next day after that . . . and so on, and so on.

Marina quickly became a friend of mine, and I kept hoping that we could become more than just friends. However, there was one seemingly insurmountable issue. Marina was considerably younger than me, and I felt that I was just living in a dream world thinking that we could have a relationship beyond the table. After a couple of months, she asked me for my phone number.

I started to write it down for her, and she said, "No, you can't pass anything to me. Just tell me, and I'll remember it."

I told her my number and waited for her to call me. I waited, and waited, and waited some more. Then one evening after I was playing at her table that afternoon, she called. We talked for almost a half hour or so when I got the courage to ask her out to dinner. Astonishingly, she accepted my offer, and we met for lunch at Smokey Bones. We had a great time (at least I did), and it seemed to me there was a possibility for a deeper relationship beyond, "hit me."

My adult son, Daniel, and I had made reservations at Disney World to spend thanksgiving and celebrate my birthday, which fell on thanksgiving, November 26. Marina and I spoke many times on thanksgiving that year because she was cooking a duck for dinner. Every time we spoke during that afternoon, there were more problems cooking that duck . . . it just wasn't getting cooked completely. She tried many things in cooking that stupid duck and called me often asking for suggestions. I had none. Finally, as I recall, she just cut up the duck, fried the pieces, and made duck soup. We really established a relationship on those phone calls. I couldn't wait to see her again. I called her as soon as I got back to St. Louis, and we met for dinner at Outback.

After dinner, she said to me, "You know, if we see each other outside of the casino, you can never play at my table."

I realized that and told her that it was her call. She had to make the decision.

She paused for a short time, then said, "I don't want you to play at my table again."

I must explain how different we are in age, and I guess how I come by it naturally. My grandfather was born in 1836 and that is not a misprint. Not my great-great-grandfather, but my grandfather was born in 1836 and fought in the Civil War as a scout for (as he told my father) Robert E. Lee. He married my grandmother, and my father was born when his father was seventy-one and his mother was thirty-three. Their age difference was thirty-eight years. Marina is thirty-seven years younger than I am, but I guess if it's okay with her, then it is okay and very thrilling to me.

Marina and I have been together for almost ten years, and she is even more beautiful that she was when I played that first hand of blackjack at her table. I hired her for my company, Missouri Brick Company, and she is a spit re of delight to our employees as well as our customers. Marina is easily the greatest thing that ever happened to me in my later years. She is gorgeous, and we have been living together, along with her mother (who is younger than me), her daughter named Ramina who is a junior in high school, two cats, and a dog named Bella who has a world-class insatiable appetite. Marina is indeed a pleasure to live with. However, now when I say "hit me," I have to duck.

Very Hot Stuff

I have always enjoyed hot spicy food, especially Mexican and Asian foods. I have two very good friends, Don Hussman and Dwight Dickinson, who are prominent and very successful architects in the St. Louis Metropolitan area, and they enjoy the spicier Mexican flair as well. We enjoy many lunches together and spend most of the time laughing while lunching. There was a new restaurant in Kirkwood (one of the 110 independent communities surrounding St. Louis) named Caliente', and we were up for trying it out.

During lunch, while awaiting our lunch specials of enchiladas, frijoles, and tacos, I started relating my love for hot spicy foods, and of one particular dining experience that I had months previously. There was a restaurant owned by ex-footballers with the St. Louis Football Cardinals, Dan Dierdorff and Jim Hart, named Jim and Dan's Rio Grande. It was one of the latest restaurants created by them and managed by my good friend Kenny Bland. Kenny was the food expert, and Jim and Dan were the money experts. A beautiful combination indeed.

Since it was very close to a movie theater that Susan and I frequented, we decided to try it out before the movie. The menu was Tex-Mex flair and all the dishes sounded scrumptious. I am a chili lover, and they had four choices from which to choose: American Chili, Tex-Mex Chili, Grandma's White Bean Chili, and Buzzard's Breath Chili. Buzzard's Breath Chili rang the proper bell for me, so I ordered a bowl. It was delivered to the table, I took a spoonful, it tasted just fine, so I took another spoonful, then the fire attacked. I am telling Don and Dwight about the horror and killer power of Buzzard's Breath as our lunch plates arrived. The plates were very attractively presented, and there was little red pepper on the side that was placed on the outside edge of the plate. I continued relating the Buzzard's Breath experience to them in telling them of my heroism in swallowing that second spoonful, and that it was the hottest thing I had ever tasted in my life.

I told them that the next morning, I called my friend Kenny Bland and left a message to call me in room number 402 of the burn unit at Barnes Hospital and left my cell phone number. Kenny called me very concerned shortly thereafter and said, "My god, Don, what happened?"

I said, "I had a bowl of your Buzzard's Breath Chili. There may be a lawsuit!"

Then as I am telling this story, I bit in half that little red pepper on the side of the plate. My entire life started flashing before me, but I was way too macho to readily admit that death was rapidly approaching. So, I continued momentarily before it became apparent that if I didn't have a fire extinguisher immediately, my life was over. I could barely breathe and was gasping for air as we all summoned the waiter. He responded, looked at my wretched condition, and noticed the half-eaten pepper on my plate.

He said, "You didn't eat that, did you? It was a fresh Habenero pepper. We just got them in this morning for plate decoration."

"Wait a minute," I said while gasping for air, "this is lunchtime. I ordered food. It was on my plate. What am I supposed to do with it . . . say hi?"

Dwight and Don realized that if I died at that time, the lunch check was theirs, so they made every effort to save me and ordered a large glass of milk and a scoop of ice cream to assist in my survival. Thanks to them, I survived and I am able to relate this story.

Kenny Bland, in defense of the Buzzard's Breath of Death said that it was made with a combination of Jalapeños and Habeneros, but I was the only one who ordered it that day. It was made at 11:00 a.m., and this was 6:00 p.m. It sat cooking down all day and all that survived were the peppers and a scant amount of meat and beans. Luckily, I survived that as well.

Yankee Doodle Dixie

In the early seventies, St. Louis began a very short-lived trend of bringing top names in the entertainment industry to appear in small venues such as barn dinner theaters, restaurants, and nightclubs. I say short-lived because it came and went so fast that it was almost over before it started. Barbara Streisand appeared at the Crystal Palace on Gaslight Square, and the Smothers Brothers also appeared at that venue. e Four Freshmen performed at the Ramada Inn, Patti Paige was at the Barn Dinner eater, the World's Greatest Jazz Band was at the Chase Hotel, and Rich Little (my lookalike) was at the Cheshire Inn. Carlos Montoya (great guitarist) was at the United Hebrew Temple, and Andres Segovia (greater guitarist) performed at the Kiel Opera House. What a great period of time for entertainment in St. Louis. Just as a side story regarding the Segovia performance, the theater was packed, and Segovia walked on stage carrying his guitar, sat on a folding chair on stage, and started playing a Bach fugue. Less than a minute into his performance, someone in the audience coughed. Segovia stopped playing immediately and rested his guitar on his knee while someone else coughed, then another person, and then it seemed like the entire theater coughed. When there was total silence, Segovia continued playing that Bach fugue exactly where he left off.

Another performer during this great glut entertainment salvo was Chet Atkins, whose performance at the Barn Dinner eater was absolutely remarkable. Chet's style was alone in its greatness at that time in the country guitar world. He used his thumb as base accompaniment to the other fingers on his right hand. It was almost like that thumb was a third hand that was totally independent of the other fingers on his hand. The further remarkable aspect of his playing was that in the most intense and exciting part of whatever he was playing, he appeared totally relaxed. I don't think he ever broke a sweat. The most incredible part of his performance was his playing of "Yankee Doodle Dixie" at the same time on the guitar, with his fingers playing Dixie while his thumb was playing Yankee Doodle. It seemed totally impossible, yet I saw him do it. We were in the second-row center, and I watched him carefully, and no digits became detached.

I made a living (sort of) in a vocal trio with two remarkable musicians, Lon Gilbert on guitar and Barry Oxenhandler on banjo and guitar. I also played guitar. I was actually a French horn and trumpet player, and barely adequate on the guitar. Susan, a very talented guitarist, gave me a beautiful Martin O-18 guitar for our fifth anniversary. It was far beyond my musical ability, but nonetheless a gorgeous musical instrument. e day after the Chet Atkins concert, I sat on the balcony of our apartment and attempted to play "Yankee Doodle Dixie" at the same time, just as Chet. A foolish attempt at best. I struggled for over three hours and finally got the opening phrase of Yankee

Doodle with my thumb (Yankee Doodle went to town) and the opening phrase of Dixie (I wish I was in the land of cotton) with my fingers. I was incredibly proud of myself and called to Susan to hear it. I played it for her, and it actually sounded correct.

She said, "How did you do that?"

I said that I first started out playing Dixie with my fingers, and while I was playing that by note, I thought Yankee Doodle and worked it in with my thumb.

She said, "Good grief, Don, you could drive yourself crazy and tie your brain in a knot."

I replied, "You are right, baby, my head is tied in a knot at this very moment!"

Susan said that I shouldn't think of it as two different songs, that I should write it out and just play it as one piece. She took a piece of manuscript paper, wrote the two different melodies as one piece, she then took my guitar, and played it perfectly on the first try that took maybe twenty seconds.

I was so embarrassed. I got up and left the apartment without even saying goodbye. I don't recall talking to her at all for several days.

I Don't Gamble. I Play Poker

From the time I was a child, I enjoyed playing card games. My mom, dad, and brother played a game called pit, which as I remember was a game with cards that you traded commodities like flax (I never knew what that was . . . and still don't), wheat, oats, rice, etc. It was a somewhat a wild game with hands grabbing, cards flying until someone would yell "cornered on corn!" We also played a card game named authors, which I remember to this day regarding who wrote what. It was a very fun learning experience.

When the entire nation went goofy over a card game called Canasta, which was played with a double deck, and our whole family played it nightly for a while. My dad loved a game of cards called pinochle, which we played with his friends. I was always invited to play because of my card sense as my dad called it. We also played hearts, which was a game where you could wipe out all the opponents if you collected all thirteen hearts along with the kiss of death queen of spades. Every heart penalized you one point, and the queen of spades penalized you thirteen points. Unless you got all hearts and that dreaded queen, then all other players got charged twenty-six points against them. When you amassed one hundred points, you lost the game. I have a pretty good memory for cards, and a lot of my friends call it card sense. My brother, when I was just six or seven, would play a game with me called concentration, where all fifty-two cards were laid randomly on the table face down and you would expose one and try to match it with another—six with a six, eight with an eight, one at a time. Every time one card was exposed, you had to remember where the match was in the unexposed face down cards. So, if another matching card was picked from the pile, you knew where its partner was. Whoever ended up with the most pairs, won the game. I consistently beat my ten years older brother.

In my twenties, there was a weekly (or maybe multiple times weekly) poker game with friends that floated from house to house. We played for high stakes of a $.25 limit— that is 25 cents being the most you could wager any time.

Also, a massive wager like that was a rarity. If you lost $25, it was a major catastrophe, except for one night at L. D. Brodsky's house.

We were playing seven card stud, and on the first five cards, I had a club flush. Terrific, eh? Not so fast. Barry on the first five cards had kings full. I was clearly toast. The other three players kept calling whatever we bet. I knew for certain I had won the pot. Not true. At that moment, I was a very sad second.

In seven card stud, the last card is face down, and it was dealt. I didn't look at mine, and neither did Barry look at his. We both knew we were golden with our hands. He bet everything he had, which was a little over $55 bucks (which was allowed on the last card). I knew I had won with my club flush, and I had around $60 dollars, so I called. He turned his cards over and revealed his king's full house. I knew I had lost, sadly. I turned my cards over, and the last card down was the seven of clubs, giving me a straight flush, a big surprise to us both. Barry, mustering as much control as he possibly could, stood up, smiled, and said, "I am never playing poker again!" Which was very true until the next week when we played again!

Now with the immense popularity of Texas hold 'em, I have developed a friendship with a very congenial group of friends, and we play every Sunday morning after breakfast at the Hollywood Casino in Maryland Heights, Missouri. Poker is an enormous challenge and greatly unpredictable. Just this afternoon, I had a diamond king high straight flush, which is extraordinary, and in the pot was only $10; however, I received an additional $325 from the house. The games are different, and every hand is unique. Poker is not a game playing against the house. You are playing against the other players. There are two exceptional players, Matt and Mike, who seem to win with remarkable consistency, and six or so others— Darryl, Goldie, Brian, Gregg, and Inky. There are very few major disasters, and generally a good time is had by all.

The worst hand I ever had was pocket queens and the flop was QQK. I had four queens, I bet $5, and everyone dropped. I didn't sleep for a couple nights as I should have checked, and let the hand develop.

Poker is a great game and somewhat addictive. I still remember cards as I did play concentration with my brother.

Three Quickies with Susan
(I Just Loved Quickies with Susan)

Susan and I were on a road trip traveling for a couple of hours when we saw a road sign advertising "Stuckey's next exit." We were both getting a little hungry, and maybe some good rural home cooking might just fill the bill. Stuckey's stores were small diners with huge stores that contained forgettable trinkets. I don't know if any still exist, but they had great pecans and home-cooked meals. We pulled onto the lot and entered the store. The diner was to the right, and all of the trinkets were to the left. We turned right, entered the dining section, and found an unoccupied booth. A "Flotype" waitress came up and took our drink orders. Behind the counter of the restaurant, there was a menu describing all of the dining options. One of the options said "Fried ham Sandwich." I thought, well, I guess that is some sort of country specialty until I realized that the letters were all scrunched together.

I asked Susan if she had ever heard of a "Freedom Sandwich" (carefully planting the mispronouncing in her mind), and she said, "No, I never have heard of a freedom sandwich. I'll ask the waitress." (Aha . . . I got her.) The waitress returned to take our order, and Susan said "Ma'am, what is a Freedom Sandwich?"

The waitress replied, "I don't know."

"What do you mean you don't know? It is on your menu board." The waitress looked at the board and said, "Mah'em, that is a Fryhed Hahem."

Susan realized how I set her up and really laughed at her mistake.

Another quickie . . . .

Susan was a very proper lady and even knew which side of the plate the knife and spoon went, as well as the napkin and fork. She was very well schooled in proper decorum. We were dining at a very trendy white tablecloth restaurant in the Central West End area of St. Louis named Balaban's. We placed our orders, and the salads were brought with a dressing cruet on the side. My salad had some large leafy lettuce that needed to be cut up somewhat. I took my knife and fork and started to cut when, I guess, the knife caught a large piece of lettuce, and my salad exploded all over the tablecloth. I knew Susan was looking at me, but I never looked nor even caught her eye. I very carefully took the salad dressing cruet and started dolloping the lettuce where it landed on the table. I was doing it very precisely, not spilling any of the dressing on the tablecloth, just dripping it perfectly on each piece of lettuce on the table and never looking at Susan. I knew she was embarrassed but loving it.

I heard her saying while laughing, "Oh no."

The third little quickie... Susan loved a chocolatier in St. Louis named Bissinger's Handcrafted Chocolatier. In Susan's words, their raspberry creams were "to die for."

Susan's birthday was April 13. So, for her birthday one year, I gave her a two-pound box of those overly sweet confections. It became a nightly ritual that around 9:30 p.m., I would bring her the box, and she would remove three or four of the chocolates, not removing the little paper wrappers holding them. Every night, she would rummage through the empty wrappers seeking a few more chocolates, never removing the wrappers from the box. When it was obvious to me, but not to Susan, that the chocolates were getting fewer and fewer, I returned to Bissinger's and bought another box. I secretly added a few chocolates to the original box, and Susan kept exhibiting great joy when she discovered a few more left. Eventually, the new box needed replacing, so I went back to Bissinger's and told them the story about the nightly hunt. I bought another one-pound box, and they thought it was so funny, so they gave me another box for free. I continued secretly reloading the original box until that two-pound box became over ten pounds of chocolates . . . with Susan never noticing. Every night, she would forage and get thrilled finding a few more. Finally, after running out of finances to satisfy her raspberry cream addiction, I had to tell her what I had done.

She laughed with that ever so delightful way of hers and said, "Well, I guess I was the perfect victim of your loveable prank. You are free to do that again whenever you wish."

Fernando Tatis and the Incredible Feat

The date was April 23, 1999, and the Cardinals were playing a night game that Friday in Los Angeles. The Cardinals were batting in the top of the third inning with the score 2-0 Dodgers. The Cardinals loaded the bases with two singles and a hit batter making every base occupied and bringing up Fernando Tatis who then crushed a pitch thrown by starting pitcher, Chan Ho Park, into the left field bleachers for a grand slam home run, making the score 4-2 Cardinals. After a series of unusual events, the Cardinals once again loaded the bases with Tatis coming up to bat again with the bases loaded. The score at that time was 7-2 Cardinals against the same pitcher, Chan Ho Park (I have never understood just why he was still pitching), who hung a curve that Tatis crushed once again to the left field bleachers, very close to where the first grand slam ended.

Two grand slams in the same inning! That never happened before in Major League Baseball and will probably never happen again, especially off the same pitcher! I asked both of my good friends, Jack Buck, the Cardinals broadcaster (who called both slams), and Marty Hendin (Vice President of the Cardinals) if that opportunity ever occurred before in a major league game, and they both doubted the possibility, especially off the same starting pitcher. Sensible thinking would dictate that after seven runs allowed by the starting pitcher, that pitcher would have been pulled before the opportunity presented itself once again. Without question, I firmly believe that is the only time it could possibly occur, and will probably never happen again, certainly against the same pitcher. The final score was 12-5 Cardinals.

I, as a baseball art photographer, had the exclusive rights to photograph Mark McGwire's seventieth home run baseball as well as Sammy Sosa's sixty-sixth home run baseball. I created a photo of each of those baseballs in a limited-edition print. Therefore, I had a reason to make the following call the morning after Fernando Tatis hit those two grand slams in one inning. This fact was all over the news media, and a big, big deal. I called my gallery at the moment it opened. Darlene Williams, the gallery director, answered my call.

I tried to mimic Fernando's accent, I said, "Hallo, ees Mr. Markaese dere?"

Darlene said, "No, I'm sorry he isn't, who is calling, please?"

"Deese ese Fernando Tatis."

"Oh, Mister Tatis, I am certain that Mr. Marquess would love to talk with you, why do you want to talk to him?"

In my strong Fernando Tatis accent, I said, "I want him to photograph my balls!"

There was a long pause and a complete silence for several moments when finally, Darlene said, "Oh, Don, why do you do this to me?" And then laughed hysterically. As a matter of fact, I laughed a lot as well! I got her again.

Just another quick story about Darlene who was a very beautiful lady with a terrific sense of humor who could speak with anyone at their level, from a truck driver to a corporate executive. She was with Anheuser Busch at their world headquarters in St. Louis, and was an excellent lady for my gallery. She had that very rare talent to relate to any person entering the gallery and they all liked her immediately.

One morning, while driving to work, I saw a sign in front of Webster High School announcing Blood Drive Today. I called the gallery to speak with Darlene about various topics regarding sales of my prints, and at the end of the conversation, I told her that I had donated a pint of blood to the Red Cross for their blood drive.

She said, "Don, that is great."

I said that the nurse would be at the gallery at 4:00 p.m.

Darlene said, "OK, I'll see you then."

I said, "I will try to make it, but maybe not. I donated a pint of your blood, not mine!"

Once again, while laughing, "Oh, Don, why do you keep doing this to me?"

The Great Gippo

I have been very fortunate in my life to have had many friends. Most of them were very intelligent and talented. A very select few stand out as being extraordinarily talented. The "Great Gippo" is one of them. Jan Gippo was the piccoloist (piccolo picker) for the St. Louis Symphony for thirty- five years or so. I once introduced Jan (pronounced "Yahn") to a friend of mine and described him as one of the top two piccoloists in the world.

Jan, being ever so humble, said, "No, I am probably one of the top three. Rampal and Galway are very good flutists and play the piccolo also. I must be behind them." at is Jan, always deferring to other greats of the world. Jan commissioned the highly respected composer, Lowell Lieberman, to compose a piccolo concerto for him. When Lowell Lieberman completed the composition, Jan performed the world premiere of that concerto at the National Flute Convention in New York City, with the orchestral ensemble being members of the New Jersey Symphony.

I am always using silly accents when I call Jan on the phone and always get him laughing.

One early Sunday morning, Jan was awakened by a phone call from a man with a very strong Irish accent who said, "Good morning, Mr. Gippo."

Jan said, "Marquess, that is the worst Irish accent I have ever heard." The caller was James Galway, the premier flute player in the world who was born in Belfast, Ireland, and was blessed with a beautiful Irish brogue. Jan apologized to James and said he thought it was a friend pulling a prank. Jan embarrassedly called me later and told me about his blunder. James Galway wanted permission from Jan to record the Lieberman composition.

Later that morning, when I was certain that Jan was at his Sunday morning radio broadcast From the Garden Live, I called his number, got his voicemail, and said in a French accent, "Oh ho ho, Monsieur Gippo, do not let that Irishman record your concerto. Fleese ees Jean Pierre Rampal. I must have fleet for myself to record."

Later that evening, the phone rang at home. Susan answered it in the kitchen, and I could hear her laughing.

She then called out to me from the kitchen: "Oh, Jean Pierre, Monsieur Gippo wants to speak with you!"

As mentioned earlier, Jan Gippo was incredibly brilliant and an extremely talented musician. But like all gifted individuals, he was somewhat absentminded and a little confused from time to time. This next story is one of those instances where a "you would have to be there" statement would apply. Nevertheless, I will make an attempt to describe it. We were in the car together. He was driving, and we were passing by Washington University. I asked him if he would be available for a poker game Saturday night at my house.

He said, "I don't know. I will have to check with Allen."

I said, "Who is Allen?"

He said, "I didn't mean Allen, I meant Carl."

I said, "Who is Carl?"

He responded, "Jane Allen is a terrific piano instructor. Jane Carl is the lady I am almost engaged to. How I got that so confused with both of their first names being Jane is very confusing to me. If I could have a picture of my brain at that moment, it would be quite a blur. Where that came from, I don't know."

I responded, "Third base." (For those of you that understand that remark, no explanation is needed. For those that don't understand it, an explanation is impossible.)

Jan, who is a little over six feet tall and at the time several thousand pounds overweight, gave a concert at the Royal Academy of Music in London, which was a great success.

The next day, the writer of his rave review started the review by saying, "Jan Gippo, a very large man with a very small instrument . . . ."

One of my favorite writers is Max Shulman (Many Loves of Dobie Gillis, Rally Round the Flag Boys, etc.), who had a character named Crip in one of his books (I think it was Sleep to Noon) who was so named because he always had a broken limb, a sprained ankle, or some other ailment in that he was always on crutches or had some part of his body in a cast. Jan, who was always very healthy, developed a series of physical problems late in his life that greatly reminded me of Shulman's Crip. Jan, who was an insulin dependent diabetic (he had a stomach stapling for weight control) told me that he was diagnosed with a fatty liver that is similar to cirrhosis but not alcohol-induced. It was cancerous and he needed a new liver. But before that could be accomplished, the doctor detected some heart issue that needed to be taken care of, which required several hospital stays. Something in that operation required additional surgery, and it seemed to me that almost weekly there was some other domino falling that required something else, after something else, after something else. Finally, all was clear for a new liver for Jan. The operation was a success.

His old liver was removed and a new liver was installed. Happy Day! Jan is of Norwegian Jewish ethnicity, and like much of the Jewish population, he possesses a great sense of humor, so I felt that my homecoming gift from the hospital for him would be accepted with the proper spirit. After I determined that he was going to continue to live and everything worked out well, as a gift for his arrival home, I contacted a Jewish deli and ordered a chopped liver on rye with a little onion and Gulden's mustard.

The owner of the deli, whose name was Saul, after being told what I wanted to do and why, said, "Ooh, I have got to be a part of this!" He couldn't stop laughing.

I requested that Saul would have a note inserted for the delivery with the chopped liver on rye that stated, "Welcome home . . . . I don't know where this liver came from, but I have my suspicions! From your friend and mine, Don."

Dogs Are Truly Man's Best Friend

As a pre-teen, I had my best friend, Sarge, a collie/mutt blend. My grandmother had a neighbor with a beautiful collie that looked just like the big TV star, Lassie, who just had a litter by some non-pedigreed vagabond who apparently saw the beautiful collie in the backyard, became enraptured with that collie's irresistible body, jumped the fence, and left his calling card. Itinerant dogs carry no papers, so it was just a drive-by impregnation. My grandmother told my mother that the lady across the street was selling these tainted puppies for $10 bucks each. My mom told me that if I wanted a marked down doggie, it would cost me $10. I had saved $16.50 from my paper route, so I had the pick of this embarrassing litter. Sarge was the best looking and most intelligent and friendly puppy of the litter, so he became mine!

Sarge was my constant companion with his white fur, brown ears, and a few brown markings with a fluffy collie tail. I bragged to my friends and created a story that I almost believed about a timber wolf being Sarge's daddy. Sarge was my bodyguard and best friend. I had a friend, Dick, and he and I rode our bikes almost everywhere with Sarge running alongside. Dick saw Sarge every day and felt very comfortable around him. One day, Dick left something accidentally on our dining room table. It was summer and hot as hell in the middle of July. The dining room window was partly open. Dick pushed it open and started to climb in. Bad idea. Sarge denied his entry, barked, snapped, and growled with a menacing tooth-baring snarl that made Dick reconsider entry. The next day, Dick told me about the encounter, but he and my guarding Sarge were close friends once again. Sarge knew his job as a house patrol officer, and as long as you didn't invade his protected responsibility, you were just fine.

In much later years, after being married to Susan for thirty years or so, we had a black and white Cocker Spaniel named Murphy that became my spiritual adviser. No matter what happened during the day in my business, I would come home, and Murphy was always happy to see me regardless of any of the bad happenings in my business, or in the world for that matter. Murphy was always thrilled and happy to see me. The stock market could take a major hit, but Murphy didn't seem to care. Murphy would jump on my lap. I could tell him my misfortunes, but he still had his very positive and very fun outlook. He always looked at me with an expression that said, "Hey, nothing matters. If I have you and my milk bone, what is there to worry about?" He always convinced me to look at the brighter side of life. Truly my spiritual adviser.

I have always loved Old English sheep dogs but have never owned one. It always seemed to me that it would be best if a neighbor owned one that I could visit from time to time. As luck would have it, our neighbor Art Tonkins had a loveable one named, Daisy, that was eternally a puppy. Even at eight years old, she had the temperament of an eight-month-old puppy. We developed a strong friendship though separated by our backyard fence.

Another kind of dog that I thought was beautiful but never knew the name of the breed—I described it and Susan told me its name—was a Weimaraner. I really liked its short tannish brown coat that had a definite mauve tone, and I thought that was a definite artistic attribute. Also, Weimaraners had a nose that matched the body. A Weimaraner's nose definitely made that breed a beauty. Luckily, Susan thought the same and did extensive research to find the perfect Weim pup. There was a breeder in Florida named Bagshaw Breeders, and they had a litter of pups that were for sale. The strain of Weimaraners that they had was called Magnum, and they were bred for temperament and size. We picked one from the photos they sent by FedEx and picked one with the most intelligent and friendly face. They flew our choice male to St. Louis, and we could not have chosen a better one. Although he was only five weeks old when we got him, he seemed to have an inner instinct that his bodily functions were for the backyard only. He never made a mess inside. We learned later that the Magnum strain meant big! Our cute little puppy that we named Toby grew to an incredibly powerful 118 lbs. He was one strong hunk of dog flesh. Every night when I came home from work, I would hold his rawhide chew bone and he, with his incredibly powerful jaws, would gnaw on it until my arms tired out. He was great with kids in the neighborhood, and Donny and Danny, our boys, loved him as well. We felt that little kids could almost ride on his back and would never feel in danger. Toby was indeed a gentle giant. However, bad guys, beware, he could remove an arm or two if provoked.

Toby had a strong conscience and was greatly remorseful if he did something wrong. At those rare times of infraction, he would get very low on the carpet, come toward me very apologetically, and plead with me with his amber eyes and beg for forgiveness. If Toby had something in his mouth that he thought might be frowned upon by us, he would take it to the dining room and hide in plain sight under the dining room table.

For our fifteenth anniversary, Susan gave me a beautiful Rolex Cellini watch that was eighteen carat gold with a beautiful brown leather band. I came out of the shower, and the vanity counter where I left it was bare. No Rolex. I went downstairs to the dining room, and there was Toby chewing away with the leather band hanging out of one side of his mouth. He had his guilty dog expression when he saw me, and stopped chewing, and allowed me to rescue my watch. One side of the watch leather band was gone and the other side with the clasp was slowly disappearing. Toby allowed me to pry open his mouth and retrieve the watch. I managed to save the clasp, which was eighteen carat gold as well. The jeweler told me it was lucky I saved it because to replace it was over $120. Toby was guilty as hell as well as remorseful. I still have the reminder of his felony by a tooth mark on the backside of my watch. (At the time of his infraction, I was tempted to give him a memory of my tooth mark on his backside.)

When a service man would come to the house, Toby would place his 118-pound body between Susan and the serviceman, and just sit calmly on guard between them with the unspoken advice: "One false move, Buster, and you will regret it!"

I took Toby to see Dr. Clark at the Clark Animal Hospital for his annual checkup and the waiting room was packed. Toby was very well behaved, no matter where he was, and sat in front of me with his usual noble position with his chest in its normal kingly stance. All of the other dogs were sitting on the floor with their masters. Everything was under control in the waiting room. Then a man walked in with his coal black Scottish Terrier who proceeded to disrupt the peace and quiet of the waiting room, as he barked at every dog there, and then all of the dogs started barking and whining and total chaos erupted. Toby didn't change position, but very loudly let out a giant woof! All of the dogs, including the disturber Terrier, kind of bounced in the air, and total silence filled the room.

Toby was indeed a wonderful animal and my best friend for many years.

Now Bella is our wonderful animal with a beautiful face, a great heart, and an insatiable appetite. When I come home, Bella is always happy to see me, and even happier if I have a treat for her, and I give her a ten-minute-or-so neck massage.

Dogs are just flat the greatest. They seem to love me just as I love them!

Michael Barnes And The Seventieth Home-Run Ball

I had achieved a degree of success with my baseball art photos. I read in the paper the day after Phil Ozersky, a scientist at Washington University Medical School, caught Mark McGwire's seventieth home-run baseball and he hadn't decided what to do with it. I found his name in the phone book (remember those?), called him and left a message saying that I had an idea that could be pro table for him, and he could still retain the ball and decide what to do with it later. I would just need the ball for a few minutes. At that time, I had an exhibit of my photos at the Cardinals Hall of Fame and had achieved a certain degree of credibility. I left my phone number and hoped that he would call me back. He didn't . . . but his attorney, Michael Barnes, who was handling the merchandising of Phil Ozersky's good fortune, left a message that I should call him with my proposal. At this moment, I hadn't totally formulated what my proposal was, but I felt that I should call him back and tell him what I planned to do, and how much money he, Phil Ozersky, and I could make from my (yet to be determined) proposal. I formulated what I felt was a great idea for all parties and went over and over it in my mind in the hope that he would agree and we could have the contract produced. I was very nervous about the entire situation because I knew that it could be a career-enhancing move. I kept rehearsing my call over and over in my head and finally had everything straight for my idea and had the courage to pick up the phone to call Michael Barnes.

I called, and his phone call was answered with his message: "Thanks for calling Michael Barnes, sports attorney. Leave a message, and I will return your call as soon as possible."

I said very strongly (this was really important to me) in my rich radio voice, "Hi, this is Michael Barnes . . . . No, wait a minute, you are Michael Barnes, and I am . . . . Well, it no longer matters who I am . . . . Goodbye." I blew it.

I called again the next day, and Michael himself answered. I told him who I was and that my proposition was as follows: I would photograph Mark McGwire's seventieth home-run ball, produce seventy signed and numbered Cibachrome thirty-by-forty-inch prints selling for $2,500 each with $500 donated to Cardinals Care, and the remaining $2,000 to be split equally between Phil Ozersky and the Marquess Gallery. Also, I would produce a total of seven thousand eighteen-by-twenty-four-inch special prints selling for $70 each, with $10 of each print donated to Cardinals Care and the remaining $60 to be split equally between Phil Ozersky and the Marquess Gallery. Michael Barnes thought it was a terrific idea and said that I should have my attorney draw up the agreement. The eighteen-page document was produced and signed by both parties. As a postscript, Phil Ozersky auctioned the ball at Guernsey's in New York, and Todd McFarlane (the cartoonist of Spawn) was the successful bidder at $3.14 million dollars. Barry Bonds, several years later, greatly devalued that investment when he hit seventy-three home runs.

Some People Can Tell a Joke, Some People Can't

Humor has a way of making a cloudy day sunny. I can be in a very down mood, but reading several pages of my collection of Gary Larson (the Far Side) cartoons, makes me feel much better. A Mel Brook movie can have the same effect. Young Frankenstein is one of the best ever. Humor indeed soothes the troubled soul. I am offering a few of my favorite humorous stories.

1. A man was doing an article on prison life and attended a large prison in cen Kansas. He completed his morning tour and was invited to join the inmate's lunch. There may have been 150 or so inmates. After the meal, one of inmates stood up and said very loudly, "Seventy-four!" and everybody laugh Another man stood up and yelled, "Twenty-four!" then everyone laughed ag Then one other stood up and said loudly, "Twelve." The reporter asked warden just what was going on.

The warden explained, "Most of these inmates have been here for a long time and have heard most of the jokes many, many times, and the lunch break is rather short, so they compiled a list of 150 of the funniest jokes they have ever heard. They wrote them all down and compiled them in a booklet, so in the interest of saving time, the inmates will just call out a number for their joke of choice instead of taking the time to tell the entire joke." The reporter was amazed and asked if he could read it and come back for dinner with the inmates in the dining hall. He was given the booklet and read all of the jokes and found the funniest one. He went to the dinner to join the inmates.

After dinner one man stood up and yelled, "Sixty-two." Everyone roared with laughter.

"Fifty-four," another yelled, then a hearty laughter erupted. The reporter saw a pause, stood up, and yelled "Forty-six." Dead silence, no one laughed at all.

Once again, he stood up and screamed even louder, "Forty-six!" Still no response. He told the warden, "I have read the entire list of jokes, and that one is the absolute funniest I have ever heard. I yelled it twice and no one laughed. Why?"

The warden said, "Well, some people can tell a joke . . . some people can't."

2. It was late at night when the phone rings in the army motor pool. The priv answers the phone and says, "Motor Pool."
The voice says. "What is available in the pool tonight?"
The private says, "Four jeeps, a couple of pickups, and a big Cadillac for the fat-assed general."
The caller says very loudly, "Do you know who you are talking to?"

The private says, "No, I don't."

The voice says, "This is the general!"

The private says, "Who wee, do you know who you are talking to?"

The general says, "No, I don't."

The private then says, "Well, goodbye, fat ass!"

3. A very wealthy rancher went on a safari and was enraptured by the zebras. thought they were the most incredible animals he had ever seen. He wants to bring one back to his ranch. He arranged and purchased one, then brought back and let her run freely in the meadow on his ranch.

A bull noticed this new animal running around in the field, and walked up to the zebra and said, "What in the world are you doing on this ranch?"

The zebra said, "Well, I am just supposed to run around here and look beautiful. What do you do around here?"

The bull replied, "Take off those striped pajamas, and I'll show you!"

4. An elderly man and his wife were taking their daily walk and noticed that a n insurance company had opened in their local shopping center.

The wife says to the husband, "You know, Charlie, maybe you should think about getting some life insurance."

He said, "You know, you are probably right, let's go and check it out."

They walk into the office, and Charlie's wife sits in the waiting room, while the husband goes in to talk to the agent.

He says to the agent, "I am considering purchasing a life insurance policy, what will it cost?"

The agent looks at the obviously very old man and says, "I don't know, sir, how old are you?"

Charlie says, "I am ninety-two years old, but I feel great. My wife and I take a walk every day, I mow the lawn every week and shoot baskets with friends of mine every Sunday afternoon. The old ticker is in great shape!"

The agent says, "Do you have a doctor?"

"Of course I do"…

"What is your doctor's name?"

Charlie says, "My doctor's name, my doctor's name . . . my doctor's name… what is that flower that has a long stem with thorns and beautiful red petals?"

The agent says, "Rose?"

"Rose, that's right. Rose! What's my doctor's name?"

5. Dave, up in years, calls his doctor and says, "Doc, I am feeling great and I h fully recovered from that cardiac incident I had months ago, and Margie a greatly miss those intimate moments we used to have. Is it possible to have prescription for Viagra?"

Doc says, "I don't think that is wise, Dave, you know you have just recently recovered from your heart incident."

"But, Doc, Margie and I really miss those intimate moments together . . . Please, Doc!"

"OK, Dave, but let's do it this way, take Viagra for a week, skip a week, take Viagra another week, skip another week, then call me."

Weeks go by and Dave doesn't call, so the doctor gets worried and calls his number. Margie answers and the doctor says, "Margie, how is Dave?"

"Oh Doc, I am so sorry, Dave died last week."

The doctor says, "It was the Viagra, wasn't it?"

"No, Doc. It was all that skipping."

6. A man was sitting on an airplane next to a very well-dressed elderly lady, the sun caught the ring on her finger the reflection of it was almost blinding, the man kept looking at the incredible diamond and just had to ask about it said, "Ma'am, I am a jeweler in Manhattan and I have never seen such incredible diamond, it looks almost as big as the Hope Diamond."

She says, "Yes, it is almost the same size, it is the Klopman Diamond, but like the Hope Diamond, it carries a curse."

The jeweler says, "A curse? What is the curse?"

She says "Mr. Klopman."

7. After Quasimodo fell to his death, Notre Dame was in the market for a new ringer. So, posters were put out with the notice. After several days, a m applied who had no arms and wanted the job. He told the man in the bell to that Quasimodo was a hero to him, and he wanted the job as bell ringer our respect for him.

"But how can you do that? You have no arms," he said.

"I'll show you."

He backed up to the door started running toward the bell, smashed it with his face, slipped and fell out the window, and crashed to his death on the ground. A crowd gathered around as the custodian ran downstairs and one of the crowds said to him, "Who is he?"

"I don't know, but his face rings a bell."

Two days later another applicant comes to the bell tower and asks for the job. He said that his armless brother fell to his death last week, and out of respect for his brother, he wanted the job.

The custodian said, "OK, let's see how you do."

The man backed up to the door and took off at great speed, grabbed the rope on the bell, his hands slipped, and he tumbled to his death on the ground below. The custodian ran down the stairs and a crowd had gathered around and asked him who the dead man was.

He replied, "I don't know, but he is a dead ringer for his brother!" (Sorry about that one)

8. Sidney and his wife of ten years were invited to a party, and Sid says to wife, Sarah, "Now these are guys that I play poker with every Wednesday, they are bringing their wives, so just be nice. Please, don't start making stories to make you sound important, just be a nice person and listen."

After a wonderful evening with great food and friends, they get back in the car, and as soon as the door closes, Sidney says, "Well, Sarah, you did it again! The subject of classical music came up and they started talking about Mozart. You had to jump in the conversation and say, '"Oh, Mozart was such a nice young man, we met and talked at the Fifty-Seventh Street subway station many, many times,' and you kept talking about it and repeated it many times! How could you be so dumb? You know the train doesn't stop on Fifty-Seventh!"

9. A nice, young Jewish boy comes home after graduating from college with degree in economics. And he says, "Mom, I got a job offer and I am work for Jesus."

The mom almost faints and says, "Oh no, my son . . . How could you do that after all your fine and educational times at the temple and in this kosher household?"

He says, "Don't get excited, Mama . . . Kraft Jesus, Kraft Cheeses!"

Las Vegas
(We're Gonna Kill 'Em)

A very good friend of mine years ago was a man named Lon Gilbert. Lon was a very fine guitarist and had an incredibly rich baritone voice. Lon, Barry Oxenhandler, Susie Drozda, and I sang in what I considered at the time to be an excellent folk quartet that was destined for greatness. Our group achieved marginal success for a while, then split up, and went our individual ways. Lon loved to gamble, however for the most part, that love was unrequited. Lon was skillful, however very unlucky. I have always considered myself luckier than skillful when it comes to gambling, which is a situation that most gamblers prefer.

Lon Gilbert married a very beautiful and statuesque lady named Donna Daugherty, who could have very easily been a top model. They were getting married on a Saturday in early April, and he wanted to spend their honeymoon weekend in Las Vegas. He invited Susan and I to come along, and I was just fine with that. Lon had never been to Las Vegas, but I had been there several times and just loved it. They got married, and the next weekend we were going to Vegas. Sadly, in the middle of the week, Donna got the flu and just couldn't travel. Without Donna, Susan decided that she wouldn't go either, so Lon and I went to Las Vegas anyway to celebrate his honeymoon. Very strange indeed, but the trip to Vegas excited both of us enough that we were going anyway . . . without the girls!

It was to be a very short trip, leaving Friday morning and returning Sunday night. As we were on the plane, Lon asked me how much money I was bringing, so I told him that I was taking just a little over $400. He said that was strange, as it was the same amount that he was taking. This was 1970, and that truly seemed to be a considerable amount to take for just a weekend.

Lon then stated, "We are going to kill 'em." Of course. e plane touched down at 10 a.m., and we got to the very long taxi line and finally got into a cab. Lon asked the driver where the cheapest hotels are in Las Vegas, and the cabbie told him that they were downtown, definitely not on the strip.

Lon said, "Great, take us downtown."

I hadn't spent much time downtown, as the several times I had been there, I stayed on the strip. e hotels downtown that I remember at the time were the Fremont, the Mint, the Four Queens, the Las Vegas Club, and the brand-new Union Plaza Hotel. All of the hotels had signs in the windows advertising their breakfast specials, which you won't believe: two eggs, hash browns, bacon, toast, and coffee for thirty-nine cents. It is true, you can look it up (Casey Stengel). We checked in to the cheapest hotel we could find (we didn't want to waste any of our gambling money), which was the Las Vegas Club Hotel. It cost $18.75

per night, which included two free breakfasts. What a deal! We got to the room that had two twin beds (thank goodness), a shower only, and in the upper right corner of the room there was a black-and-white TV chained and secured with a padlock. I had no idea that anything like this existed in Las Vegas. There was also a McDonald's restaurant downtown, which we frequented several times.

So, we went across the street to the brand-new Union Plaza Hotel to take all their money. This was around two o'clock in the afternoon. We still had our $400 each. We hadn't lost a dime. I found a $5 blackjack table and proceeded on my quest for untold fortune. After about an hour or so, I had taken the casino for $35 and was a very happy player. Lon came up to me and asked to borrow some money. An hour plus at the tables and he blew his entire $400 or so. I loaned him my $35 winnings, and he went away, only to return a half hour or so later, broke again. I was very lucky again and loaned him my latest $40 winnings. Therefore, a pattern was set. Once I loaned it to Lon, I couldn't lose it, so I inadvertently opened up a savings account in Las Vegas. I wasn't continually a winner, but I was doing much better than Lon. Remember, we had only been there a couple of hours and had a full couple of days ahead. In Las Vegas, if you are playing at a table, the drinks are free. Lon would sit at a table, order a "free" drink, and before it got delivered, he would lose another $15–$20.

I told him that it would be much cheaper to just go to the bar and order his gin and tonic, but he said, "Hey, they are free at the tables." The weekend progressed with roughly the same pattern. I had only about $250 of my $400 left, but Lon owed me about $450, so it was a pro table trip for me. We played and played until it was crunch time for the plane's departure. We caught a cab to the airport. Lon had no money to pay half, so I paid the entire cab bill. We then got to the airport and literally ran to the gate just in time to make the plane. When we got back to St. Louis, we couldn't have gotten my car off the lot were it not for me. Lon is a very intelligent individual with a bachelor's degree, but somehow or another, he leaves that intelligence elsewhere when he enters a gambling venue.

His honeymoon was very enjoyable for me, especially, and I enjoyed depositing the $485 check he wrote to me. Viva Las Vegas!

John Curry Marquess

My father was Robert Lee Marquess, named after Robert E. Lee, the great Confederate general. The reason? My father's father fought in the Civil War. If you do the math, that seems impossible; however, here is the explanation: My father was born in 1907 when his father was seventy-one years of age. My grandfather, John Curry Marquess, was born in 1836 and fought for the South in the Civil War. (I have the muzzle-loading rifle that he carried.) As my father told me, his father was a scout for Lee. This is not known to be a provable fact, however, that is what my grandfather told my father. Upon further conversations with Civil War historians, he was probably a spy for the South, whether directly reporting to Lee or not. The reason for that statement is that he told my father that most of the time, he did not wear his uniform when he went beyond enemy lines, and that determined that he was a spy. My dad told me many stories of his father hiding out in barns and keeping himself warm under hay. My dad also expressed disbelief that many nights his father kept from freezing by covering himself with leaves and piling snow on top of the leaves.

My grandfather survived the war and purchased one thousand acres of tobacco land in western Kentucky in a teeny-tiny town named Pee Dee. From what my father told me, he probably owned the town. He was the largest taxpayer in Christian County, Kentucky. When his first wife died, he became a very desirable widower. Trying to do the extrapolation from what my father told me, as well as researched records, my grandmother was thirty-three years old when my father was born. The first child from their marriage was stillborn, and my father was their second child. My grandfather's first marriage was childless. My grandmother, Frances Redd, was twenty-nine years of age, and my grandfather was sixty-eight when they married.

I have a letter written in beautiful script in February 1861 by my grandfather to his brother, James Marquess, stating that there definitely would be a war. e US government, so my grandfather felt, lied to the South and ignored the Mason–Dixon Line agreement in considering to allow California to enter the Union as a free state. Per the Mason–Dixon agreement, all states above this imaginary line would be free states and those below would be slave states. The state of California spanned that line and wanted to enter as a free state. My grandfather felt that the South would not allow this without a fight. Therefore, war was inevitable. The South was greatly dependent on slave labor for the production of cotton.

Furthermore, you hear stories of the Civil War in which brother fought brother. My grandfather's brother, James Marquess, who lived in Ohio and fought for the North, was captured by the South. My grandfather interceded and got his brother released, but James had to sign a document to "Fight no more." In my family, brother really did fight brother.

Another interesting part of my heritage is that my sixth-generational grandfather was a pirate who was hanged for treason. John Curry Marquess was the son of William Kidd Marquess II. William Kidd Marquess II was the grandson of William Kidd Marquess, who was the grandson of Captain William Kidd (1655–1701), the pirate (privateer, according to my family) who was hanged for treason at the age of forty-seven. The lineage is directly to me in that he is my great-great-great-great-great-great-grandfather. My brother, Robert K. Marquess, my father's cousin, Wes Marquess, and my wife, Susan, all researched the history of William Kidd and came up with identical results.

I truly don't know if this has any connection whatsoever, but I have never been seasick in my life. I have been on a small boat with four sailors in the Pacic Ocean when a vicious storm attacked and all four sailors got extremely sick, but not me. I was on a cruise ship when the stabilizers stopped working and 90 percent of the passengers were greatly ill, but not me. I am not fully aware of whether my ancestry has anything to do with that, but it is a curiosity.

Kennenbunkport, Maine

Susan, before we were married, worked for BOAC (British Overseas Airline Company) in Denver, Colorado, as a travel agent booking flights and trips worldwide. Susan was born in New Jersey and traveled throughout New England, a location that she felt needed to be photographed by me. She used her extensive travel agent abilities to book our New England trip. She booked spectacular bed-and-breakfast inns for the four of us—Susan, Danny, Donny, and me—and the trip was perfect. We went to see Niagara Falls and stayed at the Asa Ransom House in Clarence, New York, where the room was terrific and the food was spectacular. We visited Boston and enjoyed Durgin Park with the surly waitresses and the terrific food. The New England Aquarium was worth the entire trip alone, and we were having a wonderful time indeed. We stayed at the Ramada Inn that was owned by a friend's cousin, and the accommodations were comfortable indeed. As I remember, the hotel was on Soldiers Memorial Parkway just off Storrow Drive. e drive to the New England Aquarium was a short forty-minute drive from the hotel.

We got lost heading back to our hotel from the aquarium driving on Storrow Drive when for the first ten miles there were signs saying "Storrow Drive Left" or "Storrow Drive Right." Then we came to a fork in the road with no mention of Storrow Drive at all. Apparently, we chose the wrong time of that fork because Storrow Drive was mentioned no more. Being a typical guy who never asks for directions, I drove on for about another half hour or so (it only took us forty minutes to get from Ramada Inn on Soldiers Memorial Drive to the New England Aquarium, but so far, we had been traveling back two hours or so trying to find it). Susan finally convinced me to stop and ask for directions . . . definitely a nonmacho thing for a man of my stature. Guys just don't stop to ask for directions. There was a gas station ahead, so I pulled over, went inside, and asked the attendant how to find the Ramada Inn on Soldiers Memorial Drive. As he was giving me directions, another customer came in, interrupted the clerk, and asked me what we were looking for. I told him where we were headed, and the clerk continued giving me directions. The customer looked at the clerk and said to him, "What kind of idiot are you? They will never get there that way." The clerk said, "Who are you calling an idiot? I know this is the best way for them to find it." The customer yelled at the clerk and used several imaginative couplings of four-letter words. The clerk yelled back at him, and, fearing that it might come to blows, I left, went to the car, and started heading in the general direction that both of them seemed to agree upon. When I got to the car and told Susan what had happened in the filling station, she wasn't surprised at all.

She said that, "Helpful Bostonians are like that."

An hour or so later, we saw the red neon sign that said Ramada and hoped it was the one that had our clothing in the room. Lucky us, it was.

Our next stop was the Ralph Waldo Emerson Inn in Rockport, Maine, which was situated on the beach of the Atlantic Ocean and had a great restaurant that had terrific food and a great view of the sea. So far, Susan had mapped out the perfect trip for us. We then proceeded north to Kennebunkport, which was a very scenic ocean "fishing village" for, I guess, the super wealthy.

Kennebunkport was extremely picturesque, and Susan booked a room for us at the Kennebunkport Inn, which was a converted several-hundred-year-old mansion. It couldn't have been more beautiful (nor more expensive) and, as I recall, sat at the top of a hill overlooking the quaint shops of the port. One of the major attractions of Kennebunkport was a point on the sea a couple miles north of the village, where Spouting Rock and Blowing Cave were located. Susan and the boys wanted to spend time at the beach, so I armed myself with my three cameras and headed to the point on the rocks where I could make "great art." I reached the point and there was a small sign that said, No Climbing on the Rocks. The sign was small, and I figured, what the hell, great art lies ahead. I was the only person anywhere around and felt I could be wherever I wanted. I climbed out onto the rocks, and there was an opening in the rocks where a pool of ocean water was located. I started using my cameras to photograph whatever I thought would make interesting "art." From out of nowhere, two guys in stocking caps and turtleneck sweaters stood next to me on the rocks overlooking spouting rock. I was a little frightened, but they asked me for my identification and wanted to know just what in the hell I was doing there. I showed them my driver's license as well as my photography business card. They frisked me and treated me like a criminal suspect. I asked them what was going on, and they pointed out a beautiful home right across the inlet. There was a flag raised, and they said that that meant that the vice president, George H. W. Bush, was in residence. His summer home was on Walker Point, which was just across the inlet. After convincing them that I was just a guy taking pictures, they left me alone on the rocks. They were Secret Service men protecting the vice president of the United States. Apparently, I convinced them that I was harmless and no threat to the veepee, so they went away and left me alone on the rocks. Anyway, after they left, I stood on the rocks with cameras in hand ready to take some magnificent photos. It was an overcast day and the light was somewhat gloomy, but I was there anyway ready to make the perfect photograph. I looked down at the pool of water surrounded by these massive rocks, and the water came in and made a little "bloop."

The water spouted about six inches several times, and I thought, "Well this is a tiny area away from most entertainment, and the people here must be starved for any small bit of excitement they can find."

I started shooting when I heard a giant "roar." Aha, I thought, "Blowing cave!" Loud roar, probably greater than most ocean roars, but no big deal. As I was waiting for the next little "bloop," another intense roar occurred and the spouting rock spouted! A geyser exploded and spewed water probably six feet above me through the rocks. I was almost washed off the rocks and into the sea. I was soaked, and my cameras were soaking wet. I guess the fact that I was in danger and about to be going to Davy Jones' Locker didn't concern the Secret Service guys. As long as I had no high-powered rifle, I was on my own.

I made it back to my car and headed to the beach to spend some quality time with Susan and the boys.

Susan asked if I had gotten some great shots, and I said, "I'll tell you later!"

I spent two days later on a deep-sea shing boat, which was a great thrill as well as being very productive. I must have caught ten or more large cod and had a whole lot of fun doing so.

After Kennebunkport, we headed north for Bar Harbor (pronounced Bah Habah), where Susan had not booked any place for us and we were just going to wing it. Winging it never took flight because everything was booked, so we went inland and spent the night in Bangor, Maine. With no further excitement in Bangor, nor Bah Habah, we started the long drive home.

Hotel Colombi

In the Missouri brick business, we represented the largest manufacturer of split tile in the world named Gail Tile, which was located in Giessen, West Germany. We were very successful in securing sales for that company, and I was invited to their factory on many occasions. Gail had developed an incredibly strong ceramic that was only one-eight-inch thick but could be extruded seamlessly for twenty feet or more. I was invited to the plant to view this new and very innovative product.

The USA representative and very close friend, Bill Haslett, was there for the unveiling, and Bill and I were offered a new Opel station wagon to use for a week to tour Europe. This was an incredible opportunity for us. Bill and I purchased a new Michelin Guide and mapped our trip. Since Bill was a gourmet and I loved to eat, we carefully mapped our trip based on the number of toques (chef hats) shown after each restaurant review. We had a culinary experience awaiting.

Our first stop was Rothenburg ob de Tauber, which was a walled city untouched by World War II bombings. The Isenhut (White House) was our first stop for a hotel and dining. I took care of the room negotiations since we were looking for a deal for two rooms. Since it was off-season, we got a very good rate for both rooms. The dinner was spectacular, and the tour of the tenth-century village was great. We both walked the wall.

The next stop was Brussels, Belgium, where the waffles were absolutely the very best in the world. We traveled south from there to Luxembourg, where the capital of Luxembourg is Luxembourg, and stayed in a terrific very old hotel and dinned at a gourmet "Chinese" restaurant.

The next morning, leaving Luxembourg, the fog was so thick that the sides of the Autobahn were invisible. I was driving and felt very nervous traveling when it was difficult to see fifty feet ahead. I was driving at eighty kilometers (forty-eight miles per hour), and cars were ying past us at very high speeds. I guessed that they were used to driving blind. When we reached the border of France, all traffic slowed to a crawl. A gendarme stopped us, and I asked what happened.

He stated, "Two hundred car crash, four dead." The highway closed, so we took an alternate route past Cherbourg to our destination, the Colombi Hotel in Freiburg. The hotel was one of the top hotels in Germany, and the restaurant showed five chef hats. It was our top dining adventure of the trip. We both ordered the chef's selection, which was a terrific meal including dessert for the costly price of $125 for each of us. Bill ordered a bottle of wine, which the waiter placed in an ice bucket behind Bill's chair. Dining at a table next to us were a very elegant appearing couple celebrating something. The man had snow-white hair and resembled Spencer Tracey in his later years. e lady was beautifully dressed in a very formal light orange gown.

As we were still dining, the waiter filled Bill's wine glass for the fourth time or so and emptied his bottle. Unknown to Bill, the waiter poured two glasses of wine for the couple next to us and then placed their bottle in the ice bucket behind Bill. Bill finished his last glass of wine and looked for the waiter to fill it. The waiter was nowhere around, so Bill just got up, went to the ice bucket, picked up the bottle, filled his glass, then placed the bottle back in the bucket, not seeing the glare of Spencer Tracey watching Bill, the ugly American, stealing his wine.

Bill sat down, took a sip, and with a very wild look in his eyes, said, "Ooh . . . that's really good!"

I saw the entire thing develop and just waited to see what would happen. I told Bill what he just did, and he looked over at the now-steaming man at the table next to us. Bill got up, walked over, and apologized to the man, who fortunately spoke English, and the man laughed and graciously accepted the apology. Our waiter came to the table, and Bill explained what happened and requested that our waiter offer the man a cigar from the cigar case. He did, and Spencer lookalike smiled and accepted the offering. The bill came for us, and Bill said that that was the first time he has ever seen a cigar that cost fifty-two dollars.

The Fabled Waters of The Sea of Cortez

Jim Sullivan, who was the president of Gail Tile, USA, put together a group of Gail distributors, who happened to be the top sales companies for Gail, and called it the "board of directors." It was actually the board of directors of nothing, it just had a neat sounding name. Once a year, Gail would host some lavish meeting of "the board," and in 1982, it was to be in a brand-new resort named "Los Arenas" on the tip of the Baja in Mexico at the mouth of the Sea of Cortez. I received the invitation letter and jumped at the opportunity.

The itinerary was to fly into Los Angeles and spend the night at Jim Sullivan's yacht club, the Balboa Bay Club, then travel to La Paz, Mexico, which was located on the Sea of Cortez side of the Baja, and then take a private plane down to the tip of the Baja to Los Arenas for three days and four nights of delicious food and fishing. The Balboa Bay Club was super posh, and Jim's new forty-five-foot cabin sailboat with sleeping berths below was dwarfed by the other craft at the club. Jim Sullivan was a sailor, as were the other two of the three of his guests. Phil Stalcup from Seattle had his own sailboat, as did Harry Atherton from Boston. Three of the four of us were seasoned sailors. Harry, Jim, and Phil had their fishing gear in PVC tubes to be carried on the plane with us to Los Arenas. These guys were serious deep-sea fishermen. Our plane for La Paz was leaving late in the afternoon, so we had time for a morning sail in Jim's brand-new sailboat. It was great fun especially for me since I had no experience and basically nothing to do, so I could just sit and relax and enjoy the beautiful morning's sail. The three other guys were doing what sailors do when sailing, which seems to be a lot. After the morning's sail, a wind came up as we approached the harbor returning Jim's sailboat to its slip. Jim thought that with three sailors on board, sailing the harbor sounded like it would work. Well . . . it didn't. With all of the jibbing and rigging and such, the wind was so strong that we collided with another sailboat that was leaving the harbor. Jim and the other two sailors thought that it was much funnier than the collided boat owner did, but apologies were made and there were no adverse consequences.

We then boarded the plane for our flight to La Paz, where we were taken to a private airstrip and a very small plane awaited our arrival. There was a pilot, but no copilot, so I occupied that seat. The pilot spoke no English, but he knew where we were headed (I hoped). The instrument readings were covered in dust and the pilot kept wiping them clean with a very dusty rag, and I thought that this flight might not make it to Los Arenas. After a while, a dirt runway appeared, and we landed and were taken to the resort by some sort of jeeplike vehicle. The resort was indeed very picturesque and brand-spanking-new. However, apparently the owner ran out of money when it came time to hire a cook and must have just found someone hiding behind a cactus and said, "Can you cook?", and hired him. e dining at the resort was a cut below Taco Bell. Sadly, it was the same with our shing vessel. It was a twenty-two-foot boat with one outboard motor and one captain named Manuel.

We arrived at the beach at dawn where the boat was in the sand, with Manuel standing in the back. There were slots in front of the seats to rest the shing poles, but not much of anything else . . . no seat belts. The four of us got on the boat, and my shing pole was there for me. The other guys brought their poles (PVC pipes, remember). I never had much of a chance to deep-sea fish, but I was very open to the adventure. Our knowledgeable captain, Manuel, knew just where to go for us to catch "bait." At one point, all four of us had a fish on the line. We were catching bonita, which I understand to be of the tuna variety, however much smaller. The biggest fish I caught, Manuel cut up for bait. After an hour or so, we had enough bait, so Manuel hauled anchor and we headed further out to sea.

I considered it a very unfair competition, but we all put $10 in a "big fish pool." Those guys were taking advantage of me, but I really didn't care. This was fun, and I was loving it. Manuel prepared my line with bait, and we all dropped our lines hoping to lure a big one. We all caught several fish, and at the next location where we dropped our lines, I felt my line grow taut and thought that I had caught my hook on a rock or something. I leaned forward and wound the line tight again and kept repeating that for twenty to thirty minutes. This was no rock that I snagged.

As I kept reeling it in, Manuel shouted, "Rojo, rojo." Then I saw the bright reddish orange scales surface. I continued reeling him in, and Manuel screamed, "Rojo rojo," then pointed to me, flexed his arms, and called me "El Magni co."

It was a 45½ pound red snapper. at was the biggest one he had ever seen. I was so proud of that fish that I carried it through the dining room of the resort and proudly showed it the diners. "Yep, I caught this fish all by myself. Isn't it gorgeous?"

I had heard many horror stories about the outrageous costs of stuffing a caught fish (Fish taxidermists, I assume) and sending it back home. I thought the best thing to do with that red snapper was to eat it at the resort.

One of our group, Phil Stalcup, said, "I am not going to let their cook screw up this sh." So, he filleted it and sautéed it with lemon, garlic, and butter. To this day, it was the best fish I have ever tasted in my life. After dinner, as I collected my $30 reward for the big fish pool, I reminded the guys of my newly dubbed title: "El Magni co." Unfortunately, they voted and came up with another name far too fierce to mention.

The next morning, same routine, same bait catching, and then moving on to catch the big ones. Another "big fish" pool. I won it again with a sizable catch, not as large as big red but impressive anyway. at night, after collecting the big fish pool once again, I reminded them of my "El Magni co" title. They voted and came up with that same insulting name from the night before.

The third day, we had no "beeg feesh" pool. Nevertheless, I caught the biggest fish. Then also, this third day, we went around the tip of the Baja and ventured far from shore into the Pacific Ocean. Toward the end of the day, a storm came up, and I was certain we were goners. Ninety percent of the time heading back to shore, the waves were so choppy that the propeller of the outboard motor was out of the water. (As one saving grace in our time of great peril, I thought that it would be a great legacy for my descendants to speak of me as perishing at the mouth of the Sea of Cortez in a deep-sea shing boat . . . that certainly sounds more macho than getting crushed by a Good Humor truck while crossing Big Bend Boulevard, doesn't it?) e three sailors on our little shing boat got very sick; however, I didn't.

I guess the nomenclature "El Magni co" was very apt. (Tastefully, I neglected to remind my companions of such. But then again, those guys had been guzzling beer all day, and I guess they would have been just as sick in a much calmer sea.) The last morning, we were driven to the dirt landing strip.

After waiting for forty-five minutes, a large Jeep vehicle met us, and the driver said, "Sometimes, the plane, she makes it, and sometimes she doesn't." is time she didn't. We jeeped back north to La Paz.

We made it back to La Paz, and our linguist (?), Jim Sullivan, explained to the cabbie at the hotel that he had heard about a saloon in La Paz that had a forty-foot bar that was made out of sterling silver and the bar stools were sterling silver saddles. It appeared that the driver understood, so we left the hotel and loaded in his cab. As we were driving, the bright lights of downtown La Paz faded in the distance. We were leaving the city. From Jim's description, the bar sounded like it was in the heart (maybe the pancreas) of activity of downtown La Paz. But then again, we really didn't know much at all regarding the nightlife in La Paz. Jim Sullivan was the only one of us who heard of this saloon, so trustfully we waited. Well, at this time, the bright lights of La Paz were so far behind us that they appeared as very foggy yellow mist in the rear-view mirror. We were definitely in the boonies of the Baja. Burning smudge pots appeared in the road ahead of us, but the driver didn't break speed. He just continued on the shoulder of the road and continued less than a half mile ahead, and an even more primitive dirt road was on the right. The cabbie made an abrupt right and continued his speed with the dust almost obliterating our view of anything. Shortly ahead, there was a parked large truck with a canvas top open in the back and four armed federales sitting in wait. We were entering a compound of some sort.

Mentally, it crossed my mind that the ransom note to the US government would say, "We got 'em, you want 'em? Send eighteen billion U.S. to La Paz, and you can have 'em back!" (A pipe dream of grandeur, to be sure. The figure would probably be closer to eighteen bucks American.) The compound was a long circle drive with individual lean-to cabins each containing one bare lightbulb with a Mexican piruja (a Mexican woman who sells her body for money or things of value) standing by with a "comehither look." There must have been ten or so of these little huts. One of the "girls" very closely resembled a large pigeon. Whoops, Jim Sullivan's fluency in Mexicali linguistics brought us to this very precarious situation.

He was apologetic and kept saying, "So sorry, guys."

Jim slipped the driver another $20, and we headed back to La Paz, where we dined in the relative safety of the hotel cantina!

Arriving back in St. Louis, I boasted to Susan about my world-record red snapper and my newly dubbed nickname, "El Magni co." She said that she knew that that was a proper name for me even before we got married and said that it was a very appropriate title. (At least that is what I think she said.)

Henry Mancini, The Gentleman

One of the most beautiful shopping areas in the United States is the Country Club Plaza in Kansas City, Missouri. The architecture of the buildings is of Spanish influence developed by the J. C. Nichols Company after J. C. Nichols returned from a visit to Seville, Spain, in 1920. The shopping area is the first designed with the concept of auto transported customers. It consists of eighteen separate buildings comprising of over eight hundred thousand square feet of shopping area. It contains several boutique hotels and a very large and beautifully designed hotel originally named Alameda Plaza Hotel (now the Intercontinental Hotel) that was designed by architect Ward Haylett. Ward told me that the budget for the hotel was almost unlimited when he designed it for its opening in 1972. He told me that it was where "God would stay . . . if he could afford it."

I had a trip to Kansas City in 1981 several years after it opened, and Ward Haylett arranged for me to have a very beautiful suite that even had a grand piano in the room. It was terrific, needless to say. I had lusted for years for a Hart Schaffner Marx, Christian Dior three-piece suit, which I finally purchased for my visit. The suit was of a deep teal blue color and made of some sort of luxuriously soft cotton, and I felt very important wearing it. I considered myself very hot stuff.

On my day of checking in as I was walking through the lobby, Henry Mancini came walking toward me. Music has always been a very large part of my life, and Henry Mancini's compositions and arrangements were included in my short list of fabulous musical creations. His music for Peter Gunn and his music created for the movie Hatari! remain among my favorites even to this day. Henry's music for all of the Pink Panther movies for Blake Edwards is timeless. His compositions for many movies resulted in many Grammys, and his collaborations with the lyricist, Johnny Mercer, became some of the most popular musical compositions in history. My friend, Jan Gippo, who was with the St. Louis Symphony for over thirty-five years, told me that in a conversation with Henry Mancini, Henry told him that the royalties from "Moon River," paid for everything—his house, his cars, the education of his children, just everything. All other revenues were just "gravy."

As a related side story to this side story, my friend, Jan Gippo, the (almost) world's greatest piccoloist who related this story, was in the orchestra for a pops concert that Henry Mancini was guest-conducting the "Star-Spangled Banner" march was on the program, and the very famous piccolo countermelody was ready to be performed with Jan Gippo standing and preparing to play when Henry Mancini asked to use Jan's piccolo and played it perfectly, probably not quite as well as the (almost) world's greatest piccoloist but nevertheless flawlessly. Jan told me that that proved to him that Henry Mancini was not only an incredible composer and arranger, but also a fine musician. He thanked Jan for the use of his piccolo and then returned to the conductor's podium.

At any rate, when I saw Henry Mancini heading toward me, I momentarily lost my scruples and said, "Hi, Hank, it's been a long time. Good to see you again!"

He stopped and said, "It has been, hasn't it . . . how have you been?" (My outright lie just went past him, and he was such a gentleman that he didn't confront me with "Who the hell are you?")

We stood and talked for maybe ten minutes, and he invited me to the Starlight Theater for his performance with the Kansas City Philharmonic Orchestra. Sadly, I had to decline due to a business meeting that I had that evening.

But then he said, "Good seeing you again. Keep in touch."

I said, "Hank, you do the same."

I will always carry that guilt with me, but he was so cordial and considerate as well as very respectful toward me that I will also always carry that wonderful moment with me.

I will also wonder who he thought I was.

What Happens in Port St. Lucie Doesn't Stay in Port St. Lucie

In March 2008, I was with John Rooney again at spring training. Mike Shannon invited John to dinner that night to meet his newly found girlfriend, Lori Bergman (who later became Mrs. Shannon), and John asked me to tag along. I was thrilled at the opportunity, as a good meal at a fine restaurant is a difficult event for me to pass up. The restaurant was a white tablecloth restaurant with tuxedoed waiters, and the menu looked terrific.

The waiter came to the table to take our drink orders, and Mike Shannon asked me what I wanted.

I said, "Club soda, Mike."

He said, "Don't be shy. They have a terrific wine list. Just order what you want . . . I'm buying."

"Seriously, Mike, I drink no alcohol whatsoever. I have an allergy to it."

He pressed me further: "You can't be serious. You were a friend of Jack's (Jack Buck) and you don't drink at all?"

John Rooney chimed in and said, "No, Mike, Don doesn't drink alcohol at all."

I explained further: "Mike, I hate the taste of alcohol. I have no moral aversion to it. I just hate the taste, plus I get a shooting pain just above my eyebrows with just one taste and I feel nauseous. I see no reason to suffer through that."

He kept shaking his head, saying, "I can't believe it."

At any rate, my club soda was very refreshing and the meal was terrific. We ended the evening early because John and Mike were doing a Cardinals/Mets game in Port St. Lucie the next day and they both liked to arrive a couple of hours before the game.

John and I picked up Jim Jackson (the world-class broadcast engineer, and without Jim, there would be zero spring training broadcasts) and then picked up Mike Shannon, and we were on our way to Port St. Lucie for the game. It was really interesting to me because of conversations regarding compensation for pre- and post-game interviews . . . who does this and for what pay. I was like a little fly on the wall hearing inside information that I never thought of before.

Before the game started, John Rooney and I were in a broadcast booth next to the visitor's booth when the national anthem started playing. John Rooney did a perfect Enrico Palazzo (Leslie Nielsen in Naked Gun) rendition of the anthem and had me laughing so hard that I almost teared up. Then he did a play-by-play of Porky Pig broadcasting a baseball game.

That was the funniest broadcasting rendition of a pretend game that I ever heard. John could do stand-up comedy and bring down the house.

The game now is in progress and we are in the Cardinals (visitors) broadcast booth when Mike Shannon at the mike notices a "tiki hut" bar in the concourse in the left field stands and says something about it. I thought I heard my name, but then maybe not. I was to the left of John Rooney and one broadcast person away from Shannon. They both had headphones on and I didn't.

After the inning ends, Mike Shannon leans over past John Rooney and says to me, "Get ready for your phone to ring, big boy." (Mike's term of endearment for almost everyone.)

Several moments later, the phone rang, and it was my beautiful wife, Susan, listening to the broadcast in St. Louis, who said, "Well, what happens in Port St. Lucie doesn't stay in Port St. Lucie."

Mike Shannon, during the game, said, "There is our good friend, Don Marquess, in the tiki hut with a Bud Select in one hand and two tiki hut girls in the other hand."

When Mike gets on a subject, he doesn't let up easily. There were many more references to me being over there with the "beer and broads." He was having very hard time accepting my lifetime sobriety.

After saying those totally untrue things about me, he said to me, "I just made you a hero, big boy."

I thought Susan may be the only person listening to the broadcast who knew that it was a total fabrication.

From that time on, Don Marquess and the tiki hut adventure became a subject anytime a reference to the Mets in Port St. Lucie was brought up during any broadcast. Mike and his future wife, Lori, were in Key West and found a coconut that was very primitively carved in the shape of a hula dancer with a little grass skirt and bright red lips, which they brought to me as a gift because it was remindful of the tiki hut girls. It was mentioned numerous times during Cardinals broadcasts.

Susan, who was having as much fun with the tiki hut adventure as Mike and John were, found a photo on the internet of three oldish fat ladies in bikinis (super el yucko), had it printed, and enclosed it in an 8 ½ x 11 envelopes with a note for Mike Shannon, saying, "Don has had so much fun with you and John talking about his "tiki hut" escapades. He is opening his own "tiki hut" in St. Louis. He put me in charge of hiring the waitresses. Here are my first choices. What do you think?"

The Cartier Watch

In my years as an architectural representative for my father's brick company, I developed many friendships with architects in the area. Two of my very good friends, Frank Riedman and Tom Wilkins, formed a new architectural firm named Wilkins Riedman Architects. Tom and Frank had worked together on many projects including the Anheuser-Busch corporate headquarters. Their first project together was the St. Louis Soccer Park. Frank Riedman had always loved Cartier watches and purchased one to celebrate their new project.

Frank and I had become close friends, and he told me this credible story.

Frank was driving a prospective client to look at a building that the new client admired at the University of Missouri's School of Mining and Metallurgy located in Rolla, Missouri, which is located around one hundred miles southwest of St. Louis, about a two-hour drive. Frank and the new client were deep in discussion regarding the new project when Frank took off his new Cartier watch, wound it (this was in the seventies, and his watch had to be wound, no battery involved), and after winding it, unrolled his window, and threw his watch out the window. Frank smoked, and looked in the ash tray and saw his cigarette in the tray. Apparently, he was so deep in discussion with his new client that he had a momentary brain freeze and thought he was throwing his cigarette out the window. Frank was mortified and pulled off the interstate at the next exit ramp.

The client asked, "Why are we pulling off the highway?"

Frank said, "I accidentally threw something out the window." The client asked, "What did you throw out?"

Frank, trying to avoid admitting his momentary stupidity, especially in front of his new client, thought for a few moments, and said, not wanting to lie to the client, "I threw my brand-new Cartier watch out the window about a mile back!"

"What? You threw your watch out the window? How in the hell did you do that?"

Frank replied, "I have no idea. I guess I thought I was throwing my cigarette away, and I was so engrossed about your new building, I guess I had a momentary brain freeze." The client was speechless.

They searched and searched, but never found his watch. Surprisingly, Frank got the new project with the client, who told Frank that that story was worth every bit of his design fee.

Oh Deer

St. Louis in 1991 had no casinos; however, directly across the Mississippi River in Alton, Illinois, a casino named the Alton Belle had opened. It was a very small riverboat casino offering one-hour cruises in order to comply with Illinois regulations. Our very close friend, Lon Gilbert, who loved to gamble, had never been there; and Susan and I offered to take him there in early October 1993. I might also mention that I loved to play blackjack and didn't have to fly the three-and-a-half-hour flight to Las Vegas to do so. This was to be a fun evening . . .

St. Louis was settled as a major river port in 1764 and was at the confluence of two major rivers: the Missouri and the Mississippi. This was very wonderful for traders because pelts were transported by boats from both the north by the Mississippi and the northwest territories on the Missouri river. However, all of the water surging together at the confluence of those rivers made that area susceptible to periodic flooding. In 1993, St. Louis had a major flood, but the highway to Alton was dry and clear; however, the adjacent area to the highway was severely flooded. Traveling to the Alton Bridge to enter the town that had the Alton Belle, the road, Highway 67, was raised enough to be passable; however, both sides of the road were nothing but trees and water, much like the cypress swamps in southern Louisiana. There was a concrete median on Highway 67, and as we were traveling in the center lane next to this median, a white truck slightly ahead of us in the curb lane swerved and wobbled as if he had blown a tire. I looked at that truck for just a brief moment, and when I turned my vision back to my lane, there were three deer hopping and jumping in front of my car. It was dusk and my headlights were on, and the three deer in front of me looked like aliens in a Steven Spielberg movie, all three trying to get over the concrete median. In that very brief moment, I didn't know exactly what was behind me or to the side of my car, so I just slammed into them. One of the deer went over my car and his hoof damaged my trunk. One was completely smashed by my car. The third one escaped, and I assumed, unharmed. The hood and front bumper of my 1992 white Lexus ES300 was smooshed and very bloody. I called the highway patrol, and a car with a trooper arrived in a few minutes.

I explained in detail to the trooper how it happened, and he said that that happens with regularity with deer trying to escape the flooding. However, to get three at a time hadn't happened before. Susan, my beautiful wife, who was the nurturing mother of all living creatures, was crying about the death of those deer.

The officer said, "Ma'am, your husband saved your life. Many drivers slam on their brakes and are hit from behind by another car, or swerve into a different lane and cause a major collision. Your husband did the right thing and saved your life." (The more he spoke, the taller I got.)

I became the heroic driver of the month in my mind and just felt great that he said all of those great things to my wife. I really felt bad about hitting and killing them also; however, I also felt pretty horrible about the damage to my Lexus, knowing fully well that those deer had no liability insurance (the repair bill was $6,700). I told the trooper that the deer were his if he wanted them. He said he did and thanked me.

We never made it to the Alton Belle that evening, but I did get a couple of bucks regardless. (Sorry about that.)

Irving B. Mestman

During my first year at the University of Missouri in Columbia I became friends with a fellow freshman named Irving Mestman. Irving was a really nice guy and, like me, a non-drinker. In college life that was almost unheard of. My non-drinking was not due to any moral conviction, it was just due to the fact that I hated the taste of alcohol. Just a sip of anything that had alcohol in it just was an abhorrent taste to me. Neither of my parents ever drank so I guess I didn't get the alcohol gene. Later in life from a couple of doctor friends of mine I learned that I have a definite allergy. Just a ship of it gives me a shooting pain across my forehead and a definite queeziness in my stomach. Irving seem to have the identical similarities.

One early evening Irv stopped by my room to tell me he was invited to a purple passion party from a friend of his that was in a fraternity. Irv told me that the purple passion a combination of Welch's grape juice and grain alcohol. He said he would probably not drink much but it would be something he had never had before. I told him it would be very interesting to me to see how he would react to the purple passion Joy juice. He promised to stop by on his way to his room to let me know how the party was. He left my room around 7 PM.

Just before 9 PM my roommate and I were in our room studying (of course) when there was a heavy thud on our door. I opened the door and a zombie entered and collapsed on the floor of our room. It was only a couple of hours after he left for the party. Irving was completely passed out and totally incoherent on the floor of our room. My roommate Roger, and I, carried Irv to the bathroom down the hall, and luckily, we got there just in time for him. Neither Roger nor I could revive Irv to even speak or acknowledge our presence. We got a couple of volunteer students down the hall to help us take Irv to the hospital on the campus. Irving's stomach was pumped and he spent two days in the hospital.

The first day after his hospital stay he came into my room again to give me the details of his unfortunate purple passion party. After he had a cup of the grape juice heavily laced with grain alcohol, which he said didn't really taste bad, he remembered pouring another cup, but that's about it. He had absolutely no recollection of coming to my room or anything leading up to then, or anything afterwards. He did however remember waking up in a hospital bed, and not much other than that. To me that was further proof of the demons contained in any alcohol.

For years later, every so often I would receive à letter with the return address being IBM and the letter starting off 'To the man who saved my life". Irving was working and was loving his job and had never again had even a ship of grape juice nor the alcohol contained their in.

Hooray for my friend Irving!

What An Unbelievable Trip!

The year was 1984 and the longest trip ever was presented to me as an invitation for meeting and merriment in San Diego, California. Simple…. Just fly from St. Louis to San Diego, have a great dinner sponsored by Gail Tile on a boat named the Mauritania. It was for a tile distributorship meeting including a day tour of SeaWorld. Simple you say, and loads of fun. Loads of fun yes,… simple no. Susan my beautiful wife would not get on an airplane, so it was a driving trip from St. Louis to San Diego, only about 1850 miles, no big deal right? Nay, Nay, I say. Susan said "oh that's great we can take the boys and visit my sister in California as well". Susans sister, Natalie, however lived in Sonoma California, a mere 540 miles or so from San Diego. Already this quick little Trip ballooned to 2,500 miles or so, just one way, and we would have to get back to St. Louis. This trip for a dinner and meeting in San Diego has now grown to three weeks or so. Susan said oh this is great we can take in the famous San Diego Zoo and then spend the day or so at Disneyland, then take a spin through San Francisco and spend a couple of days with my sister in Sonoma… just the thought of all this driving gave me a weary weary headache. Susan never had, and never would, drive on a highway…so all 5 to 6000 miles of driving awaited me. Goody goody.

Truly without question my favorite road trip of all is on the old route 66, now Interstate 44, heading Southwest through Oklahoma City, Mighty pretty, Gallup New Mexico, Albuquerque and other points Southwest. However, this trip was going to be a doozy. We loaded my 82 Toranado to the gills and started our journey. Danny was nine years old and Donny was twelve (I need not elaborate how the two of them got along in the backseat on the trip, as it would probably cause you to stop reading), at one point when we got to Yuma Arizona and finished our meal at the McDonald's we were truly tempted to leave one of them there, however reluctantly, we once again had them both in the backseat getting along like nine-year-old and 12-year-old brothers do… not at all. We finally arrived (still alive with no murders committed) in San Diego and got a beautiful and very large room at the highly recommended Sea Isle Hotel. We found a babysitter through the concierge at the hotel, and was a lovely young lady who entertained our boys for the entire evening of our meeting. The dinner and cruise was delightful and needless to say, Susan and I enjoyed the evening away from our loving sons.

The next day we went to the beautiful and lush with tropical plants, the San Diego Zoo which was a delightful and wonderful excursion. St. Louis has one of the largest and most respected Zoos in the country, but San Diego has the extra added benefit of lush tropical plants and palm trees. One more meeting with the tile folks that night and then the next morning we were off for Los Angeles and

Disneyland. The boys actually got along well because of all of the excitement of the zoo the day before in San Diego, and then a full day in Disneyland, which kept them as well as Susan and I well entertained. Then we continued our trek north to San Francisco… this is where the totally weird part of our trip comes in.

Susan and I had never been to San Francisco in our 15+ years of marriage, and my brother and his wife had never been to San Francisco either. We discovered they were there on the same day we were there. On a call back to St. Louis, my mom told me that my brother and his wife Millie were there on the same day, and they were in a hotel directly across from ours. We didn't realize it until were on the way north to Sonoma. It gets stranger.

In St. Louis about three weeks before we started our trip, I was working on a project for a new building designed by HOK architects. The project designer was Peter Hoyt who told me he was going to be on vacation shortly and he wanted to get his selection done before he left. We got that worked out, and HOK specked our Gail Tile for the new building.

When we finally reached Sonoma, California on our trip to meet with Susan's sister Natalie she directed us on a trip through Northern California passing through Bodega Bay, where the movie The Birds, a Great film directed by Alfred Hitchcock was filmed, and then she lead us to Muir Woods, a beautiful forest with giant redwood trees. Upon arriving I carried my three cameras and low pro camera bag with me to shoot some major photos. We walked through the woods for about an hour or so, when Susan, her sister and the boys were quite tired. I had to change film, so I sat on a bench and started loading more film into my cameras and there was no one in eyesight except one man carrying a backpack and walking on the trail directly in front of the bench where I was sitting. I looked at him and I said "Peter?" and believe it or not, it was Peter Hoyt, the architect that I was working with in St. Louis over three weeks ago, | walking with his backpack through Muir Woods.

I got a very cold feeling up my spine and started shivering. All of the above things seemed so weird and coincidental that I immediately thought of Irwin Allen and his many disaster movies. Irwin Allen was termed the disaster master, and I started thinking how he structured his movies with individual stories of people all coming to the same point where a major disaster was about to occur. Irwin Allen produced and directed the Poseidon adventure and the Towering Inferno among many other memorable films. I thought "if I start hearing Maureen McGovern singing, I'm running for safety". I felt that the big earthquake was going to hit San Francisco and we had better get away as soon as possible. I told this to Susan when we got back to the hotel and she shared my thoughts but we didn't tell the boys and we skedaddled out of Northern California and started our trip back home.

Fortunately, it was just a strange feeling on my part, as the big earthquake never occurred, but it was one of the strangest moments in my entire life. Gleefully, when we returned home after almost 6000 miles driving, and I think I actually kissed the front lawn when we got home.

Why Black Coffee is Part of My Life

There was a student gathering place next to the Library on the quadrangle at St. Louis University called the campus club. It was a great place to see friends and to drink coffee and have a snack or so. One afternoon between classes I saw a very attractive little redhead at the counter, ordering something or another. She was very cute and perky, and really caught my eye. I hurried to the counter, hoping to start a conversation with her, as her coffee order was delivered, she commences to put three or four spoonfuls of sugar and a large dollop of cream. This was just the way I liked my coffee, however, to start a conversation with her, I said" how can you ruin a great cup of coffee by putting all that stuff in it? It appears that you are making a milkshake rather than a cup of coffee'. She turned and looked at me, gave me a big smile from ear to ear, and I could tell that she kind of liked me as well. Her name was Leslie Davenport, possibly the prettiest and cutest student in all of St. Louis University, at least that's what I thought at the time. We both went back to my table and sat down and talked for a very lengthy time. Afterwards, I just barely made it to my logic class, but we made plans to meet after class at the campus club. I offered to take her home after school and she gratefully accepted my offer.

We had a very lustful relationship for over a year. We spent so much time together we both missed parties, movies, friendships, etc. because we enjoyed each other's company so much. We had great seats for a Bobby Darin show at the Chase Hotel in St. Louis, but we never made it. Togetherness was the choice., constant choice of our evenings. Someone at some time or another must have told Leslie that she resembled Doris Day. She picked up many of the mannerisms of Doris Day, which really enhanced her beautiful appearance.

I never told Leslie about my black coffee lie, and had to drink my coffee black for our entire year together. At the time I thought the bitter taste of black coffee was well worth my experience, very delightful experience, with the beautiful and very cleverly constructed Leslie Davenport. As a matter of fact, I grew to love, black coffee and still drink it that way to this very day….

I would write more, but my Starbucks is ready now.

The Unbearable Being of Weight

Puberty hit me pretty hard, and it was a major battle to keep weight off. I would gain 10 to 15 pounds and then stop eating for a while and lose it. Then I would gain 10 to 15 pounds again, then stop eating again and lose it. Following that cycle and using my Jethro Clampett method of ciphering, my calculations tell me that I have lost 1326 pounds in my lifetime. Fortunately, that pattern stopped for a while, which allowed me to be a normal weighted person. I am 6 feet tall and for the most of my adult life I have weighed a hefty 200 pounds or so.

Unfortunately, the fat bug raises his jowelly head once again and around the time I turned forty I started to heap on a few (?) more pounds and shot up to around 250 pounds. A good architect friend, Bob Entzeroth, who was on a diet, and aware of everyone's weight, said to me one day when I entered his office "Don, what do you weigh now?" I told him 250 pounds. He said to me "don't think of yourself as weighing 250 pounds, think of yourself as weighing an eighth of a ton". Bob was always aware of what people weighed whatever he was on a diet. I think that from time to time there are tiny particles of fat in the air, and if you happen to be in the area of someone who recently lost weight, the area surrounding them is chock full of those tiny fat particles, and all that air is very fattening…my simple reasoning for unexplained weight gain. An unproven concept, but it is a possibility!

In 1982 Susan and I attended a board of education meeting and socialized with many board members. I was president of the PTA at that time and met with a lot of people that I hadn't seen for a year or so. One particular friend was an attorney named Alan Jerger. He looked at me and in total astonishment said to me "My God... what happened to you? it looks like someone just pumped you up!" Well sadly, he was right. I was greatly embarrassed and didn't know exactly what to say. then I just blurted out ' I know, it's just driving me crazy, my doctor says that after a series of tests, I should weigh around 280 pounds. I have got to gain 30 more pounds in the next two months. I don't think I can do it. Susan is waking me up halfway through the night with the prescribed slice of cheesecake or dish of ice cream or plate of cookies, and a number of things that are very fattening. She is doing her very best trying to help me follow doctor's orders. I really don't know if I can make the doctor's requirements of my getting to 280 pounds, but I'm trying" Alan Jerger just stared at me in total disbelief, truly with his jaw hanging low. After a couple of minutes of staring at me, in all seriousness, he said to me 'I think you need to get a different opinion and perhaps change doctors'. Later that evening I told Susan of my conversation with my attorney friend, Alan Jerger. She thought my response to him was brilliant, and said that his remark to me was so embarrassing that he deserved just what I said. Susan said all that while laughing hysterically. Then she said, you know he was right, you do look like somebody just pumped you up. I replied "I Will start my diet tomorrow… and I did.

Jim Sullivan's Arrival

Jim Sullivan was the president of Gail Tile US. Gail was the largest manufacturer of split tile in the world and was located in Giessen West Germany. All of the tile they manufactured was frost proof and suitable for exterior usage in the freezing climate of northern United States. Missouri Brick had recently received exclusivity of distributorship of their tile in the state of Missouri and the closely surrounding States. We received almost immediate success with gathering specifications of their tile in our distributorship area. Very quickly we rose to the top five distributors in the United States for Gail Tile. Jim Sullivan was the excellent president of Gail for the US market, as he was very brilliant and possessed a delightful sense of humor. Jim Sullivan was coming to St. Louis to visit for the first time to see our operation and make several Architectural calls. I felt that his arrival should be somewhat special.

There was a hotel in St. Louis named the Cheshire Inn. Which was built in the style of an old English Inn. They had a Rolls-Royce at their disposal for special arrivals and I thought that would be a terrific way to welcome Jim Sullivan to St. Louis. I got his flight schedule and secured the Rolls-Royce, and the uniformed chauffeur to pick him up at the airport. A close friend of mine had a very beautiful and voluptuous wife who had a great sense of humor. I asked her if she would be willing to ride in the Rolls-Royce to the airport to welcome Jim Sullivan to St. Louis. I also asked if she would dress very professionally, but leave several buttons of her outfit open. What a terrific way that would be to welcome Jim to St. Louis. I met her the day of Jim's arrival at the Cheshire Inn and she indeed looked fabulous, as well as being very cleverly constructed. I told the hotel manager what I was doing and he thought it was indeed a fun way to welcome a dignitary to the city of St. Louis.

The rooms of this hotel were glorious indeed as they contained a Four poster bed as well as old London furniture. I imagined the wonder in Jim Sullivan's mind as to what was in his future that evening when he was greeted with the Rolls-Royce and beautiful Donna inside. The entire plan that I had was that Donna would be very professional but also somewhat flirtatious and giving Jim Sullivan thoughts of a thoroughly enjoyable evening. My complete plan however was not reached. I asked several of my friends, male friends, to pretend to be of questionable gender and stationed in the room for Jim's arrival. Unfortunately, I couldn't convince any of them to do it for me. Nevertheless, the plan was great anyway. The total caper was to be that Donna would accompany Jim and the two doors of the room, then she would say "Sorry Mr. Sullivan, but I come with the car, and stay with the car" and when the door was opened, the man who was of somewhat gender confused, would appear after the door was opened, and say "hello you beautiful man...I come with the room!". What an incredible letdown that would be from being up so high with expectations and then to have those eliminated in a heartbeat, unfortunately that last part never happened, but nevertheless it was a delightful way to welcome Jim Sullivan to St. Louis. The three of us including Donna, had a wonderful meal in their dining room and laughed continuously about his welcome to our fine town.

The Shortest Line at White Castle

White Castle hamburgers are truly unique. There is really nothing like them. Each White Castle is maybe 2 1/2 bites at the most. They are very moist, easy to chew and go down very easily. That is why they are called sliders. Maybe two or three times a year Susan and I got a great urge to have several white castles. There was a recently constructed White Castle restaurant, not too far from our house. We drove to it, parked the car on the lot while Susan waited for me to go inside and get a bag. This was a brand-new white Castle which was probably the state of the art at that time, and it was packed. There were four serving lines, which were all at least six or seven people deep, except one. There were only two people in that line so I got behind the second person quickly so people in the other lines wouldn't jump in ahead of me. The first person in that line ordered 25 white castles, which were served to him very quickly. However, the second person in line was a different story.

The man directly in front of me was about 6'4" tall, wearing a cowboy hat, and a somewhat decorated cowboy shirt. He also had a zero Halliburton case with him and he ordered 78 white castles. I said to him that I like white castles also but he had to have one terrific appetite to order 78 of them. He reached down and picked up his Halliburton case, opened it up, and it was insulated with foam. He told me that that case held 78 white castles. He said that St. Louis was the farthest west city that had a white Castle store, and every time he was going from the east to the west, he arranged a stop in St. Louis to pick up his load of white castles. He and his wife, would then meet with several couples at the Phoenix airport and they would have a white castle party. He told me all of this while grinning through his browned and wrinkled complexion and heavily tanned face. He told me what I already knew, white Castle hamburgers are unlike any other hamburger in the world. That is not an insult to McDonald's or Hardee's or any other hamburger chain. White Castle hamburgers are barely hamburgers. White Castle hamburgers are not fried nor grilled nor even roasted, they are actually steamed on a bed of very wet and watery onions, and the hamburger itself never touches the grill. They are steamed and incredibly flavorful.

I finally returned to my patiently, waiting wife, with my sack of eight, white castles, and told her the story of the tall rancher who was second in line at the counter. She said, 'thank goodness I was worried that maybe you were trampled by a thundering hoard of White Castle eaters. The sack was empty by the time we drove the 6 miles to get home. I would write more but I have suddenly been attacked with a craving for White Castle hamburgers.

Riding the Rapids

Every year, Jim Sullivan engineered a Board of Directors meeting at some interesting location, and this particular meeting was in Sun River, Oregon in a condo building owned by Bud Morris who was our host for the trip. The attendees were from many different parts of the country, Phil Stalcup from Seattle, Harry Atherton from Boston. Arnold Moses from Baltimore and me from St. Louis. Bud Morris was a terrific host and took us on a tour of many interesting points around Sun River. Bud met us all at the airport in Portland and drove us to Mount Rainier in Washington and then took us to a sight where we viewed Mount Saint Helens that erupted earlier in the year. White Ash still covered our viewpoint. Again, as always at the board meetings we had incredible food as well as terrific scenery.

Jim Sullivan and Bud Morris arranged for Whitewater rafting on the Deschutes River which was close to Bud's condo in Sunriver. He drove us to the starting point of our rafting and the guide told us with the rainfall the night before the rapids were a little more challenging than usual. He explained to us that there are six grades of rapids, with grade one or two being a float trip, and grade 6 being like Niagara Falls. The Deschutes was usually a high three level to a four level. With the heavy rain the night before, the rampage would be a high four to perhaps a low five. The guide said the rapids that day would be for more experienced rapid floaters than he thought we were, so he said if we canceled, he would understand. Five of us were more adventurous than we should've been, but the sixth one, Arnold Moses, opted to pass. Arnold was the oldest of the group and definitely the more cautious. He stood on the shore and waved goodbye to us as he also nodded his head in deep concern for his fellow directors. We all waived goodbye to Arnold thinking that was the last time we would see him…or anyone at all>

The ride started off somewhat calmly and I felt that our guide closely resembled Burt Reynolds. The speed of our raft quickly increased and we all had oars and specific duties given by our guide, fortunately for me, three of our group were experienced sailors and had ridden rapids before. As the speed of our raft increased, the experienced rafters, as well as our guide, were frantically rowing and trying to keep us from smashing into the rocks. I had absolutely no idea what I was doing but I was frantic as well, while trying to follow the lead of our guide. At one point I was certain that I was hearing banjo music played by a pale face with large ears and far distant appearing eyes. We were constantly getting soaked and we were more in the water than dry. We were flying and crashing and splashing and crashing some more, when finally the rapids slowed and the waves stopped crushing our skulls, and we started floating speedy, but safely on the Deschutes, when we came to a calm and conferring area on the river, the guide told us how to roar to the shore which we did, and then his wife met us in a vehicle which was a large Jeep like vehicle so we all piled in wearing our very wet and totally clothing. Arnold Moses was dry as a bone sitting in the front seat and grinning from ear to ear that he didn't have to suffer in wetness. We then drove around the river, and then at a point on the shore we noticed two tuxedo waiters greeting us as we arrived. There were two white table clothed dining areas and as we exited the vehicle in our soaked clothes the tuxedoed waiters, actually a waiter and his wife had just finished char grilling filet mignon and baked potatoes with several bottles of champagne and wine for our afternoon dining pleasure, of course I only had Club soda to celebrate the event, but the steak was cooked perfectly and the surprise of the T tuxedoed waiters was one of the most delicious meals of my life.

Bobby Kennedy

The year was 1960 and Robert Kennedy was his brother John's campaign manager. He was coming too St. Louis University for a rally for his brother. John Boehm, Jay Bentley, and I were students who had just started singing together as a folk trio. Folk music was extremely popular at that time, and quickly we became "Big men on Campus". We were asked to perform for Kennedy's rally, and were very honored and excited to do so. The quadrangle was packed with students and we were to perform while everyone waited for Robert Kennedy to arrive. We were his "warm up act". We had been asked to sing about a half hour before his arrival. Well, at that time we only had about 25 minutes of rehearsed material (about two sides of a Kingston Trio album) but we felt that with our loveable intros we could stretch it out to a half hour or so. We actually accomplished that…. however, no Bobby Kennedy. His helicopter had not arrived. So, we sang "Tom Dooley" again. Then did several sing a-longs and told quick little stories. Still no Bobby. We sang yet the third sing-a-long of "Michael row the Boat Ashore" …still no Bobby…

We kept the crowd that had gathered in the quadrangle entertained(?) for over an hour when we finally heard the Whirleybird's flappers and Bobby had landed. We stepped to the side of the microphone…way to the side, as Bobby broke rank from his protectors, came over to us and apologized for being late. We will never forget his kindness and consideration.

I would have voted for his brother, but at that time voting age was 21 and I was only 19. John F. Kennedy's brother was such a kind gentleman, I was ready to cast my vote for his brother John, the next president of the United States, even though I was too young to do so.

Smoking

I sadly admit …. I was a smoker. I tried to quit on multiple occasions with very limited success, essentially no success at all. Susan and I had just bought our first house and cigarettes were getting very expensive! …all the way up to .50 per pack! My house payment was $133.50 per month, I could burn up a considerable amount of my house payment, Also, Susan was pregnant with Danny, our second son. Unknown expenses were on the horizon. Cigarettes went up to fifty cents a pack! In a poker game at home, I could smoke an entire pack. Something had to be done for sure. This time I could not fail.

I made many absolute decisions to never ever light up another cigarette. Period. Never again! But I always failed. I would on many occasions throw a pack away, maybe even what was left of an entire carton. Still no success. No matter what I tried, I still failed…This time I had a method that proved to be the perfect method…. I could even patent it (if such a thing were possible).

I got to thinking that a person could take anything for a week. It was possible to tolerate almost anything for a week or so… Even relatives moving in for a week, so I decided to quit just for a week, the thought of never having another cigarette was far too difficult for me to handle. So, every time I tried to quit, after a few days, I gave in to the tobacco devil. So, giving up cigarettes for one week only seemed like a doable endeavor. That week was very difficult for me to get through, but every time I wanted a cigarette, I thought "only a few more days and my cigarette will be ready for me and waiting". I kept looking forward to that day. It was Friday at 4 PM when I would have my cigarette…that thought kept me away from my cigarette all week finally Friday at 4 PM arrived, and that cigarette was lighted with glee. It really tasted terrific. As I was delighting in the wonderful taste of that cigarette, I thought, "5well I made it for a week and didn't die. I think I can last for one more week!" so I put my cigarette out and started my second week…

The second week, I coughed and gagged for much of the week. My body started to purge itself of all of the nicotine poisoning I had built up for many years. By Wednesday that week, the coughing and gagging abated and I was actually feeling much better. Friday at 4 PM arrived, I forgot about my cigarette, it was 5:15 and I realized I had not had my cigarette, so I lit up, and that cigarette didn't taste quite as good as the one the previous Friday, but I smoked it anyway. Then I thought "well I made it through another week. I am going to go just one more week without a cigarette". The next Friday arrived, and I had no desire for another cigarette. That was over 50 years ago and I've never had another cigarette. Other than those two weeks of misery, I have never even had a desire for another cigarette.

That was an absolute perfectly way to quit smoking. I recommend that whole heartedly to all of the addicted smokers in the world….. It works!!

Oysters, Oysters, Oysters, and more Oysters

Once a year Jim Sullivan President of Gail International tile had a board of directors meeting. It was actually the board of directors of nothing, it just sounded important. His meetings were always at some interesting place in the country. We met at Santa Catalina Island, Door County Wisconsin, Sunriver Idaho, and the tip of the Baja in Mexico. Jim assembled a group of 7 of his distributors who were the top sellers in the country for his product, Gail Tile was manufactured in West Germany. and the largest producer of split tile in the world. Jim was a fun guy and the members of his board of director's meetings became very much like fraternity brothers at Jim's meetings that lasted usually 4 to 5 days, where a great time was had by all. I was the permanent designated driver, being a non-drinker, however I had just as much fun as everybody else and was totally alert for all of it.

One of the meetings was held on St. Mary's Island on the Chesapeake Bay. For this meeting he booked rooms for us at the Laura Ashley Inn on the Island. All of the directors met at a little outdoor restaurant on the Chesapeake Bay where Oyster fishermen (?) lined up their boats at the dock and started one by one shoveling oysters from their boats onto a conveyor belt which led to a large 18 wheel closed van. Another 18-wheel closed van was behind the first one awaiting to be loaded as well. When we were having lunch there were seven oyster boats lined up and two large closed 18-wheel vans we're being loaded. We were told that was the largest harboring port for oysters in the country. That night we had a scheduled dinner at the Laura Ashley inn.

There were five of us dining that evening. One of us didn't eat oysters at all. One of us (Me) was not a major oyster fan, as a matter of fact I really had no desire for them. That left three main oyster eaters…with me just being the fourth, reluctant, but willing. We all sat at the table awaiting dinner. Two waitresses carried in two gigantic platters containing 24 dozen oysters on each platter. I had never seen so many oysters at one time. They were shucked and open with many of them almost as big as my hand. I learned very quickly that adding Lemon juice horseradish and ketchup disguised the inherent flavor of raw oysters and I actually enjoyed them. As I remember, I ate close to two dozen of them…they were harvested that afternoon and couldn't be fresher. Now, thinking back on that evening with me eating two dozen, that left 46 dozen to be consumed by the other three Directors, which seems like an impossible task. Nevertheless, with that being the only course for dinner, which lasted almost 4 hours, it could have been possible.

Also, I must give credit to the man in the world who ate the first oyster, as he must've been incredibly desperate for nourishment. Seeing the way an oyster looks, eating it is the last thing that would cross my mind.

I have heard for years of the incredible power of oysters, but for me when I returned home to my loving wife Susan, only three of the two dozen worked.

Finally...a Brilliant Thought

As mentioned before, my maternal grandfather was an inventor who at the age of 80 got his 31st Patent. He passed away at 101. My grandfather, for some unknown reason thought that I would be an inventor as well, I worked for my grandfather, as all of his descendants did at one time or another, and one morning after he picked me up for work at his company, he was explaining something to me about one of his inventions, I think I was maybe 12 or 13 years old. I must've said something to him that made him think that I fully understood what he was talking about, therefore, he thought that I was the only descendent of his that had any hope for the future. To this date, I have no recollection of what he was talking about or whether I understood it or not, but apparently, he thought I had potential. As I now approach 84 years of age, the halfway point of my life, I have invented nothing. Looking at me from his perch in heaven, he must be greatly disappointed in his grandson. However, I do have a very simple, yet somewhat complex idea for harnessing power in the future.

We have tried many different versions of creating power. We have created batteries to store, solar energy, however, that can be produced only during the day when the sun is on the side of the Earth. It is also very difficult to produce solar energy during a cloudy day or a hurricane, for example. Solar energy is rather fickle in its ability to produce power.

We have harnessed wind with many windfarms, capturing the also very fickle wind is only a sometime thing. I truly believe wind power is not the answer.

Water energy is very effective by producing Dams holding back rivers and using that energy to power turbines generating electrical power for cities that are relatively close to the areas producing power. For example, the Hydroelectric power produced by Hoover dam is about 4,000,000,000 kWh of energy each year which provides power to Nevada, Arizona and California, and serves 1.3 million people every year. However, that is one small section of the United States.

Oil does a pretty nice job of powering our cars and many things needing energy. However, producing more fossil fuel will take another billion or so years after we deplete what is stored in the bowels of our earth. Our current fossil fuel will be gone sometime in the near future.

There is only one source of power that cannot be depleted and is always present.

GRAVITY.

I believe that I am correct in stating that every action has a reaction. My grandfather, I feel certain could figure out some way to harness that energy, which can never be depleted. As I approach the halfway point of my life, reaching 84 years of age, time is not in my favor to go back to school and change majors. Therefore, someone else must figure it out. If my grandfather is reading the last page in this book from his lofty place in the afterlife, maybe he will think that finally his grandson had a pretty good idea.

www.ingramcontent.com/pod-product-compliance
Lightning Source LLC
Chambersburg PA
CBHW052027030426
42337CB00027B/4894